Egyptian Revolutions

Egyptian Revolutions

Conflict, Repetition and Identification

Amal Treacher Kabesh

ROWMAN &
LITTLEFIELD
INTERNATIONAL

London • *New York*

Published by Rowman & Littlefield International Ltd
Unit A, Whitacre Mews, 26-34 Stannary Street, London SE11 4AB
www.rowmaninternational.com

Rowman & Littlefield International Ltd. is an affiliate of Rowman & Littlefield
4501 Forbes Boulevard, Suite 200, Lanham, Maryland 20706, USA
With additional offices in Boulder, New York, Toronto (Canada), and
Plymouth (UK)
www.rowman.com

British Library Cataloguing in Publication Data
A catalogue record for this book is available from the British Library

ISBN: HB 978-1-7834-8187-3
ISBN: PB 978-1-78348-188-0

Library of Congress Cataloging-in-Publication Data
ISBN 978-1-78348-187-3 (cloth : alk. paper)
ISBN 978-1-78348-188-0 (paper : alk. paper)
ISBN 978-1-78348-189-7 (electronic)

∞™ The paper used in this publication meets the minimum requirements of
American National Standard for Information Sciences—Permanence of Paper for
Printed Library Materials, ANSI/NISO Z39.48-1992.

Printed in the United States of America

Contents

Acknowledgements   vii

1 Conflict, Repetition and Identification   1

2 Living with Perpetual Insecurity   23

3 The Intimacy of Subjection   47

4 Enduring Repetition: Events, Narratives, Emotions   73

5 Female Agency: Struggling against Constraint   99

6 Power, Domination, Struggle   123

7 The Essential Endeavour: Being Accountable   149

Bibliography   167

Index   179

About the Author   187

Acknowledgements

I am grateful to Samantha Ashenden, Lene Auestad, James Brown, Lesley Caldwell, Jonathan Davidoff and Susannah Radstone for organising seminars and conferences, where I gained invaluable comments and helpful pointers. I am also thankful to the members of the Psychoanalysis and Politics Network for continuing and helpful discussion that has taken place over many years. For providing much-needed support, important acts of kindness and friendship, I thank David Ball, Jo Cassidy, Helen Crowley, Bill Dixon, Harry Ferguson, Alison Haigh, Pauline Henderson, Clare Hemmings, Sharon Jackson, Christian Karner, Hanan Kholoussy, Claire Knee, Lynne Layton, Veronica Layunta-Maurel, Rana Nessim, Julia O'Connell Davidson, Yvonne Patrick and Susannah Radstone. As always I am grateful to Amir Hawash for his continuing love, support and tolerating my absences while I have been working on this book – thank you.

Jenny Money corrected the manuscript thoroughly and with meticulous attention to detail. She also very generously undertook proof reading the manuscript and picked up numerous mistakes. I have benefited very much from the work she has undertaken on this book. Martina O'Sullivan and Mike Watson have been exceptionally supportive, tolerant of my endless delays and kindly taking the manuscript off me when I was (very) reluctant to let it go. I am very appreciative of Jenny, Martina and Mike and thank them wholeheartedly.

I am grateful and indebted to Alice Bloch, Kirsten Campbell and Suki Ali for their persistent support, careful reading of this manuscript and exceptionally helpful comments and criticisms.

This book is dedicated to the late, and much missed, Peter Horne.

Chapter 1

Conflict, Repetition and Identification

The Egyptian people are tense and apprehensive – this statement is at risk of being an overly assertive declaration; yet, events since January 2011 have caused schismatic socio-political-emotional shifts. It has been a turbulent and sensitive time. Families have been divided and friendships fractured because of differing opinions, beliefs and allegiances. It is unclear whether these splits and ruptures will ever be repaired or, indeed, healed. Egypt remains socially, politically and emotionally precarious and the future profoundly uncertain. Egyptians feel pride, loyalty and love for Egypt, and this remains constant and is well captured in the following fragment: 'And I would like to ask you in these few lines I write, to take the trouble to kiss her for me – her lotus and palm trees, her waters and her evenings – kiss all of her – kiss Egypt on the mouth' (Marangou 2001: 19).

These affectionate, if not erotic, lines embody how Egypt seizes the Egyptian people and it holds us in its grasp. This reach is generous, warm, loving and simultaneously troublesome and troubling. Egypt ensnares us through its sensuality, familial and national history, its chaos and the fun of everyday living where everything is full of noise, taste and smell (although, at times, challenging). Tangibly and intangibly we are touched and, as Ahdaf Soueif (2012: 6) writes, Cairo 'puts her lips to our ears, she tucks her arm into ours and draws us close'. Those of us who live part of the time elsewhere still gain our breath and 'aliveness' through our deep attachment to Egypt and to other Egyptians.

Our lives have been disrupted by the political events of January 2011; whether or not we agreed with the fervent demonstrations and socio-political demands, we have all been profoundly affected by them. In any case, all Egyptians were caught up in the events, watched and listened to the media endlessly, had strong opinions that were continually shared and were emotionally stirred – whether by excitement, optimism or anxiety. We could not believe what was taking place. Events unfolded at speed as the then president Mubarak resigned, the Supreme Council of Armed Forces took temporary charge, preparations for presidential and parliamentary elections were put in place and new political parties found their voice and presence in Egypt.

We miss it when we are away from Cairo; however, recently – over the past 15 years or so – we have missed Egypt *even when we are on its soil*. Oppression, corruption and the relentless daily grind have taken away Egypt and left in its place yearnings for 'bread, freedom, social justice' – though, at times, human dignity is used instead of social justice. These redolent phrases – freedom, bread, social justice, human dignity – are the demands that arose so loudly and importantly in January 2011 and were chanted with passion by protestors all over Egypt. The demand for bread (standing for an adequate material standard of living) lies alongside the necessary requirement for a society based on social justice. We were convinced, with optimism and excitement, that our lives were going to change for the best, forever. We were quickly proved wrong.

The demands for bread, freedom and social justice persist, as life in Egypt has seen no improvement whatsoever since the revolutionary activity that took place in 2011 and beyond, despite the fall of the Mubarak regime and the election of the Muslim Brotherhood as the governing party, with Mohammed Morsi as the president of Egypt (June 2012–July 2013). These socio-political demands arose from profound disaffection, anger at the persistent exploitation of and lack of opportunity for the majority of the population and, importantly, frustration at the decline of Egypt as a nation that can take its place as an international power. Egypt is a society marked by intense national pride especially in its pharaonic history and civilisation. This history fuels a commonplace passion for the nation and reinforces an insistent demand that Egypt should return to its former place of glory.

Although the above is a snapshot of the atmosphere in the country since the fervent events that occurred during January and February 2011, it cannot, perhaps, convey the insecurity and divisions within Egyptian society that have led to fractures within families and friendship groups and the breakdown of civil society. Civility that was a feature of Egyptian society is little in evidence. Fears for personal safety are high, as there are numerous accounts of robbery and theft, whether of cars or homes, and of attacks on people – especially women – and an escalation in drug and alcohol abuse. We have also had to make personal adjustments to these aspects of Egyptian society as, previously, we gave little, if any, thought to our safety as we walked in all confidence through the streets, no matter what time of the day or night.

Since January 2011 we have been thrown out of our usual rhythms of living and inhabiting our lives, as we have been thrown off balance subsequent to the revolutionary activity that has taken place since 2011. Especially in the aftermath of the election of the Muslim Brotherhood to power, many Egyptians lost their ordinary capacity to think and respond sensibly and carefully. I wrote the afterword of my previous book (Treacher Kabesh 2013a) quickly in 2012. To this day I remain troubled about what I had written as I was confused and overwhelmed by the events that were taking place, so that an ordinary and thoughtful state of mind was absent. Paranoia dominated during this time of civil uncertainty and dreadful insecurity. To illustrate this state of mind, I will draw on a personal example. Early one morning I was walking down the street where I live; there were very few people around and it was very quiet. The silence was unsettling rather than a welcome calm that can descend on noisy cities. I passed a car and noticed a middle-aged man buying bread from a cart. As he turned behind him, I imagined that he was reaching for his gun in order to shoot me. I provide this example to illustrate how charged the atmosphere was and how ordinary activity was laden with emotion and fantasy. The difficulty is that these burdened states of mind lead to troubling emotional and socio-political consequences. The afterword was written at a highly charged, emotional and troubling time, when many Egyptian people were protesting against the Muslim Brotherhood rule, leading to Morsi and the Muslim Brotherhood being ousted from power by the military under the leadership of Abdul Fattah Al-Sisi. Following this period of violence, oppression and fury (by the Muslim Brotherhood) and relief (many of the Egyptian population), were relieved that the occupation by the Muslim Brotherhood in squares across Egypt was over.

In the afterword I gave little thought to the Muslim Brotherhood, relieved that they were no longer in power. I took the stance too easily and too quickly of erring on the side of the *status quo*. I was not impartial, as I overly identified with those who wanted the ousting of the Muslim Brotherhood. I do not agree with the ideologies and belief system of the Muslim Brotherhood and think that they made many mistakes when in power. However, I now regret that I did not reach out to try to understand the members of the Muslim Brotherhood. Disappointed in my one-sided commitment, I now feel some remorse. I did not take up a position advocated by Edward Said of humanism as a 'useable praxis for intellectuals and academics who want to know what they are doing, what they are committed to as scholars, and who want also to connect these principles to the world in which they live as citizens' (Said 2004a: 6). I am attempting in this book to think anew my previous viewpoints and to move towards explicating a framework for thinking through the material and socio-political conditions that are required for social justice to be established. As Achille Mbembe (2015) powerfully points out, we must demythologise so as to 'dry up the mythic, symbolic resources' in order that we do not 'die hating somebody else'. This impassioned essay by Mbembe is a *cri de cœur* – an appeal for thinking to take place alongside different emotional responses. Revolutions, as Hazim Kandil (2012: 1) points out, 'break our hearts whether they fail or succeed'; I would add that they also fracture the human spirit.

How does a society that has been colonised recover? This ambitious question is the driving challenge of this book. In this monograph, I endeavour to trace through the damage done to Egyptian subjectivity. In so doing, I take full account of the economic, political, psychic and social effects of inhabiting postcolonialism. I argue that repetition of the past persists inexorably in the present. Alongside this theoretical and methodological stance, emphasis is placed on understanding how public life is lived and experienced at the level of the 'everyday', as I attempt to trace through the emotions, fantasies and narratives of public events and argue that this triad of 'emotions, fantasies, narratives' are inextricably linked into the way in which 'events' are experienced.

Three terms – conflict, repetition and identification – frame my concerns and drive my preoccupations. Egypt has a troubled history, and the central focus of this book is to explore how this troubling past lives on and is perpetuated in the present. History is repeated due to identification (loving and, at times, adhesive); consciously and unconsciously, it can lead to repetition. Repetition, however, is never without conflict, as the wish to make something anew lies alongside the fear and insecurity of the unknown. Conflict arises for a variety of reasons: in attempts to break away from that which is known and internalised; in the negotiations required to navigate the bonds that provide us with love and sustenance but that can also bind us; in the concern, if not anxiety, that can occur when there is divergence of opinions – even if mild – and certainly if the disagreement/s are so intense that they lead to divisions within social networks; and in the emotions that arise when divergent and irreconcilable narratives and discourses lead to conflicts that may or may not be tolerated. These conflicts operate at individual, family and community levels and occur, needless to say, between the state and individuals. The state in Egypt is extremely powerful and omnipresent and, to draw upon a commonplace depiction, can rightly be described as 'the Deep State'.

I am preoccupied with the role of emotions and fantasy in public life, and, following Jacqueline Rose (1998), I understand them not as antagonistic but, rather, as the glue of social life. This statement is, perhaps, and especially for those of us reliant on psychoanalysis, incontestable as, after all, evidence of emotions and their role in human interactions, relationships with self and other, and acting on the world we inhabit, is omnipresent. This book is about the complexities, contradictions, push-and-pull factors, messiness and challenges of everyday life.

I engage here with tracing through the effects of socio-political events on ordinary life – which, as Kathleen Stewart (2007) describes it,

is a shifting assemblage of practices and practical knowledges, a scene of both liveness and exhaustion, a dream of escape or of the simple life. Ordinary affects are the varied, surging capacities to affect and be affected that give everyday life the quality of a continual motion of relations, scenes, contingencies, and emergences. They're things that happen. They happen in impulses, sensations, expectations, daydreams, encounters, and habits of relating, in strategies and their failures, in forms of persuasion, contagion, and compulsion, in modes of attention, attachment, and agency, and in public and social worlds of all kinds that catch people in something that feels like *some*thing. (2007: 4–5)

Emotions have histories that are both private and, simultaneously, socially culturally-politically formed. The problem for me, and this is a perpetual difficulty, is how to elucidate emotions through holding together psychoanalysis and social-cultural theory (in my case, postcolonial theory) in order to provide depth of understanding? Furthermore, how can I hold together an analysis that unites psychoanalysis and social theory in a way that is fruitful and does not obfuscate complexity? The intricacy involved in tracing through emotions is that they are elusive and slippery and simultaneously provoke intensity of feeling. Ordinary affects are 'at once abstract and concrete, ordinary affects are more directly compelling than ideologies, as well as more fractious, multiplicitous, and unpredictable than symbolic meanings' (Stewart 2007: 4). The vexed question – How do emotions hinder or foster social justice? – underpins my concerns. For example, how do the emotions of fear, vulnerability, anger, hope and betrayal impede at best and paralyse at worst the making of a different and better society?

I endeavour to think through a theoretical framework based on the psychopolitical (Hook 2012), and I draw on psychoanalysis and postcolonial theory because, as Stuart Hall asserts, structural matters are connected to psychic life and cannot be separated out as we live through and identify with these structures (Schwarz 2000). Our very subjectivity, our ways of being, our emotions, fantasies and beliefs – the very stuff of who we are and how we live – are gained through these sociopolitical structures. Ideologies are lived, experienced, perpetuated and, unfortunately, go to the heart of subjectivities and cannot be sloughed off. This theoretical frame does not dismiss or sideline socio-political-historical factors – anything but – instead, it pays close attention to the interpenetration of these structures into subjectivities. Frantz Fanon's understandings of colonisation and colonised subjectivities are inspirational because he 'does not prescribe a hierarchy of relations between material reality and mental or corporeal experience' (Hook 2012: 102).

In one way this book is based on a particular version of humanism influenced by Edward Said, who writes (and it is worth quoting him in full):

> Humanism is not about withdrawal and exclusion. Quite the reverse: its purpose is to make more things available to critical scrutiny as the produce of human labour, human energies for emancipation and enlightenment, and, just as importantly, human misreadings and misinterpretations

of the collective past and present. There was never a misinterpretation that could not be revised, improved, or overturned. There was never a history that could not to some degree be recovered and compassionately understood in all its suffering and accomplishment. Conversely, there was never a shameful secret injustice or a cruel collective punishment or a manifestly imperial plan for domination that could not be exposed, explained, and criticized. (2004a: 22)

Postcolonialism, along with Western imperialism, causes untold damage and reproduces conditions that obstruct societies from recovery. My preoccupation is with how these material structures forged from postcolonialism and imperialism impact on and form subjectivities that are not injured due to private and personal biography and conditions but, rather, are profoundly social injuries. We need to politicise these injuries (Howe 1991) and our wounded attachments (Brown 1995). Postcolonial subjectivity is dense and so overdetermined that it eludes simplistic theorisation. We have no hope of understanding its complex formation unless we 'understand adequately what it sustains, what lends it potent affective qualities, what supports its most visceral aspects' (Hook 2012: 49). Repetition, conflict and identification are, I insist, central aspects of subjectivity, and these mechanisms are continually in operation in inhabiting a life and in subjection.

For my preoccupations to make sense, some context is required. The next brief section therefore summarises the pertinent events that have occurred in Egypt, while a more elaborate account is given throughout the book.

From the Present to the Past and Back Again

Adhaf Soueif pertinently points out that a 'revolution is a process, not an event. And, as you know, our Egyptian revolution is ongoing. And its path has not been smooth. How could it have been when the interests we are seeking to break free of are so powerful and so pervasive?' (2012: xiv). These persistent national and international interests have profoundly impeded the outcome of the political activity that has taken place in recent years in Egypt. On 25 January 2011, Egypt erupted in political activity. Midan Tahrir (Liberation Square) was taken over by protestors, who cut across lines of class, gender, age and religious faith, all demanding the resignation of the then president Hosni Mubarak and his government. This regime was widely perceived, with good reason, as motivated by self-interest and corruption. Mubarak and his government were perceived as severely inadequate due to their failure to tackle the acute and harsh problems from which the Egyptian population was suffering. Unemployment was soaring and the majority of young men under the age of 30 were unemployed. Inflation was high, and manufacturing was in severe decline, leading to the closure of many factories and businesses. In addition, education and health provision were in dire straits: for example, the decay of public hospitals was staggering and shocking, illustrating the inefficiency and corruption of governmental administration.

Above all, the corruption of central government, exemplified by the decision to install Gamal Mubarak (Hosni Mubarak's son) as the next president, led to public outrage that had no impact whatsoever on the decision. It was clear that the Mubarak family and their supporters could do what they wanted without consideration of the consequences for or impact on the Egyptian population. When Hosni Mubarak was interviewed on television about the increase of public political activity taking place, he contemptuously replied, 'Let them play', little imagining that the political demands would increase immensely and lead to his resignation in February 2011. In a state of excitement, optimism and disbelief, we (that is, the Egyptian population) witnessed these sociopolitical events and could not believe our good fortune. Egypt, we were convinced, was on the way to equality and social justice.

Since January 2011, the political situation in Egypt has been complex, fragile and turbulent. Yet, in seeming contradiction, little has changed. Following the ousting of Hosni Mubarak, the Supreme Council of the Armed Forces took over the country, promising that it would be an interim government. A new constitution was written and presidential elections were held that led to Muhammad Morsi from the Freedom and Justice Party (the political wing of the Muslim Brotherhood) becoming president. Quickly, staggeringly so, the Muslim Brotherhood ruled with the same repressive determination as the Mubarak regime. Within three weeks of coming to power, Muhammad Morsi was shouting on the TV, telling us that he would not tolerate any dissent from the views of the Muslim Brotherhood. Under their jurisdiction, a new constitution was put in place that excluded women and Christians and made clear that Egypt would be ruled entirely under a particular version of Islamic law.

There were promises that the Senate would be inclusive and contain Christians, Muslims who did not belong to the Muslim Brotherhood and women, but this did not occur; only men who belonged to the Muslim Brotherhood constituted the Senate. Violence against women escalated, especially against those who did not wear the *hijab*; the oppression of political views that did not adhere to those of the Muslim Brotherhood increased to a worrying degree, and there was little, if any, attempt to repair the corruption and decay of the Mubarak regime. Indeed, in November 2012, Morsi gave himself unprecedented powers, and it was clear that the Muslim Brotherhood would not countenance another election. Egyptians, on the whole, were disappointed, and many depicted the revolution of 2011 as the Stolen Revolution. Political activity, which had been ongoing, increased again, and many Egyptian people began to demonstrate with fervour and intent, and in large numbers, against the Muslim Brotherhood; the demonstrators included individuals who had previously voted eagerly and without hesitation for the Muslim Brotherhood. Ordinary citizens were dismayed by the incompetence of Muslim Brotherhood rule and, equally importantly, were aghast at its particular interpretation of Islam.

The then Field Marshal Al-Sisi offered to broker an agreement, 'but the Brothers flexed their muscles, deploying armed supporters to clear the anti-Islamist sit-in around the presidential palace in December 2012, killing and torturing dozens in the process' (Kandil 2014). The protests culminated in demonstrations which, in Egypt (if not elsewhere), were unprecedented. As Kandil (2014: 15–17) puts it pithily, 'Millions took to the streets, not once, but three times in the space of a month: to rebel against Morsi on 30 June, to celebrate his overthrow on 3 July, and to express their defiance of Islamist violence on 26 July'. In June 2013, Islamists set up camp outside the Rabaa al-Adawiya mosque in Cairo, as well as other camps elsewhere. Egyptian citizens were appalled and frightened by the presence of Islamic groups, including Al-Qaeda, who flew their black flag openly. The hate speech that poured forth from the camps against ordinary citizens was terrifying and worrying. For these reasons, most Egyptians accepted, albeit reluctantly, the massacres that took place while the camps were cleared. Since the summer of 2013, many active Muslim Brotherhood supporters have again been imprisoned and oppressed, the military is again in power and Abdul Fattah Al-Sisi is the president (there was a turnout of 48 per cent of the population, and Al-Sisi won 97 per cent of the vote). He is loved by many Egyptians and admired for his good looks, urbane dress code and ability to rule with leadership and authority. Other reasons for Al-Sisi's popularity are numerous: he is a member of the military and the military is widely respected; he is perceived as beyond corruption and as a leader who can act. Above all, it is widely believed that Al-Sisi will follow in Nasser's anti-imperialist footsteps and ensure that Egypt will be admired once again.

Many favourable analogies are made between Al-Sisi and Gamal Abdul Nasser (leader of the Free Officers who led the revolution in 1952 and was the president of Egypt from 1954 until 1969), and both are represented as 'Fathers of the Nation'. Memories of Nasser challenging Britain and winning the Suez War have been revived and provide ballast for a potent belief that Egypt will take its rightful place as *the* nation in the Arab world. These memories and narratives are reinforced by the new and massive project to extend and widen the Suez Canal in order to increase the number and size of ships able to use the canal. We (Egyptians) watched the extensive news coverage of the unveiling of these plans and, while we knew that the coverage was carefully orchestrated, we wept with relief that plans were being followed through to ensure that Egypt would be prosperous again.

The past, however, cannot simply be wiped out, despite desperate efforts by the Egyptian state and ordinary citizens to do so. As Julian Go (2013) writes, the post-independence years have been

> marked by continued exploitation, violence and global inequality. Furthermore, political decolonization did not herald the end of the West's power over the globe. While colonial relations of power officially receded, the older power relations simply took on more subtle, insidious, and even more potent forms, variously called 'neo-imperialism' or 'neo-colonialism'. (2013: 5)

The dominant discourse that Egypt has overcome the past is prevalent in political discourses and in the heartfelt narratives of Egyptian citizens, and is exemplified by the persistent use of the phrase 'Forget it'. The assertion that the nation – Egypt – has been rescued and is now a postcolonial nation has been used by different presidents with powerful effect, as interwoven with this reassuring narrative is the claim that the past has been overcome and therefore the injury and humiliation caused by colonialism have ended. At present, people speak of Nasser,

Sadat and Al-Sisi with respect and deference and refuse to utter the name of Mubarak because 'We do not want to remember'. This refusal to remember is understandable, but profound difficulties endure, nevertheless, when forgetting is preferable to robust recall, as these empty assertions at best hinder a confrontation with how the past refuses to go away despite all claims and hopes to the contrary.

Egypt at present is marked by the oppression of political dissent, the disturbing activity of the state and the persistent imprisonment of those who dissent (both activists on the 'left' and members of the Muslim Brotherhood) alongside the relentless poor material conditions for many of the Egyptian population. The Deep State is entrenched, as illustrated by the imprisonment of activists and members of the Muslim Brotherhood, many of whom are under the threat of the death penalty. The courts pass sentences with extraordinary speed – for example, sentences were passed on over 600 people who belong to the Muslim Brotherhood in less than two days and, in the case of radical activists, the judgement was passed within 11 minutes without the presence of either the defendants or their lawyers.

Egypt is divided and has been shattered by the events, experiences, emotions and broken hopes and dreams since January 2011. There are profound divisions in family and friendship networks, and it is difficult to know if these will ever be healed, as perhaps too much has been said which cannot be undone, and too much hurt caused by all concerned; the fractures are deep. In short and perhaps rather crudely, Egypt is divided across the following lines: those in support of the military and Al-Sisi, those who support neither the military nor the Muslim Brotherhood and those who are members of the Muslim Brotherhood and other fundamentalist organisations.

Injured Subjectivities

While working on an edited collection entitled *Public Emotions* (2007) my co-editors (Susannah Radstone, Corine Squire and Perri 6) and I wanted to explore the consequences of emotions on public life. We encouraged the contributors to think through the consequences of emotions without making a judgement as to whether the emotion under discussion was positive or negative. I want to revisit the matter of emotions, to place judgement much more closely at the core of the discussion and to think closely about what is transmitted, absorbed and perpetuated. The everyday is the specific focus of exploration in relation to ordinary citizens and daily living. A psychosocial studies conceptual framework is essential in order to draw out the impact on injured subjectivities, everyday practices and everyday living, with the dilemmas and complexities they all entail. I am concerned with the socio-political conditions that impede the possibility of responsible citizenship; by this I mean the compassionate, ordinary, responsive and responsible qualities that are necessary for a 'life of the mind', to draw on a redolent phrase from Hannah Arendt (1978).

I am preoccupied with the interrelationship between events, narratives and discourses, emotions and fantasy on subjectivity and everyday life. Importantly, this interlinked chain of terms, I argue, is the glue of socio-political-historical life. I attempt to illuminate the 'noncoherent, the incommensurate, and the scenic, as well as the attachment, intimacy, exhaustion, and the unlivable but animating desires for rest or for the simple life' (Stewart 2007: 7). I draw partly on novels and autobiographies to elucidate and explore that which is elusive, slippery and silenced in many official discourses and everyday narratives. As I am engaged in understanding what is troubling and troublesome about subjectivity and the socio-political order in Egypt, these novels and autobiographies provide a resource that is not usually available, and include the following: *In the Eye of the Sun* (Soueif 1992), *The Beginning and the End* (Mahfouz 1985), *A Border Passage* (Ahmed 1999), *Al-Bab Al Maftah* (Al-Zayyat 1960, *The Open Door* 2005), *Butterfly Wings* (Salmawy 2014) and *Friendly Fire* (Al Aswany 2009).

This book is my attempt to explore, understand and penetrate once again – but from a different vantage point – the various processes and socio-political dynamics, emotions and fantasies and their effect on ordinary lives. This is never just an abstract problem but is full of emotion, and I am haunted by previous generations in my family and by what Toni Morrison refers to as 'The Thing'. As Avery Gordon writes, 'Morrison is clear that *the thing* is full of the sedimented conditions from colonialism that persist, endure and have persistent effects' (Gordon 1997: 5). As Adam Phillips explores in his essay entitled 'Keeping Our Distance', writing a history and, I would add, an account of the present, 'invariably involves issues of distance and proximity' (Phillips 2012: 212). I feel too close to past and present events; they are an essential part of who I am, and I am bound both to Egypt as a country and, crucially, to my family and friends. All of this can be interpreted as overly subjective, following a commonplace or usual understanding of academic scholarship, and I hope through this proximity to elucidate the complexities of Egyptian society and what it means to inhabit everyday life there. So, while I feel too close to recent events, and have little, if any, distance from my Egyptian family, I can simultaneously wish to distance myself from certain events and am unable to bear my knowledge of the killings and torture that are taking place. It is an emotional effort for me to confront these massacres perpetrated by the police and the army in the name of the state.

Affect and fantasy are vital to understanding our investments in certain forms of representation, as 'memory and desire play their part in the construction of history for all writers, in terms of both what is sidelined and what is recuperated' (Andrijasevic et al. 2014: 5). Emotion, fantasy and beliefs have operated powerfully as I have worked on this book and have led to paralysis and anxiety about whether or not I have understood matters sufficiently, alongside the overwhelming concern that I am betraying people I love and to whom I have important attachments. I cannot bear the relentless oppression, the 'stuckness' of everyday life and the economic insecurities, the intransigence of the role of the Deep State, the fractures within families (including my own) and the unyielding pointing of the finger that leads to circulating blame – in short, the political, social and emotional upheaval.

'The Thing', with all its complexities, emotional difficulties and theoretical puzzles, will not let go. I conceptualise memory, narrative, emotions and events as part of an interlinked and inextricable chain, together with the fundamental role of fantasy and the unconscious. Avery Gordon (1997) in *Ghostly Matters* explores how haunting raises spectres, alters the experience of being in time and unsettles our viewpoint of temporalities as linear. The past, present and future cannot be separated out as they are fused in an intertwined web. These spectres and ghosts are all too real and cannot be dismissed as figments of the imagination. According to Stephen Frosh (2013a: 4), Freud was all too troubled about the way that there is something very real about ghosts. Psychoanalysis, as Frosh points out, disturbs any idea of rational communication and the illusion that there can be straightforward exchange from one person to another.

This monograph contests a tendency within postcolonial theory to understand the current events occurring in Egypt as resistance to

Western imperialism and/or the end of postcolonialism (Dabashi 2012) or a rather romantic positioning of activists (Iskander 2013) as agentic. Rather, I am preoccupied with closely tracing through the persistence of history while paying close attention to the discontinuities from the past. In short, I am deeply troubled by the events and, simultaneously, by the theoretical explanations that are provided, as the dominant understanding bypasses important matters of how history is repeated persistently and of how many people are invested psychically, emotionally and socially in Egyptian society, which remains unchanged. Adherence to that which is known and familiar may evoke conflict and distress while simultaneously providing certainty and security.

Much valuable work has been undertaken on the political conditions in Egypt (see Mitchell 2002, Osman 2010, Kandil 2012) and cannot and should not be dismissed or undermined. I aim to add to this theoretical framework through elaborating a close understanding of the analysis of an injured node of postcolonised subjectivities. I am frequently confronted by a theoretical challenge which remains unresolved, and this confrontation focuses on how to analyse or at least be cognisant of the enduring power of colonialism and its psychic effects while simultaneously recognising that subjectivities are not formed totally through the socio-political-psychic conditions of colonialism or, indeed, postcolonialism. The West and the United States, after all, are not the centre of everyone's universe, and yet lives are lived in relation to the relentless dominating power of the West. Human beings also engage with the society in which they live, and have complex perceptions of and relationships to themselves and others that are not necessarily marked by imperialism. As Hall writes, there is the deeply unresolved question

> as to how to reconcile – or at least hold in a proper balance – *both* Fanon's spectacular demonstrations of the power of the racial binary to *fix*, and Bhabha's equally important and theoretically productive argument that all binary systems of power are nevertheless, *at the same time*, often if not always, troubled and subverted by ambivalence and disavowal. Our dilemma is how to *think together* the overwhelming power of the binary, which persists despite everything in all racially inflected systems of power and representation. (1996a: 27)

Nussbaum (2008), in *Upheavals of Thought*, provides a sustained exploration of emotions and their centrality to human life and identity. I am reliant on this viewpoint and, throughout this book, I explore a variety of emotions such as loss, anger, disappointment, love, anxiety, triumph, hope and guilt, which may both hinder and facilitate the recovery of a postcolonised society and promote well-being in a society that has been profoundly damaged and which, indeed, continues to damage its citizens. Emotions are messy and contradictory and play their part in the production of narratives, interpretations of events and participation in everyday living, but this is not an adequate reason to render them absent or marginal from theoretical analysis, particularly as they can unsettle that which is known. Emotions unsettle because of the uncomfortable knowledge about the self that they can provoke and the inner chaos and ambivalences towards self and other that they can reveal. There is no reason whatsoever to believe in the illusion that relationships between human beings are smooth, simple or conflict free for, as Daniel Mendelsohn rather poignantly writes, 'Closeness can lead to emotions other than love. It's the ones who have been too intimate with you, lived [or loved] in too close quarters, seen too much of your pain or envy, or … your shame, who, at the crucial moment, can be too easy to cut out, to exile, to expel, to kill off' (2007: 160).

As Nussbaum asserts, while there is something 'excruciating' about emotions (2008: 16), we should neither neglect them nor, indeed,

> regard them as immune from rational criticism: for they may be no more reliable than any other set of entrenched beliefs. There may even be special reasons for regarding them with suspicion, given their specific content and the nature of their history. (2008: 2)

We need, however, to be cautious and ensure that theory and emotions are not split off as though there were no relationship between thought and feeling. Susannah Radstone explores the interrelationship between theory and affect in her (2007a) essay entitled 'Theory and Affect: Undivided Worlds' and argues that thought and affect are profoundly interlinked.

It is important, nonetheless, to find ways in which to speak of how 'a reeling present is composed out of heterogeneous and noncoherent singularities' (Stewart 2007: 4) and simultaneously to trace through how ordinary life can alter and at the same time be maintained and how inhabiting a life involves alternating between feeling 'stuck' to reeling from overwhelming emotions and fantasies. There is, as Stewart affirms, the persistent need to find a way of exploring emotions that

captures 'something of their intensity and texture that makes them hab-
itable and animate' (2007: 4).

Tracing Through Wounded Subjectivities

Attachment to the past is a taken-for-granted value, and this naturalised
viewpoint will be prised apart in order to trace through the consequences of this stance. I am preoccupied with tracing through how the
past, present and future intertwine to form subjectivities. My emphasis
is on elucidating how events (past and present) impact on and form
Egyptian subjectivities. I focus on everyday life and attempt to explore
the dynamics and thickness of ordinary living. I try to follow the salutary example of Pierre Bourdieu et al. (2016; his co-authors are a team
of sociologists), who trace through various everyday examples and
reveal in meticulous detail the social suffering experienced by many
people who inhabit contemporary society.

The writing of history is a troubling matter, as it requires acute attention to which events, discourses and narratives are pertinent. In addition,
it is never straightforward to trace the lines of alliances, identifications
and descent, and we need, therefore, to persistently ask 'along what
lines of conscious and unconscious inheritance histories – individual
and collected – are moulded and passed down' (Rose 1998: 42). To
say that history is important is a banal statement; however, thinking
through how to write a history of a deeply troubled society is challenging and troubling as it poses questions about what should or should not
be emphasised, about theoretical and political investments and, perhaps
above all, about how to write a narrative which conveys the complexities of a society so frequently misrepresented.

I have tried to revisit the matter of emotions, to place judgement
much more closely at the core of the discussion and to think carefully
about what is transmitted, absorbed and perpetuated. Everyday living
and experiences are the distinct focal point of exploration in relation
to ordinary citizens and daily life. A psychosocial studies conceptual
framework is essential in order to draw out the impact on injured subjectivities and everyday practices, and living daily with the dilemmas
and complexities this entails. To explore some aspects of the socio-
emotional complex in Egypt that impede at best, and/or paralyse at
worst, an effective society from being established, I concentrate on

interior life as one route through to deepening understandings of the dire state of contemporary Egypt. Dominant theorisations tend to converge on structural inequalities such as global economy, imperialism, historical events and the inglorious role played by the United Kingdom, European nations and the United States, and these understandings are valuable and valid. They do not, however, provide a full explanation, which, I argue, requires a focus on interiority. We must 'look inward, name and confront those attitudes, norms, practices and relations that cannot be simply explained away by external and structural patterns, forces and processes' (Al-Ali 2014: 123).

I will endeavour to look inward in two different ways. First, by positing that the processes of colonialism have been internalised in Egypt, which hinders full and adequate political authority from taking place because relentless authoritarianism and patriarchy exist. Second, looking inward requires me to explore matters of subjectivity in an effort to avoid perpetuating denial and the insistence that problems are all external. Looking inward, furthermore, attempts to restore full subjectivity to Egyptian citizens and to give full due to Fanon's plea that conceptualisations of interiority take into account the more disturbing and negative aspects of human beings.

Colonisation does not, alas, just float on the skin but, rather, goes to the heart of human beings, as the contempt, denigration and refusal are taken in and affect various aspects of human life: the capacity to speak confidently with the pronoun 'I', to recognise self and other, to inhabit language, to live a life with some confidence and not from a position of perceived 'inferiority' and to work towards building a good society. As Fanon expresses it poignantly, 'All I wanted was to be a man among other men. I wanted to come lithe and young into a world that was ours and to help build it together' (Fanon 1986: 85).

There are a further number of matters that impact on the development of an understanding, and I gesture to part of the context at a particular period of time to highlight a number of issues. First, how the events taking place in the present profoundly influence the questions asked and analysis gained. The past, personal and public, pulses through the present and none of us are immune from the effects of events or indeed from the emotional history we bring to our understandings of these events. Second, the influence of the events taking place on understanding is part of the texture of conceptualising the incidents. I do not know what shape this book would have taken if the context had been different, as

I have no way of knowing what histories, thoughts, doubts or imaginings would have been provoked: it is an unknown monograph. I provide socio-political context to point to how actual events provoke certain narratives and memories. It is, of course, impossible to know whether or not there would be narratives and analysis that would cut across time and place but with a different emphasis. One theoretical matter when trying to trace through 'The Thing', as Schwarz points out, is how we will know the impressions and the effects – in fact, how we will perceive them in the first place because, if

> it is hard to get a perspective on this problem, even indeed to know where to look, it is not only because of the complexities involved but also because it is a history we're still living. Its power to organize the present is not yet finished. (2011: 5)

This is an issue of temporality and an important aspect of postcolonial theory which focuses on the view that contemporary societies carry with them the active ghosts of the past.

Third, it is difficult to just write about the event *as an event* and to adopt a seemingly neutral stance. Despite my many attempts to write about the events without interpretation, this proved impossible, as my interpretations and historical-socio-cultural-affective location always leaked. I could quite easily go back over and delete any interpretation, but I want to illustrate the ease and speed with which one's understandings and histories are always potently at work. For example, I grew up with and imbibed the view of the Muslim Brotherhood as dangerous, threatening and *the* enemy within Egypt, and I find it impossible to think of them in any other way. While other authors – for example, Dabashi (2012) – conceptualise the Arab Spring as a resistance to colonialism and are optimistic that a new democratic order is on the horizon, I am much more cautious and indeed pessimistic about the viewpoint that Egypt is, or has been, on the verge of becoming a society based on social justice.

I conceptualise memory, narrative, emotions and events as part of an interlinked and inextricable chain, together with the fundamental role of fantasy and the unconscious. I want to focus on fantasy and on the complexity of temporality in relation to how colonialism haunts and to trace through a few of the many layers that constitute 'The Thing'. The effects of colonisation have been profoundly internalised and the consequences are inescapable as they form part of the socio-political-affective landscape. This raises a critically important theoretical and method-ological issue that rests on the issue of judgement. To be clear, I take the view – and I am becoming increasingly stubborn about this – that judgement cannot and should not be avoided. My understanding of judgement is based on Hannah Arendt's notes in her posthumously published book *The Life of the Mind* (1978). It is difficult to know, when analysing narratives, *the difference between 'narrative as told' and 'narrative as lived'*. By 'narrative as told', I mean the narratives we tell and believe about ourselves, other human beings, the nation we inhabit and so on – and these narratives tend to the normative, rational, coherent and socially acceptable and dominant accounts. I conceptual-ise 'narrative as lived' as paying attention to silences, absences, affect, disavowal – a narrative that cannot be spoken due to the unconscious, fantasy, irrational thoughts and feelings and those that are inchoate and cannot be known or tolerated or indeed cohered into a narrative – but these emotions, thoughts and belief systems operate powerfully and with profound consequences – they are part of 'The Thing'.

Which emotions are provoked by the socio-political conditions that we inhabit? Which emotions facilitate and/or hinder socio-political engagements? We have to guard against thinking emotions through the binary division of positive and negative, as I have argued above. Emotions and their consequences are complex, contradictory and fre-quently messy. Walkerdine and Jimenez's careful monograph *Gender, Work and Community after De-Industrialisation* (2012) explores how a particular community coped, or not, with insecurity. I take the work of Walkderdine and Jimenez as a fine example of how to draw out and elu-cidate divergent voices, belief systems and the contradictions embedded in societies that are marked by complex affiliations. They warn against simplistic judgements of good and bad affiliations to explore

> how people live and experience the historical events they live through and because there is often a split between notions of solidarity, resilience, resis-tance (good) and victimhood, trauma, pain and pathology. (bad) (2012: 11)

This monograph is composed of seven chapters including this introduc-tory chapter, which has hopefully illuminated the various themes and preoccupations that are interwoven through this book, in which repeti-tion, conflict and identification are the main strands. I am concerned with the repetitions of the past in the present and the future and with tracing through the ways that the political is personal and impacts on ordinary citizens and everyday living, and how the seemingly neutral political sphere is replete with emotions and fantasies. I hope to provide a different understanding of a postcolonial society and the impediments to its recovery. This monograph concentrates on Egypt to elucidate relevant aspects of cultural theory (postcolonial and psychosocial) that are pertinent to understanding the socio-political situation there, and to explicate aspects of postcolonial and psychosocial theory in the extended analysis that these two theoretical frames offer. As I am attempting to draw out the various threads of Egyptian society, finding a logical order for this book is not straightforward as the lines cross and loop in an intricate web. A bigger confrontation is that Egyptian society is complicated, jagged and dense (just like all societies and cultures), and through this book I am attempting to convey the complexities involved in inhabiting this particular society. Similarly, I do not take a linear approach and move across the present to the past and loop back again as I understand temporalities to be an interconnected web that cannot, and should not, be separated.

Living with Perpetual Insecurity is the title of chapter 2, which focuses on describing the vexed material conditions and dynamics in Egypt and drawing out the fear and disappointment that are felt due to unceasing poverty and insecurity, leading ultimately to shame, humiliation, profound anxiety and the corrosion of bonds. The despair can be overwhelming and can lead, understandably, to envy and a lack of compassion towards others. Egypt does not have an adequate welfare system that includes benefits for the sick, disabled and unemployed, nor an acceptable education system, the result of which is poor physical and mental health. This chapter will elucidate and explore the effects of inhabiting perpetual insecurity on people's lived experiences. The use of the word 'perpetual' is deliberate, as insecure material conditions have always existed for the poor and insecurity is now increasing for the middle classes too. Corruption has been a way of life in Egypt over many generations, and it is difficult to gauge whether it will be overcome by the present regime.

The Intimacy of Subjection is the focus of chapter 3, which explores the complex subjectivities of the Egyptian people. Belonging and connectedness are crucial and valued aspects of subjectivities in Egypt, and this chapter explores how belonging to a family, the community and the nation provides attachments that are essential for subjectivity to be gained and sustained. Belonging and attachment can, however, also impede, as perpetuating that which is known takes place through adhesive bonds. Colonisation leads to wounded subjectivities, and this chapter illuminates the injuries that persist. These injured subjectivities involve the wish to disavow the damage of the past, the denial of the internalisation of inferiorities and the persistent denigration of those who are deemed as other, alongside the desire for power, authority and status.

Chapter 4 is titled *Enduring Repetition: Events, Narratives, Emotions.* The political is always personal and leads to conflicts (inter and intra), and this chapter will focus on drawing out the impact and consequences of these various national and international dynamics on 'ordinary' Egyptian citizens. The emotions provoked – anger, humiliation, triumph and hopelessness – will be elucidated. Chapter 5 takes gender and agency as its theme; its title *Female Agency: Struggling against Constraint* hopefully illustrates the main issues that are tackled. The matter of gender (with a particular focus on femininity) will be elucidated in terms of both everyday life and political agency. Within postcolonial theory, women can be marginalised or positioned either as full of agency or – the opposite – as helpless victims of patriarchy. The opportunities and challenges presented to men and women will be traced through in order to provide both a nuanced account of gender and political activity and a more intricate conceptual framework. This theoretical investigation will, hopefully, push boundaries of understanding and provide a careful analysis of current theories of gender, religion and secularism, agency, resistance and compliance.

Chapter 6, entitled *Power, Domination, Struggle*, provides a description of the long history of political activity in Egypt which reaches back to the nineteenth century. Contrary to the mistaken belief in the West, this political activism has been undertaken by both men and women. Despite this committed political activism, a society based on social justice and equality has not been built in Egypt. Instead, its socio-political-judicial institutions and structures are forged out of corruption, inequality and exploitation. In this chapter, I will draw out the various dynamics, process and ideologies in order to enable an intricate understanding of socio-political activism in Egypt and the various gendered dynamics that take place. The consequences on Egyptian subjects as citizens will drive this chapter. Various emotions have driven activism – hope, disappointment, fear, anger and desperation – but it is critical that a romanticism of political activism does not obscure the relentless failures.

The final chapter, entitled *The Essential Endeavour: Being Accountable*, explores the necessary challenge required of human beings if they are to live a more ethical life. I am preoccupied (obsessed may be a more accurate description!) with the impact of inhabiting a society and political system that is profoundly authoritarian, deeply oppressive and repressive and marked by devastating corruption. Despite the impressive political activity and engagement of younger generations in Egypt, there is no sign of any of this easing and weakening. Indeed, the destruction of human bonds, along with that of public spaces, is deepening (Young-Bruehl 2006). Using Arendt's (1968) view of a totalitarian society to describe an aspect of Egypt at this present period (2013–2016), I am concerned with the following question: Why do we act against our best interests? This is a theme with universal resonances but, needless to say, the enquiry has to be located within the specifics of time and place, with a focus on what kind of society (as in form and compassion) could facilitate full political participation. Judgement, though, in my view, is central to any investigation and I am influenced profoundly by Arendt's conceptualisation of judgement. She argues (1978) that judgement, more than any other mental ability, is exercised in relationship with others and that, importantly, judgement forms the basis of what Kant termed 'enlarged mentality' and enables the possibility of engaged citizenship. This final chapter explores the responsibilities of being accountable in this complex and troubling socio-political society.

In short, this book addresses recent socio-political events in Egypt and explores the repetitions, identifications, failures (or lack thereof) of political authority. It builds on postcolonial theory and a psychosocial studies framework to explore and theorise the following themes: the inheritance of history, the problematic socio-political-affective loyalties in political allegiances, the impact on everyday life, gender and agency, repetition and identification, and social justice.

Chapter 2

Living with Perpetual Insecurity

In Mahfouz's (1985) novel *The Beginning and the End*, a family struggles to keep out of poverty following the death of the husband and father. The novel follows his four children as they attempt to forge a life for themselves with varying degrees of integrity. Money and sexual desire are intertwined in this novel, as the family ignores Hassan's relationship with a prostitute (he is the eldest son) and pays no heed to Nefisa (the only female child) earning money from sex work as she provides an important source of income. This distressing novel depicts how living in poverty can corrode emotionally, physically and spiritually. It represents the abjection of poverty and the desperate attempts to avoid hardship.

Egyptian society has long been marked by corruption and chronic exploitation, and Egyptians have suffered inexorably as a consequence of inhabiting this fraudulent and corrosive economic system. This chapter will explore the psychic effects of inhabiting a corrupt system that is based on chronic and persistent inequality. Many emotions are evoked, including anxiety, envy, anger, despair and shame. Everyone, I argue, is affected and tainted by having to negotiate living in this grossly unequal society; needless to say, for many, it is an endless struggle to survive.

From Midan Tahrir in Cairo and across the whole of Egypt, 'Bread, Freedom and Social Justice' was the rallying call during the January 2011 Revolution.[1] This slogan, which dominated the demonstrations, encapsulates the failures of successive Egyptian governments (led by Gamal Abdel Nasser, Anwar Sadat and Hosni Mubarak) to build a society based on social justice and equality. These political, social and economic failures led, understandably and inevitably, to profound disaffection and disappointment. Egyptians filled city centres shouting out their claims for a better life. Eroded and depleted by years of corruption, exploitation, unemployment and the struggle to survive, the majority of the Egyptian populace had reached breaking point. These words – 'bread, freedom, social justice' – sum up pithily what is required to repair the years of socio-political-economic corruption and profoundly damaging governance. 'Bread, freedom and social justice' – though it has to be pointed out that 'dignity' was used interchangeably with 'social justice' – nevertheless, these three demands express an interlinked chain that are the basic requirements for a decent life. Dignity and/or social justice are unattainable without material security and, in turn, material security is impossible without social justice.

Material conditions for much of the population are dire and the following statistics are salutary: 26 per cent live in abject poverty, many people live on $2 a day, 70 per cent of the population are dependent on food subsidies in the form of a ration card system and 31 per cent of children under the age of five suffer from malnutrition (UN 2014). In July 2015, inflation rocketed and food became extremely expensive – including staples such as bread and sugar (meat for many was out of the question). An example from my local baker illustrates the rate of inflation. This excellent baker sells bags of breadsticks (a luxury that only the middle class can afford); between January and June 2014, the cost of breadsticks doubled from 50 pence a bag to £1 sterling. The price of bread (*ayshe baladi*), which everyone can afford to buy, increased considerably, the size of the loaf became smaller and, of equal importance, poor quality of flour was used.

Still, today, insecurity is compounded by high unemployment, and it is especially difficult for young men under 35 to find work; gaining a job, any job, involves calling in favours and the skilful manipulation of social networks. Material conditions affect men and women equally but with different consequences. Women carry the burden of feeding and caring for the family and poor, and working-class women frequently undertake household tasks for middle-class families, including cleaning, washing, cooking and childcare; frequently, alas, the women are paid little. It is a different situation for middle-class women, who are not expected to contribute in any way whatsoever to household expenditure. Within Egyptian society, it is incumbent on men to provide materially for the family, and the failure to do so is perceived and experienced as shameful. Egypt does not have an adequate welfare system; therefore, there is no state help for those who are ill, disabled or elderly. Those who require material help are reliant on an informal system that operates within families and also charitable donations. Religious organisations and non-governmental organisations (NGOs) are crucial providers of material support. This lack of a material system and structure leads to poor physical and mental health. The use of the word 'perpetual' in the title of this chapter is intentional and is chosen to indicate that profound insecure material conditions have always existed for the poor and now material insecurity is increasing for the middle classes as well.

There is little information on social policy in Egypt. Past government reports have skimmed over the extreme problems of health, poverty and education, and it is unclear whether this will change under the present regime led by the current (since June 2014) President Fattah Al-Sisi. It is difficult to find adequate statistics for Egypt as these are largely massaged to provide a better image than is actually the case, resulting in a wide chasm between the actual state of profound difficulties and the false image provided by government agencies.

It is important to outline the dire state of Egypt's economy in order to provide a context for the everyday experiences and struggles of the Egyptians. The decrease in the rate of gross domestic product illustrates the situation; in 2010–2011, it was expected to be only 1.6 per cent, down from 5.1 per cent in 2009–2010 (Abou and Zaazou 2013). Egypt is in the bottom 40 per cent of all developing countries, according to the 2014 United Nations Development Report (UN 2014). It is placed 110th in world rankings; education, healthcare and transportation have deteriorated drastically. Public hospitals are slum buildings and there are many photographs, taken by doctors, that are easily available on the Internet, and which show the dreadful conditions of disrepair and filth. To illustrate this further, I was once passing a building that I imagined was about to be condemned and discovered to my horror that it was a public hospital. There are over 60 children to a class in state schools (all middle-class parents send their children to private schools). Crushing socio-economic conditions, exploitation and corruption mark Egypt. At present (summer 2016), there is little hope – inflation is rocketing and unemployment is severe and is the norm to the extent that, typically, I do not know of a single family who is not affected by it.

Egypt is an important country both geographically and politically. Situated at the borders of Europe yet in the north of Africa, it is close to the oil reserves in the Gulf. Egypt controls the Suez Canal, the world's most important trade route. It continues to play a pivotal mediating role in the Palestinian–Israeli conflict and in international attempts to achieve a resolution. In addition, as Osman (2010: 5) points out, it is the birthplace and centre of a number of trends and ideas, including Arab nationalism. Egypt, though, has a long history of being invaded and colonised, from the later Islamic empires to Napoleon's France and colonial Britain. Geography and nature have been generous but history has been harsh (2010: 15). Egypt has frequently fallen prey to invaders and, throughout its long history its inhabitants have been second-class citizens. Towards the end of the nineteenth and the early twentieth centuries, Egypt was transformed from a country that exported food and textiles into a country whose economy became 'dominated by the production of a single commodity, raw cotton, for the global textile industry of Europe' (Mitchell 1991: 16). The effect on Egypt of becoming dependent on a single commodity was profound. Mitchell elucidates the effects as follows: enormous growth in imports (textiles and food); a network of roads, railways, police stations and, of significance,

> a new relationship to the land, which became a privately owned commodity concentrated in the hands of a small, powerful and increasingly wealthy social class [alongside the] influx of Europeans, seeking to make fortunes, find employment, transform agricultural production or impose colonial control. (1991: 16)

These effects persist in present-day conditions in the country, and are the strong foundations on which exploitation, corruption and economic inequality are built.

Material Conditions

I now present an abridged account of the economic conditions and policies, both of present-day Egypt and of the successive governments of presidents Nasser (1954–1970), Sadat (1970–1981) and Mubarak (1981–2011); the consequences of these policies will be followed through in detail. Egypt under Nasser managed to overthrow, in part, some vestiges of the country's colonial past, but there was a profound failure to create and consolidate a society based on social justice at the level of internal and domestic politics. Gamal Abdel Nasser was the first Egyptian to rule Egypt for centuries, and the excitement and hope this raised cannot be overestimated. In 1953, the military government took power securely and began to change internal politics, attempting to build a fairer society. As Osman (2010: 45) points out, the economic underpinning of the Nasserite transformation was twofold: reform of landownership and reform of the public sector. Land reform, a fairer distribution of land away from the landowners and towards the *fellaheen* (peasantry), was popular and had immense social effects. The Nasserite economic revolution also created a new public sector and a new class of state-owned factories, companies and enterprises. In addition, almost all of Egypt's sizable businesses were nationalised in an attempt to remodel the structure of wealth by transferring ownership from a narrow capitalist class to millions of ordinary employees, poor labourers and struggling workers. Nasser's project was given an inclusive national appeal by its emphasis on civic notions such as social equality, identification with the poor and Egypt's role as the leader of the Arab world free of an Islamic dimension (Osman 2010: 51). Despite robust attempts by the Nasserite government to strengthen Egypt's domestic production, to enable employment for all and to build up the civil service, their fiscal policies were not successful. As Julian Go (2013: 5) points out, decolonisation promised independence from the past and 'a blessed future – a future whereby colonial exploitation would be replaced with economic "development" and social "progress"'. The Egyptians are waiting, with scant hope, for a blessed future to arrive.

Sadat enabled a more open-door financial system based on the free market, and this is perceived as either progressive or not depending on the political views held in relation to the benefits of global capitalism. Sadat introduced a more liberal capitalist system for the economy, usually described as *Al-infitah* (opening up). This move, undertaken in 1974, was designed to open Egypt up to foreign trade, investment and market economics. Sadat's economic policy was simultaneously a political project, as he endeavoured to position Egypt as one of the United States' key allies in the region. Sadat admired the Shah of Iran and, in an interview conducted in 1974, declared that the Shah 'was a brilliant and extraordinary man' (Kandil 2012: 157). Sadat disputed the view that Russia and America were two superpowers, as he perceived

the United States as *the only* superpower. In the long term, Sadat aimed
to shift Egypt from the Nasserite vision of Arab nationalism to providing

> prosperity (*rakhaa*) that would spread over Egypt as a result of a massive
> reduction in the military budget, and the transformation of the country
> from a stalwart of the Arab 'solidarity front' into a regional investment
> destination open for business, trade, commerce and high finance. (Osman
> 2010: 118, italics in the original)

This strategy enabled an expanding bourgeoisie and the upper echelons
of the military to use every opportunity for monetary gain and commer-
cial expansion. The economist and journalist Mohammed Heikel sums
up the situation rather pithily. Egypt, he writes,

> was not being transformed from a planned to a market economy but rather to
> a supermarket economy ... Egyptian society was now divided between the
> 'fat cats' and their hangers-on, perhaps 150,000 people at most, on one side,
> and the rest of the population on the other. (quoted in Kandil 2012: 164)

Following Anwar Sadat's assassination, Mubarak ruled Egypt from
1981 until February 2011. Mubarak inherited a regime that had broken
its promises, if not its obligations, to the poor and had allied itself firmly
to the bourgeoisie, who were increasingly controlling the economy for
their own benefit. At the beginning of his presidency, Mubarak was
perceived as a leader who would bring balance to Egypt. He seemed to
manage this, and his

> 'speeches, his choice of words, the way he described himself and his
> vision for the country's future suggested a man who was concerned less
> with his legacy or with how he was viewed as a leader and more with his
> capacity to deliver. Mubarak seemed pragmatic, wholly concerned with
> Egypt's immediate economic problems, the inheritance of *al-infitah*'.
> (Osman 2010: 167)

The economic situation was very severe, and, without significant
intervention, the trajectory would continue to be problematic for many
reasons: massive debt, a growing population, increasing unemployment
and, significantly, a manufacturing industry that produced little. There
was no attempt to institute rules, regulations and laws that might have
facilitated a successful economy (Cook 2012).

Egypt's economic situation was, and remains, dire and the current need for a different economic order arises from a number of various and interlinked matters: chronic insecurity, enduring exploitative and corrupt economic practices alongside 'official indifference to [the] increasingly grim circumstances' (Cook 2012: 184). It is unclear whether the present regime is as indifferent or as incompetent as previous governments.

Belonging, Exploitation, Denigration

Egypt is a society with a long history of colonisation and marked by insecurity and precarious economic conditions. Due to its history of colonisation, as with other colonised societies, insecurity and coercive violence are a constant presence.

As Timothy Mitchell (1991) and David Graeber (2014) argue, material conditions and the moral socio-political order are interlinked, as a fair economic structure provides material security while, simultaneously, a moral order is based on social justice. Contemporary neo-liberal conditions and a history of colonisation that persists in the present are interlinked profoundly and demand discipline in relation to individualism, regulation, productivity and obedience. Walkerdine and Jimenez (2012) provide an important account of the effects of neo-liberalism on people and argue that under neo-liberal conditions people have become extracted into the abstract category of labour. It is money, not human beings, that is the dominant value, as David Graeber states:

> Underneath the essential fabric of our institutions today – state and market, our most basic conceptions of the nature of freedom, morality, sociality – all of which have been shaped by a history of war, conquest, and slavery in ways we're no longer capable of even perceiving because we can no longer imagine things any other way. (Graeber 2014: 14)

The history of war, conquest and slavery must also include the conditions of colonisation, characterised by 'the usurping of raw materials produced by the colonized countries, the exploitation of their cheap labour, and the marketing of finished products produced by the colonial countries' (Amin 2006: 23). Colonisation, historically and in the present, produces violence, degradation and exploitation simultaneously, both for the individual subject and for societies that have been colonised. These latter are positioned by coloniser societies as being in need of 'development' due to the perceived inherent socio-political structures that apparently were, and are, 'backward'. This argument runs along the following lines: economic 'development' is seemingly impossible, as Egyptian society prevents progressive movement. Moreover, Egyptian national culture is said to 'inculcate a fatalistic attitude to life, excessive respect for the past, resistance to change' (Amin 2006: 24).

Violence and cruelty occur due to the denigration of colonised societies and because the discipline of contemporary political economy requires a set of psychic and ethical dispositions and a social body that is forged out of neo-liberal subjectivity. James Ferguson argues stringently that thinking about the social world we inhabit, which is built upon massive and extreme inequality, requires dealing 'with (rather than denouncing) this reality … going beyond pious wishing for equality to ask how *in*equalities are socially institutionalized, and whether such modes of institutionalization are politically or ethically preferable to others' (Ferguson 2013: 232).

Neo-liberalism demands that human beings be autonomous, free from constraint and obligation, disciplined and in thrall to the work ethic, productive and accepting of any work conditions, no matter how exploitative (see Davidson and Rutherford 2011, a special issue on many aspects of neo-liberalism). Violence, denigration and contempt, I insist, occur because colonisation is about the perceived necessity of bringing the colonised to the point 'where they can become political subjects in a modern sense, capable of self-submission to the *regularity* of law and of attachment to abstract principles rather than affective ties' (Lloyd 2003: 212). Symbolic violence occurs because the colonised subject has to comply with the demands of neo-liberal capital in order to achieve success in the labour force.

While neo-liberal societies require individualism and autonomy, Egyptian subjectivities are built out of relationality and interdependence (Joseph 1999). Subjectivity is made from, and sustained through, relationships with others, since social connection and interdependence are fundamental aspects of identity. All subjectivities are formed through interdependence (see Benjamin 1998 and Butler 2004 for sustained discussions on intersubjectivity), and for Egyptians these social connections are explicitly valued as part of social identity. Moral value is not accorded to autonomy, nor is individuality valued, as people are understood, and understand themselves, as nodes in systems of relationships. In short, subjectivity is constituted by and through relationships with others. Dependence and belonging are fundamental aspects of identity in Egypt, and Egyptian society is a social system that is made through collective affiliations. Dependency should not be understood as constraining but, rather, as providing valuable bonds and connections. However, it is more profound than that because '*being* someone also implies *belonging* to someone' (Ferguson 2013: 228). Belonging, though, does entail paternalistic and hierarchical relations of authority, and, while this may be problematic, these relationships provide deep, important continuities with the past (as I have already mentioned in chapter 1 and this point will be taken up more closely in the following chapters) and are a resource and, importantly, a source of pride.

Postcolonial theory does not address the everyday effects on the emotions evoked by economic systems. In Walkerdine and Jimenez's (2012) study of an ex-mining town in South Wales, the participants did not speak about their work in terms of structural conditions and/ or exploitation but, rather, provided explanations through a narrative based on personal biographies. They tended to resort to explanations such as 'My father taught me this', and an account based on personal and family biography was accepted without question (Walkerdine and Jimenez 2012). The situation is similar in Egypt, as much pride and sustenance are gained from continuities with the past and from identification with a close member of the family (this can be one or both parents, grandparents, uncles or cousins). Dependence is not the problem; it is rather its absence that is really terrifying and this visceral fear is caused 'by the possible severing of the thread, and the fall into the social void' (Ferguson 2013: 232).

Poverty and the fear of hardship, if not destitution, provoke feelings, actions and defences. One example is the middle-class anxiety that the social conditions are such that they will become downwardly mobile. This fear, I wager, leads to fending off vulnerabilities and yet we need to bear in mind 'the awareness of everyone's vulnerability to the workings of time and decay, the quiet suffering that attends our ordinary condition of mortality, and for which perhaps the only compensation is our tenderness for each other's vulnerabilities, for what Adam Zagajewski (2001) calls "the mutilated world"' (Hoffman 2010: 414). Needless to say, most of us, even those who live in the more prosperous West, suffer under the conditions of neo-liberal capitalism, and, while this is obvious, the indignities, humiliations and anxieties experienced by most of the Egyptians are significant. Indignity is a feature of everyday life and, at the risk of being tautological, indignity is also caused by being disposable (Khanna 2007).

Being dispensable can lead inexorably to the emotions of humiliation, shame and indignity. Egypt is an honour-based society with all the meanings, values and ways of being that accompany the injunction to think of, and care for, other human beings. Humiliation, shame and anxiety are felt profoundly if material conditions hinder or make providing economically for the family impossible. At present, there is much anxiety that the socio-economic-political conditions will not improve. In Cairo, it is all we talk about in endless circular fashion: we have much to be anxious about and interlinked with persistent worry about money is the disquiet that feeling humiliated and ashamed is only just being fended off.

Humiliation occurs across many economic spheres – external pressures and institutions (for example, the IMF), the forces of global capital and international aid. Interlinked with these external forces and pressures, there is the humiliation that occurred due to the deeply corrupt Mubarak regime. As a report from Chatham House states, corruption 'is a serious problem in Egypt, contributing to high levels of poverty and unemployment. ... Corruption is understood to have taken a heavy toll on Egyptian society' (2012: 2). Mubarak's regime lacked vision: instead of a programme of financial initiatives that would have aided Egypt's population, most of whom live in poverty, a society based on corruption and exploitation prevailed. The political system descended to frightening, worrying and staggering levels of corruption, coercion, oppression and cruelty under Hosni Mubarak's rule. Any governmental procedure required bribes otherwise any progress with the necessary paperwork stopped. Careful negotiation and knowledge of the correct amount of the bribe was vital – too little and the procedure halted; too much and suspicions were raised. I know of businesses that were closed because the bribe was miscalculated. It was impossible to function without being embroiled in and tainted by corruption and bribery. It is unknown whether corruption will cease or not under this present regime.

The middle class can hold onto positions of economic privilege – I have witnessed many arguments with taxi drivers over the cost of a taxi fare and have heard frequently the statement 'I hate taxi metres' (taxi metres make it impossible to argue over the cost of the fare). They can also fight over the cost of fruit and vegetables with poor farmers who are selling their wares from a donkey cart. Corruption and exploitation are such a feature of the texture of everyday living that we, whatever our class position and economic resources, are all tainted, whether we participate actively or not in such abuse.

The need to inhabit a secure life and indeed to be someone of importance can lead to naïvety, and this is illustrated by a male character – Abdel Samad – in Salwamy's (2014) novel *Butterfly Wings*. Abdel Samad is desperate to be more financially secure and becomes the victim of an Internet scam whereby a 'woman' apparently living in Kuwait promises him marriage and financial security; despite never meeting 'her' or knowing 'her', Abdel Samad hands over 5,000 Egyptian pounds borrowed from friends and family – the average yearly salary for many people in Egypt. Destitute and humiliated, he wanders the streets of Cairo as he is unable to return to his family home. Desperation and insecurity lead to gullibility – which can lead to placing hope in disastrous fantasies.

I have previously written about the following incident and think it is worth repeating here as it illustrates diverse responses to begging (Treacher 2006). I was walking through a very well-to-do area of Cairo – Zamalek – where, incidentally, Edward Said grew up. I'd had three hours sleep and, befuddled, dazed and tired, was not at my best. A young, stunningly handsome young man approached me and, in startlingly good English, said, 'I am a student'. With these words, and his good looks, I was caught. He spoke about his poverty and how he needed medical help. He rolled up his trouser legs and I was forced to look at the most ulcerated legs I had ever seen in my life. The ulcers were weeping and a complete mess. He begged me for money. I gave him some – quite a lot – and walked away. He came after me, begging for more, and started to cry. I could not bear his abject poverty, the sight of his weeping ulcers, and his dispossession and I, too, began to weep. He carried on begging and I gave in and handed him some more money – in fact, I gave him the equivalent of about one month's salary in Egypt – £20. A crowd gathered to watch the drama and I felt protected by them and knew that they would step in if the young man crossed a line. I walked down the street not only rattled by the incident but also because I know I gave him the money to get rid of him – I could not stand being near him.

Being a good Egyptian I have to talk about this and the following three responses are interesting in their political and social content. They are all from women. The first person I told is an extremely rich young woman – I knew her from left-wing politics, which she has resolutely left behind. She berated me and spoke, accurately, of how I gave him money to assuage my guilt. She then carried on by saying that capitalism is the only way to help the poor and deprived. The next person I told was another young woman who launched into an attack on beggars: 'They are rich', she declared, and went on to assert without any doubt that 'they make their legs look like that'. The third person I told was an old friend of mine – we are practically the same age – and she looked at me sympathetically and said, 'What else could you have done?' Three very different social and political responses to the profound problem of poverty, begging and being surrounded moment by moment by people struggling on the edge.

The Persistent Struggle to Survive

Vulnerability and precariousness are part of the human condition and frequently provoke contempt, disavowal, distance rather than concern for the other human being. Cairo is full of examples of vulnerability and insecurity as poverty is everywhere (the rural and the urban merge, the poor inhabit affluent areas, female refugees from Syria sell baked goods from rickety tables on the street). Poverty is inescapable, is in the air we breathe and touches us at our very core no matter what we declare to the contrary. Instead, alas, of reaching out with concern and thought towards an alternative mode of thinking about inequality and social justice, we have closed down on thinking. This is not to say that we (and by 'we' I mean the secular left and many of the Egyptian population) would have to agree with the Islamic movements, as there is much of their thought that is profoundly problematic; instead, we could have risked opening up another register of thought and judgement which would entail thinking through which aspects of their ideology, such as the resistance to neo-liberal capital and subjectivity, may enable a more socially just society.

Humiliation, shame, disappointment and anger are provoked by the lack of economic governance as well as the inexorable demands of global capital and economic institutions. Fiscal matters not just are an internal concern but also involve international institutions; Egypt, as with many other countries, is trapped within a global system that is based on neo-liberal capitalism. This reliance leads to an 'an alliance with a transnational capitalism whose rapacious, brutal, and destructive past is continually reproduced in the present' (Ferguson 2013: 219). Forced alliances or not, from 1838 'Muhammed Ali, the "founder of modern Egypt", saw his project of state-led growth frustrated by a British–French coalition' (Shechter 2008: 571). International interference is repeated when Nasser 'experienced the crumbling of his endeavour after the 1967 war' (2008: 571). As Shechter points out, economic nationalism was long perceived as part of Egypt's national project as it was seen to be the necessary route through to developing independence from other nations. Economic and political independence were perceived to be interlinked as the growing middle class argued that foreign imports should be replaced with domestic production. Shechter writes, 'modern industry was evoked as a stepping stone to a new economy and a symbol of the broader socio-cultural transformation of the Egyptian nation' (2008: 571).

Contemporary Islamic movements can be seen as a refusal to be dominated and coerced into global capitalism. The turn to the era of the Prophet Mohammed is the rebuttal of the demands of global neo-liberalism and an attempt to heal the violence that has gone before, during which Egyptian subjects were told repeatedly, either explicitly or implicitly, that they were not good enough or, indeed, that they lack the required attributes to be successful subjects. As Lloyd (2003: 217) points out, a 'colonized culture is thus denied any orientation to the future other than one dictated by a colonial modernity that must annihilate not only the complex tissues of its actuality but even its very potentialities'. Islamic movements refuse the persistent orientation towards a particular version of modernity, and, excluded from the future, they look to the past for inspiration for a mode of being that provides full subjectivity.

My argument here is that the Islamic movements had powerful appeal for many of the Egyptian population as they saw the possibility of being liberated from the daily struggle to survive and of gaining freedom from exploitation and corruption. Islamic movements, especially the Salafi movement, provided a counterpoint to this corruption; they argue for an economic system based on Islamic principles, as set out by the prophet Mohammed. While the discourse of Islamic financial practice can appear nostalgic, it is a principled framework for thinking about a different moral order based on fairness and is a counterpoint to the corruption that has been long standing in Egypt. For many of the Egyptian population, this practice was appealing (at least 25 per cent of the population voted for the Salafi movement in the election held in 2013).

Economic decline, however, began in the 1960s, especially after the 1967 war. Since then, Egypt has changed from being economically stable to being a country reliant on aid, international grants and loans – such as the US\$1.3 billion from America for military aid in 2015 or the €5 billion package of grants and loans conferred by Europe in 2015 – in order to subsist. To further underline the economic difficulties and the historical shifts – in the 1950s and into the 1960s, E£2 bought £1 sterling. Now, in early 2016, £1 sterling buys E£11!

In 2012, the Ministry of Planning and International Cooperation published a strategic document and outlined a ten-year strategy to tackle the dire state of the Egyptian economy. This framework is of note, as it is the first strategic plan published in Egyptian history. The document outlines the initiatives that should be embarked upon to improve human development (education and health), employment prospects, low incomes and social injustice. It is unknown whether or not this strategy will be successful and/or will improve Egypt's economic prospects, but, at present (early 2016), there are few hopeful signs.

The current president, Fattah Al-Sisi, instigated a massive project to build another Suez Canal, an important material endeavour that was completed in August 2015. International relations concerning the Suez Canal will be taken up and explored in detail in chapter 6 of this book; however, for now, it is worth pointing to and underlining the importance of the Suez Canal in terms of revenue and Egyptian pride. The building of a new Suez Canal was heralded as 'Egypt's Gift to the World' (to quote the official headline) and despite, maybe, our better judgement, we watched the carefully orchestrated ceremonies with deeply felt optimism that Egypt may be on the verge of recovery. The symbolism of the ceremony, alongside the fervent hope that Egypt has embarked on material revitalisation, has led to suppression of any doubt about the feasibility of the project, and of any profound disquiet that the international financial investment (countries from the Gulf) might lead to colonisation from a different geopolitical region. Egypt is the recipient of enormous amounts of aid from the Gulf region – since

2013, the country has received more than $20 billion and, in 2015, Saudi Arabia, Kuwait, the United Arab Emirates and Oman pledged a further $12 billion. This 'dependence' repeats colonialism and I would argue that it is such fiscal imperialism that perpetuates an international system of exploitation and corruption.

These disastrous and worrying economic conditions impact on the lived experience and perpetuate the wounds caused by inhabiting a society that is chronically hierarchical and exploitative. For example, in Mahfouz's (1985) novel *The Beginning and the End*, the two younger brothers return to school after the death of their father and have to come to terms with their impoverished material conditions. While one brother (Hussein) is represented as sad about the death of his father and realistic about the family's impending poverty, his younger brother (Hassanein) pretends that they are wealthy and conceals their impoverished circumstances. Concealed poverty and the pretence of plenty are responses to the humiliation that can be evoked by living in societies that are structured through competition, hierarchies based on wealth and where money is one of the important values.

In Egypt, these feelings of shame and humiliation impact on men in relation to their role within the family. Men have to shoulder the main financial responsibility for the family and to be the primary providers – a socio-cultural imperative (although many women also carry financial responsibility and this will be explored below). Egypt does not have a welfare system; therefore, state support is not available for those who are poor and/or unemployed. Egyptians rely on an informal welfare system through which family members support one another if at all possible. Material support takes many forms, from giving money and/ or food to allowing a family member to live in your household. It is difficult to find the right word in English, here, as personal boundaries do not exist in quite the same way. Therefore, the use of words such as 'allow', 'tolerate', 'consent' or 'permit' do not fully capture the situation as, on the whole, people meet these obligations without question and do not perceive them as onerous demands.

There are, though, obligations on those who are reliant on their family for material support. Those who require financial help are obliged to shoulder their responsibility primarily by looking for work, taking whatever is on offer, no matter how menial or, indeed, how poorly paid. In a typical discussion, a young man in his mid-30s, whose employment prospects were very bad due to his lack of educational qualifications, was criticised heavily by other family members as he was perceived to not be fulfilling his obligations; the accusatory question, 'Are you not embarrassed to take money from your father?' was frequently asked. Comparisons were made with other young people who travel long distances to their – often menial – jobs, work exceptionally long hours and so on.

Fulfilling Responsibilities: Neglecting Obligations

Egyptian subjectivity is, of course, complex and contradictory because, while autonomy is not valued, people are still expected to be self-possessed and to fulfil their obligations to other human beings. There may, however, be a gap between prevailing discourses of responsibility and what actually takes place. For example, I know of one family where the eldest brother is a multimillionaire and will not help any of his siblings, even though at least two of them are in desperate situations. The short story 'Dearest sister Makarim' consists of a letter from a brother to his sister (Al Aswany 2009). This letter appeals to his sister to understand his poor health and overwhelming financial responsibilities and it is for these reasons, he laments, that he cannot provide the much-needed financial aid that his sister and his mother require. This letter illustrates a particular and prevalent appeal to women to understand, excuse, endure; covertly, through the use of a religious discourse, women are told to make the best of it.

There is, I am suggesting, a contradictory ideology at work here which focuses on responsibility and dependency. Maturity is based on being able to look after and respond to others while, simultaneously, material dependency – which requires excessive demands on other human beings – is frowned upon. It is men's responsibility to meet these material obligations and demands. The novel *Taxi* (Alkhamissi 2006) consists of a series of vignettes culled from conversations with taxi drivers. The author recounts an occasion when he is in a taxi and the driver keeps falling asleep because his economic circumstances are such that he has worked non-stop for three days. In response to Alkhamissi pleading with him to take a break, the taxi driver says, 'We live from day to day, and meal to meal. I mean, if I went home I'd find 101 disasters. I'd find the children hadn't eaten and their mother at her wits' end. No, Sir, no way' (2006: 14). The driver goes on to say that he has to pay an instalment on a loan and, once he has the money to do so, he will go home. One interpretation is that this taxi driver was avoiding the inexorable demands of domestic life and stayed away in order not to witness, or to be confronted by, the material needs of his family – this may well be true. Alongside this understandable avoidance is his knowledge of his obligations to his family as, after all, moral worth in Egypt is forged from upholding duties and responsibilities.

Social membership is gained from meeting obligations and is an important value in its own right. Fulfilling obligations is an important aspect of the social-affective ties that bind human beings together. It should be recognised, however, that these aspects of moral person-hood have arisen within, and are constituted by, a society that has been colonised for centuries and in which exploitation has been a persisting reality. Egypt is a society marked by loss, insecurity and precarity and its culture is 'constituted around and marked by an unworked-through loss' (Lloyd 2003: 215). Egypt, as with other colonised societies, is one where insecurity and coercive violence are a constant presence. In short, colonisation is about power, as Timothy Mitchell (1991) points out, and it is disciplinary power that the colonial order sought to impose on Egyptian society. The discipline required to be a complaint subject is a crucial aspect of the globalised economy.

In order to provide a textured account of the impact of the global economy, I now provide examples from Ma'adi, where I live. Ma'adi is a suburb of Cairo and is roughly 30 kilometres from the centre (or downtown, to use the most common depiction). Ma'adi, like all districts of Cairo, is an area that encompasses diversity, as exceptionally poor areas abut outstandingly rich neighbourhoods; intermixed are districts inhabited by those of us who are comfortable but certainly not rich nor indeed poor.

Road 9 in Ma'adi is iconic and is about two kilometres long.[2] It runs alongside the metro line and, walking down this main road, you pass food shops, bakeries, butchers, coffee shops, shops selling electrical appliances, equipment for plumbing, gift and book shops, and shops selling jewellery – mainly made of silver. Egyptians living in the area buy their food from local shops and the market and the men go to *ahwas* – traditional coffee shops where men (only men) sit to drink coffee, tea and/or soft drinks and smoke *shisha* (the traditional water pipe). Sitting together they watch the omnipresent large TV screen, and, if there is a football game on, the volume is so loud that conversation is impossible. These are places of popular homosociality and time seems to lose its urgency. The *ahwas* are extremely popular in the evenings, reflecting how much social activity takes place often late into the night.

Not far from the *ahwa* we begin to encounter 'Westernisation', as the cafés change and become, for example, a McDonald's or a series of coffee shops such as Beano's, Costa and so on. These places are exceptionally popular with young men and women, and provide safe meeting places for mixed-gender groups to get together. Needless to say, only the middle classes can afford to frequent these coffee shops, which now fill many middle-class areas of Cairo such as Zamalek, Heliopolis and Mohandiseen; the cost of the coffee is approximately the same as in the United Kingdom.

The coffee shops are full of affluent people and, even though they are sitting with others, they are often using their laptops and mobiles (a commonplace scene, nowadays, no matter where!). As Anouk de Koning (2006) points out, these coffee shops are always referred to in English to distinguish them from the *ahawi baladi* or traditional, male-dominated cafés described above. These coffee shops provide new public spaces where mixed-gender groups can meet and which, what is more, provide an important public space where women can socialise. Koning describes the phenomenon thus; the 'absence of alcohol and the specific and gender markers inherent in the transnational formula help define the coffee shop as a civilized and distinctive space that is marked as safe for women and decent mixed gender sociability' (2006: 229).

These popular cafés illustrate a shifting oral culture where burgers, cappuccinos and toasted sandwiches have replaced more traditional and cheaper Egyptian food. These shifting oral cultures make apparent class markers of taste and affluence. Distinction, as Koning points out, lies in both the knowledge and taste – the cosmopolitan referents for the speciality coffees and salads – on offer. These cafés are also staffed by waiters who speak English (as in all popular holiday resorts) and English (as the language of colonisation) is now the language of social interaction in these cafés, which 'do not only create new commonalities, they also divide. While creating a sense of cosmopolitan belonging, they simultaneously distance themselves from surrounding spaces and the majority of the Cairenes' (de Koning 2006: 228). Spaces such as these coffee shops, upscale supermarkets that sell products for the international and affluent communities and the large-scale (and overwhelming) shopping malls are now a feature of Cairo (Abaza 2001). A different discipline, which focuses more on consumption, is required for the affluent middle classes, a hierarchy of the senses that is more European in terms of enjoyment of the visceral space and place and the shifting taste towards a changed palate.

Abutting Ma'adi is an exceptionally poor district that is densely populated, with dire sanitation, electricity that cuts out continually and poor living conditions (they do not have Kindles or iPads to see them through electricity cuts). The buildings are very close together and are barely wide enough to allow a car to pass through and, while the area is full of people going about their daily lives, the effects of perpetual struggle are abundantly clear. There is no respite from the daily grind and from the exertion required to inhabit an area without a solid infrastructure.

Living in these conditions is potentially especially harmful to men, whose subjectivity and self-esteem are forged from work and providing for the family. In Egypt, the effect of mass unemployment is palpable. Most of us know of at least one person who is struggling to find work and the consequences of that fruitless endeavour are painful to witness. Unemployment, ill health and poor living conditions can be an overwhelming cause of anxiety, as men struggle to fulfil their material duties. While these obligations are not perceived as burdens, they are, nonetheless, a profound cause of stress. While men may be particularly prone to feelings of humiliation and shame, women may also experience these corrosive emotions of anxiety and concern; indeed, many women bear much of the responsibility for providing for the family. Female subjectivities in Egypt are valued due to what are deemed to be the natural attributes of care, nurture and self-sacrifice – putting the family first. Responsibility for the family is primary and caring for the family while also working for a living is a double burden for women. Their contribution to the family income is frequently concealed, and so it was quite by chance that I discovered that one of my aunts worked partly out of financial necessity as well as for self-fulfilment (she was a professor of sociology at a prestigious university in Cairo). We – that is, the family – all assumed that she worked just for self-fulfilment, and none of us realised that financial considerations also played a strong part in her decision to work.

As with attempts to learn the real reasons why some women work, it is also difficult to gain an accurate picture of their salaries and earnings, because women frequently conceal how much they earn for a number of reasons. First, they do not wish to humiliate their husbands and reveal that the latter cannot support the family without their wives' contributions. Second, women frequently give money to their birth families, sometimes without their husbands' knowledge. Third, they put money aside as an insurance in case they divorce and are left without adequate financial support.

Women work most frequently in the informal economy, which also makes it difficult to accurately discern how much they earn. Women work in the domestic sphere and they clean, cook, undertake child care and generally support middle-class women. This work is hard and often involves tolerating or 'putting up with' exploitation and harassment. There is no room for complaint because, if the women or their husbands voice any protest, the men are then fired without notice and the family is left homeless without any source of income.

Some women breed chickens on the roofs of apartment blocks and sell the eggs. They were thus adversely affected by the outbreak of bird flu, as an important source of income was destroyed. Some, like the two women who sit on the pavement at the end of my street, sell agricultural produce such as herbs and salad leaves. These products are cheap and barely enable the women to make a living; nevertheless, the women sit there day in, day out, whatever the weather, and appear patient, sanguine and resigned. In addition to the burden of undertaking tedious work, most women have to struggle to feed the family and provide cheap and sustaining food. Cooking is time consuming and involves preparing food, especially chicken, in such a manner that it will stretch a long way. Meat in Egypt is very expensive and the poor cannot afford to buy it (this is one reason why Ramadan is enjoyed by the poor, as the affluent middle class provides good-quality food as their charitable contribution). Much food – such as *fuul* (stewed brown beans) and *tami-yya* (the Egyptian version of *falafel*) – is very filling and the ingredients easily accessible. Home cooking is another matter; it is time consuming (especially for women who also work outside the home): for example, stuffing vegetables (believe me, this is time consuming and I have never quite mastered the skill) or making soup as a filling staple. The onus for providing for the family rests with both men and women – for men they have to earn the money so that food can be bought, while the women are responsible for cooking nutritious food within the resources available.

Inhabiting Loss

These vexacious material conditions and dynamics lead to shame, humiliation, profound anxiety and the corrosion of bonds for all persons. Egypt is a deeply religious society and everyday language is replete with references to God and to spirituality. Islam is a practice that is deeply embedded in Egyptian subjectivity and everyday life. Islam is a resource which can lead to a sanguine acceptance of the material conditions that prevail and to acceptance of the emotions provoked. The despair, however, can be overwhelming and can lead, understandably, to envy and a lack of compassion towards others – sentiments which are based on fantasies of who has an easier life. An Egyptian idiom – the hand in the water cannot feel the hand in the fire – is frequently drawn upon to rationalise feelings of envy and indifference. These two emotions can quickly slide across from one to the other and can be perceived as negative states of mind that should be overcome. One way of making the emotions of humiliation, shame and envy partially tolerable is to turn to religion as a resource. Because these emotions and fantasies are troubling, as they unsettle an illusion that many of us hold that we are generous, benevolent and free from envy and jealousy, it is commonplace for Egyptians to turn to the following explanations: 'It is God's will', 'God knows me and He wants it like this to protect me against my negative impulses', 'God is sympathetic and He will ensure that I survive' and so on. There are many prevailing religious injunctions in Egypt. The first, and maybe the most important, is to feel gratitude towards God for giving life. Interlinked with this primary command is the active belief that He will always provide and protect the believer. Religion is a resource and, as a belief system, provides explanations for things unknown, dignity, hope and optimism.

These inexorable material conditions of relentless, unceasing poverty and insecurity produce chronic anxiety, fear, humiliation and disappointment. Interwoven with the aforementioned emotions is the persistent experience of loss that is due to 'the body's longing for home, to be at home, to be at home in one's land, a land conquered, impoverished and plundered for its raw materials' (Walkerdine and Jimenez 2012: 2). The loss, according to these authors, is immense, whether it is sensed, spoken of or silenced, or indeed an 'unthought known', to draw on a poignant phrase of Christopher Bollas (1987).

The effect of inhabiting loss is complex and impacts on ways of relating and relationships with others and with how the injury of loss is embodied. Inhabiting injury produces 'affective responses of which we may not be aware: bodily dispositions, chronic illnesses, ways of being and defending against the anxiety, hurt and pain of what is experienced' (Walkerdine and Jimenez 2012: 9). In 2012, it seemed as though many men under the age of 60 were dying suddenly (the official mortality rates report that men die, on average, at the age of 69 and women at 73). For example, my husband was on his way to the funeral of one of his cousins, who was aged 58, when he received a call informing him that another male cousin had also died aged about 57. There seemed to be more deaths of middle-aged men than usual, leading my niece, aged 23 at the time, to declare that she was 'too young to be wearing black clothes all the time'. Needless to say, chronic poverty and insecurity affect women; poverty is palpable and written across the body. Women, frequently, look much older than their actual age. Poor diet, difficult, overcrowded living conditions and chronic and hazardous pollution age them dramatically.

Stress, inequality and shame lead to a worrying degree of illness that encompasses physical and mental health. Richard Wilkinson and Kate Picket (2010) convincingly argue that social inequality corrodes and leads to chronic anxiety and insecurity. Shame, they argue, is particularly corrosive as it involves comparisons with others who are perceived as having a higher status, leading to people feeling inferior, foolish, incompetent and vulnerable (2010: 41). Poverty, social injustice and material insecurity get under people's skins and the consequent emotions of shame, humiliation and anxiety (to name but a few) cannot simply be shrugged off. These persist emotions can frequently be passed onto the next generation. Transmission does not just take place through verbal communication but frequently through silence, tone of voice, gestures and the slight but perceptible change in body language, the unconscious sigh that is emitted, despite the attempt to keep emotions hidden – concealed and silent

> because the experiences of the parent generation are so painful that they cannot bear to talk about them. These intergenerational dynamics can be very effective because they operate in psychosocial ways as a kind of affective and collective continuum, in the sense that a continuous series of events can blend into each other gradually and seamlessly, making it hard to say where one ends and the next begins. (Walkerdine and Jimenez 2012: 10)

Walking through the streets of Cairo, we are surrounded by poverty, with both adults and children begging on the street. While the adults are grateful for any contribution, the children are resilient and know what they want. They ask for 'McDonalds' and are persistent. In Cairo the poor live cheek by jowl with those who are affluent; they are surrounded by the material conditions of those who are comfortable and whose possessions include TVs, computers, comfortable rooms and physical space. These children understandably want what they know is available to others and will never be accessible to them, unless there is a complete revolution at all levels of Egyptian society. These children and young people witness their parents' struggles and know of the perpetual risk of indignity and humiliation that their parents endure.

Just because anxieties cannot be named does not mean that they are not known or felt. Emotions, along with intransigent material conditions, do have significant effects. Chronic insecurity in relation to opportunities and resources passes down through the generations. It is, as David Lloyd poignantly writes, a 'chronic narrative' (Lloyd 2003: 224).

Notes

1. This chapter is based, in part, on an essay entitled 'The Egyptian economic crisis: insecurity, affect, nostalgia', to be published in Karner and Weicht (2016) *The Commonalities of Global Crisis: Markets, Communities and Nostalgia.*

2. There is a lively short film showing Road 9 on You Tube – https://www.youtube.com/watch?v=SD9ezwDtbX0 – recommended if you want to see Road 9 for yourself!).

Chapter 3

The Intimacy of Subjection

Postcolonial subjectivity is a conundrum, and it is almost impossible to find the thread from which to begin to elucidate and explore the various strands that interlink closely and constitute this complex matrix. Events, identification, repetition, fantasy, intergenerational transmission and conflict coalesce to comprise subjectivities, whether from the Middle East or the West, male or female, middle or working class. Having said that, specific subjectivities are formed and inhabited within socio-historical and political structures. While all subjectivities are psychopolitical (Hook 2012), in this chapter[1] I attempt to understand the specificities of subjectivities that have been colonised – in the case of Egypt, the violence of the colonial and postcolonial period – and the 'movement of epistemic, cultural, psychic and physical violence makes for a unique kind of historical trauma' (Hook 2005: 479). We cannot escape these political-cultural-historical-psychic structures that make and break us, despite our wish for it to be otherwise. Subjectivities are formed within and inhabited through the nexus of history, present-day events, emotions, memories, phantasies and identifications which persist in an interlinked and redolent chain. These psychic-political-social structures are intertwined and impact profoundly because, as Stuart Hall (Schwarz 2000: 270) asserts, reflecting on a time in his life and the interrelationship between social structures and psychic life:

> I could never understand why people think these structural questions were not connected to the psychic, with emotions and identifications and

feelings because, for me, those structures are things you live ... they have
real structural properties, they break you, they destroy you.

This chapter focuses on the intimate familial sphere, exploring how history and socio-political discourses are internalised through this intimate
sphere; I explore some of the emotions (such as love or loyalty), states
of mind (for example, obedience and responsibility) and narratives that
are transmitted, absorbed and perpetuated. Importantly, the intimate
sphere provides love, security and vital attachments that support and
sustain human beings while simultaneously being full of contradictions, as the bonds and alliances that are felt, experienced and imagined
can also cause conflict within the self and between the self and other
human beings. The intimate sphere is intricate, full of contradictions
and replete with dense and thorny dynamics.

Subjectivities are formed through the spectres of known and unknown
events, diverse understandings, various emotions and phantasies and
other human beings, whether they are alive or not. It is now commonplace within cultural studies and psychoanalytic frameworks to argue
that temporalities are intertwined, as the past, present and future form a
complex web of time, experience and identity. The past is inescapable
as we are born into a complex of socio-cultural-affective relations that
form profoundly subjectivities. The past and, indeed, the future and the
present cannot be made anew as if histories do not resolutely form and
impact on the present. In Egypt, there exist profound contradictions in
relation to temporalities, as the past can be idealised and attachment to
the past is seen as natural; simultaneously, the past can be dismissed
with the heartfelt assertion that the past is resolutely behind us.

The viewpoint that the past is over and done with is exemplified in
the novel *Butterfly Wings* (Salmawy 2014), where the central female
protagonist – Doha – is represented as struggling to break free of the
constraints of her life and, importantly, of her past. Doha becomes
preoccupied with transforming her life, and, while there is an acknowledgement that change is painful, there is not a hint of doubt that transformation may not be possible. In this novel, the past is represented in
a variety of ways: as that which traps and constrains, as inspiration for
beautiful designs (clothes and architecture) and as a necessary resource
with which to face the present. Temporalities are represented as distinct
and the novel represents the viewpoint that it is possible for human
beings to live in the present without the hefty weight of the past.

Despite the assertions and maybe the hopes that the past can be dispensed with, I am positing that a colonised history endures in present-day Egyptian society, in socio-political structures and the formation of subjectivities. I am preoccupied with how to make Egyptian culture complex and I understand this endeavour as tracing through the inscriptions of colonialism that remain imbricated, embedded and embodied within subjectivities. It is important to say that this endeavour is not a simplistic endorsement but, rather, it is designed to enable a shift that is convincing and which, following Fanon (1986), is attentive to the difficulties and challenges of understanding and analysing subjectivities. Fanon, pithily but powerfully, writes: 'The Negro is not. Any more than the white man'; this broken sentence indicates powerfully the precariousness of identity for all subjectivities, whatever the gender. The palimpsest of colonialism operates inexorably at intertwined political and psychic levels and to focus solely on the political effects is partial because, as Hall (1996a: 17) asserts, 'An account of racism which has no purchase on the inner landscape and the unconscious mechanisms of its effects is, at best, only half the story'.

My attempt to think through and understand the vexed matter of colonised subjectivities is troublesome and troubling and is frequently blocked, as I am filled with anxieties, fantasies and unprocessed thoughts. I can be filled with pain as I think of people I know, some of whom I love, some whom I am fond of and others I like or even am indifferent to, but I cannot bear witnessing that which I perceive to be the enduring suffering caused by colonisation. I am not arguing that other subjectivities formed within and through other socio-political-cultural times are not troubled and are free of suffering and released from the corrosive effects of the past; this would frankly be meaningless and I am far too reliant on psychoanalysis to even contemplate such an idea – I reiterate a quote from Fanon: 'the negro enslaved by his inferiority, the white man enslaved by his superiority' (1986: xiv). There is nothing inevitable about the persistence of the effects of a colonised history and I want to be clear that this is not a natural state of affairs because Egypt as a society and the Egyptians are backward and locked in tradition; rather it is because, for a complexity of reasons, it has been difficult for Egyptian society to overcome the consequences of its vexed history.

These difficulties are compounded by the socio-political injunctions that we should deny the damage that has taken place alongside the

anxieties about who we are, what we have become and what we may
be perpetuating. This, needless to say, is unconscious, but this does not
mean that denial as a state of mind does not have powerful effects on
inter- and intra-relationships. Hope can be a state of mind that over-
comes thinking and that can function as 'cruel optimism', to draw on
a phrase by Lauren Berlant (2011). Silences can function within and
through human beings to conceal and disavow the damage done to,
and perpetuated by, the socio-political orders and, in turn, the destruction inflicted on human beings by other human beings. We are, on the
whole, silenced by our loyalty and visceral need for life to be different,
better and more optimistic than it actually is, and we are too deeply
embedded in the 'habit of disavowing the personal and cultural damage
that is in part the legacy of our colonial past' (Lloyd 2003: 205).

De Alwis' phrase 'absent presences' offers an important understanding
of the way in which events, histories, memories, narratives and subjectivities are undeniably replete with traces that are inescapable and simultaneously enigmatic, as the trace is undecipherable, being neither fully
present nor fully absent (2009: 238). These absent presences, I argue,
are silent but omnipresent shards that persist, unbidden and unwanted, in
beleaguered psyches and in socio-political formations (Treacher Kabesh
2013a). Avery Gordon, in her subtle book *Ghostly Matters: Haunting and the Sociological Imagination* (1997), explores haunting – as a
word, a concept, an experience and a state of mind – and she asserts the
importance of listening and tracing through that which has been lost and
is absent in the sociological imagination, societies and individual human
beings. That which has been lost or, indeed, is absent, however, remains
present no matter how elusive, subtle and intangible. People, no matter
their history, geopolitical location or individual biographies, are always
tied 'to historical and social effects' (1997: 190). A central theme of
this book – Egyptian Revolutions – is that subjectivities are 'always and
inevitably haunted by the social and most especially by those repres-
sions, disappearances, absences and losses' (Radway 2008: xi) caused
and perpetuated by colonisation and postcolonial structures.

Emotions and fantasies unsettle any imagined boundary between
self and other, psyche and body, private and public, as emotions and
fantasies leak and are porous in that they perturb narratives that may
be imagined as settled. In no society do boundaries exist – something
which I take as a universal given. What is more, people in Egypt gain
their selfhood from their relationships with others and their sense of self

is formed through relationality, obligation and responsibility. In short, identity is claimed through what can be described as a 'we-self'. In a similar way, interior and exterior environments mingle, such that a meaningful distinction cannot be discerned between people and place. Identification, as Diana Fuss (1995) points out, cuts across and through the interior and exterior as identifications take place through various others – parents, grandparents, aunts and uncles, siblings, cousins and friends – and are all significant.

I am relying on a psychoanalytic framework in order to understand subjectivities. My starting position is that human beings are capable of love, affection, enjoyment, generosity and kindness even while being conflicted, jagged and fragmented. Subjectivity is gained through the narratives, fantasies and emotions of other human beings who, in turn, are full of other human beings (Freeman 2010). The dynamic unconscious is permeated by cultural norms, as is the conscious mind. The emotions, fantasies and narratives that relate to intimacy, familial relations and friendship networks will be elucidated, as will the impact of this triad. Subjectivities are formed through internalising and identifying with others, and, while these complex identifications are essential for subjectivity itself to be gained (our psyches are social spaces), it can also bind human beings into the past. It is our relationships to others, specifically to primary carers, that incorporates us into and inaugurates the rules of social order. Our phantasies, wishes and complexes are marked by history. Intergenerational transmission is crucial (Abraham and Torok 1994; Gordon 1997).

Anxiety is at the core of human subjectivity. We worry about our needs and desires that can frequently cut across social sanctions and feel shame about who we are and the distress that we imagine we bring to others, together with the difficulties that we can evoke for other human beings. Our relations with others are never simple; rather, these interrelationships are full of anxiety, need, demand and desire – as Julia Segal expresses it: 'Nothing is neutral. In phantasy all kinds of things are going on, in our heads, in our bodies, in our "inner world". We do not always know it "isn't really like that"; we really do "see it that way"' (Segal 2000: 30). As the unconscious pervades all thinking, writes Stephen Frosh,

> then there can be no unbiased realistic perception, no simple distinction
> between what we are 'imagining' and what we know to be real. Restlessly

pursuing expression, unconscious phantasies keep welling up, to such a
degree that wherever one looks in a person's life – their dreams, their
plans, their pictures, their judgements – one finds evidence at least of
some unconscious component. (Frosh 2002a: 51)

Human beings may strive towards integrity and attempt to act in their
own and others' best interests, but alongside these efforts, aggression,
violence, contempt and degradation operate. Identities are always
based, indeed are dependent, on the exclusion of that which has to be
disavowed, as it is unwelcome and profoundly unsettles any equilib-
rium within the self. Hall explains it thus:

Identities can function as points of identification and attachment only
because of their capacity to exclude, to leave out, to render 'outside',
abjected. Every identity has its 'margin', an excess, something more. The
unity, the internal homogeneity which the term identity treats as founda-
tional is not a natural, but a constructed form of closure, every identity
naming as its necessary, even if silenced and unspoken other, that which
it 'lacks'. (Hall 1996b: 5)

There is always a relationship between that which is said and that which
is unsaid and a dynamic between that which can be spoken and that
which is silenced and rendered absent. I am concerned with exploring
the underbelly of that which is said and claimed, alongside that which
is silenced; in short, the gap between the prevalent discourses of acceptable selfhood and intricate subjectivities. That which is known and
articulated is always complex, as 'double consciousness' – to draw on
W.E.B. DuBois (1989[1903]) – and the 'unthought known' – following
Christopher Bollas (1987) – are continually in process. Emotions may
be elusive, weak and slippery, but their effects are, in contradiction,
powerful, as they pulse through, and between, human beings. Double
consciousness operates in similar ways, producing knowledge which is
simultaneously known and yet disavowed and shunted away. As Kathleen Stewart (2007: 40) writes: 'Ordinary affects highlight the question
of the intimate impacts of forces in circulation. They're not exactly
"personal", but they sure can pull the subject into places it didn't
exactly "intend" to go'.

The matter of belonging pulses away, whatever our intention about
our direction and perhaps, especially, if we end up in a place that
we never had anticipated, hoped for or envisaged. Belonging is not

a neutral matter, as it is overdetermined, troubling and replete with personal yearnings that are rife with political ideologies. Belonging matters and belonging is full of matter. As I have previously argued (Treacher 2007), the need to attach and belong are historically, socially and politically laden and burdened with fantasies and discourses. Nira Yuval-Davis (2006) explores how belonging is about emotional attachment, feeling 'at home', and I would add that the fantasy of belonging provides an illusory but important sense of feeling secure. Yuval-Davis traces through how people can belong in many different ways, to many different objects of attachment, and how belonging always involves acts of self-identification alongside the identifications of other people on the self. Furthermore, belonging can be stable, contested and transient and always be 'a dynamic process, not a reified fixity' (Yuval-Davis 2006: 199). Belonging is not just a cognitive matter, as it is laden with emotional investments and desires.[2] Belonging is not destiny, as it involves and is imbricated by social-geographical-political location, individual attachments and identifications, and the positioning of the self by others, saturated with ethical and political values and beliefs. Despite the commonplace belief that the home is a private sphere outside the political reach, it is, nonetheless, a place and space that is 'intensely political both in its internal relationships and through its interfaces with the wider world over domestic, national and imperial scales' (Blunt and Dowling 2006: 142).

Home is a specific and important locality; within Egyptian society, homes are open to all as boundaries between home and outside are porous, just as who is and who is not perceived and loved as a family member is similarly fluid. Home as a place is a site full of contradictions – it can be a space where nurture, care and sustenance can take place alongside a site of conflict, disagreement and dissatisfaction. Home, as Annette Kuhn writes, is 'a (or *the*) prime site for negotiating inner and outer worlds, and the home itself can take on the qualities of a transitional object and a transitional space, where *edges* – the boundaries and borders between inner and outer – assume considerable emotional and imaginational weight' (Kuhn 2005: 408, italics in the original). 'Home as a place that can provide care and sustenance' is the focus of this section, while 'home as a site of conflict and harm' will be taken up in the following chapters. Homes in Cairo both cross the liminal space between home and not-home and provide for some a fortunate space of respite and ordinary care – often much needed as Cairo as a city can be 'too much'. Yet, as much as we moan (a lot!) about the traffic, dirt, rubbish, pollution, noise, density of people, heat and heaviness of the air (the list of complaints can feel endless), we also love Cairo 'not for any purity but precisely for the lamentable want of it' (Pamuk 2005: 188).

Les Back (2003: 325) explores the importance of belonging to argue that home 'means simply the centre of one's world, not in a geographical but an ontological sense, a place to be found, a place of Being'. This profoundly Winnicottian sentiment (see Winniccott 1990) is further elaborated as Back goes on to assert that being at home is not simply about living at a particular address or residence but is achieved 'through the interconnection of habitation, memory and ritual', and, citing John Berger, 'Without a home at the centre of the real, one was not only shelterless, but also lost in non-being, in unreality. Without home everything was fragmentation'. Being at home with all the sounds that are produced and enjoyed provides a constant sensory and ontological centre. We take places and our senses with us, as André Aciman explains in his 1997 memoir *Out of Egypt*. Aciman poignantly describes the viscerality of belonging and explores how human beings internalise places; we take them with us and inside us, even as we are on the move or inhabiting another location. In a sense we never leave anywhere behind, as the mind is constituted by relations with other human beings and, simultaneously, is a palimpsest of places and senses. In this chapter, I will explore how the senses, place (especially home), the family and emotions come together to form subjectivities.

The Necessity of Belonging and Connectedness

We have to be careful not to imagine that we know all there is to grasp about the family, whether that family is formed in the Middle East or in the West. Sally Alexander argues pertinently that a failure of the imagination can take place when it comes to the family, as, seemingly we 'know already, we think, all there is to know about domestic and family life; this knowingness is one of the deepest psychic political sites of conservatism' (1994: 233). This certain knowledge operates in Egypt, where any questioning of family and domestic life is met with incredulity, as it is apparently a concept which is certain, known and straightforward. It is difficult to question family life in Egypt; it is upheld as sacrosanct and this results in silences and the absence of the lived texture and complexities of being a member of a nuclear and extended family. There is profound difficulty in questioning subjectivity and/or the family; while silence about the intimate sphere is not limited to Arab culture (Al-Nowaihi 1999), it is, I argue, particularly strong in Egypt and elsewhere in the Middle East. The family is the site of obligations, bonds, responsibilities, attachments, conflicts [spoken or not], emotions and fantasies.

Suad Joseph and Martina Rieker (2008) write that it is important to acknowledge that families are a crucial aspect of understanding the complexity of contemporary social process in the Arab world. It is my hope to explore the dynamics of these relationships in terms of historical transmission and the absorption of socially acceptable narratives, beliefs and values. Families are, as Joseph and Rieker comment,

> woven into the fabric of almost every aspect of social life, family has been understood to be critical to social projects of all sorts – colonialist, anti-colonialist, nationalist, pan-Arabist, socialist, modernist, religious, and feminist. Movements from all political directions have claimed the space of family as their own, elevating its purpose and production to almost sacred principles. Relationships, ethics, and idioms nested in family discourse have been mobilized to link political, economic, social, religious, and cultural institutions and processes. (2008: 35)

The family is assumed to be the site of harmony, belongingness and nurture, and it is habitually presumed, frequently without thought that, without marriage and family life, human beings cannot function within socially sanctioned bonds.[3]

It is important to comprehend families in specific localities at particular times and to seek to grasp the changing relations within families and the shifting narratives and discourses of family life (Joseph and Rieker 2008). The family in Egypt is a kinship group that may or may not share the same household; importantly, it is marked by fluid classifications. To give just one example of this: imagine a person talking about, perhaps, his or her niece and declaring with heartfelt sincerity, 'She is like my daughter'. The 'like' is both an indication that the niece is felt to be a daughter and, simultaneously, an acknowledgement that she is not. There is a fluidity in Middle Eastern cultures as to who constitutes the family and various words are used to describe the household: '*usra*', '*aila*', '*beit*' – kin, family, household (Joseph and Rieker 2008: 36).

The family is the basic social unit of Egyptian society, and it 'provides shelter, food, clothing, protection, identity, reputation' (Abudi 2011: 30). The family is fundamental to a person's sense of self. It is important to stress, too, that the family takes precedence over the individual as it provides belonging, allegiance and commitment and, simultaneously, demands obligation and loyalty. The family as central to social life and as the source of cultural values is underlined by both Christianity and Islam. Islam, as Abudi (2011: 29) points out, pays more attention to the family than to any other institution, and many verses in the *Qur'an* are devoted to the family (marital relations, the obligations of children to their parents). Both Islam and Christianity share a belief that the family is the foundation of society and that it is the duty of parents to ensure that the family is stable and harmonious and, above all, that every member of the family is moral in every aspect of life. In short, the family is both the central regulator of everyday life and the source of identity.

Suad Joseph describes subjectivities in the Middle East as relational and based on the importance of connectivity. While exploring the culture of the Middle East, her insights are pertinent for thinking through Egyptian culture and subjectivities. She describes Middle Eastern culture as 'a culture that embeds persons in familial relationships. Personhood is understood in terms of relationships woven into one's sense of self, identity, and place in the world. One is never without family, without relationships, outside the social body' (Joseph 1999: 54), as identity is always relational and embedded. Furthermore, the self is not sealed within boundaries separating self from others, as to be whole is to be part of, connected to and absorbed through others. Central to the demands of personhood is inviting the engagement of others, and maturity is understood as embracing the self in the other and the other in the self. It is, in short, the 'connective self', to draw on Joseph's depiction.[4] Value is placed on being connected and, importantly, being a part of an interlinked web. Self-esteem, therefore, is gained from constant affective exchange, where high levels of empathy and receptivity are nurtured, and from strong identification with the family, groups and elders (Joseph 1999: 5).

It is worth explaining Egyptian subjectivities more fully, as selfhood is based on inter-relatedness and interrelationality. Autonomy is neither sought after nor seen as of moral worth. Joseph describes Middle Eastern subjectivities; selves, she writes, are woven through intimate relationships that are lifelong, which transform over the course of personal and social history and which shape and are shaped by shifts and changes of the self. It is about notions of maturity that valorise rather than pathologize the embeddedness of self and other. (1999: 2)

Pride is gained from identifying with other members of the family; people often declare that they are identical to a parent, grandparent, aunt, uncle or cousin. As Nüket Sirman (2005) argues, this is the production of a subject that desires a particular form of family – extended and close, both physically and emotionally – and, above all, a subject that desires that others be like the self. People also want to stay close together, and physical proximity is seen as desirable. A personal example may illustrate this more fully: in our previous home, the shape of the sitting room was somewhat awkward as it was rather long and thin. As we had three sofas, I suggested that we put one sofa at the end of the sitting room, and then if someone wanted to read, they could do so undisturbed by the sound of the television. When I suggested this, both my husband and my stepson looked completely aghast and, as one, declared wholeheartedly, 'But we will not be together' and refused to even consider my suggestion. Isolation and loneliness are states of being that are shunned and dreaded, while connections and proximity are desired and valued.

Wishing to be the same as others and the need for others to be the same as the self may be a particular form of subjectivity but, within a psychoanalytic framework, none of us can become a human subject without identifying with other human beings. In short, it is through identification that we become human subjects. Within such a psychoanalytic framework, according to Lucey et al. (2016: 131),

we unconsciously internalise aspects and encounters with the external world (including relationships, experiences, ideas) which then become deeply fused with our own subjectivity. What is emphasised here is the flow and interchange between inside and outside; the ways in which we dynamically take on aspects of the outside world and also how parts of ourselves are experienced as existing out there, in other people and objects. Identification is therefore constructive of the self.

Identification places us and provides our identity, security and connections within and across generations and across time. None of us,

regardless of our heritage, can achieve selfhood outside of identifications, and this is particularly apposite for those of us who have been
formed within Middle Eastern societies. Identification with others is
actively encouraged and esteemed.

The question 'Who am I?' is not of concern, as people in Egypt on
the whole do not probe who they are for two reasons. First, the strong
belief that people are as God made them and who God wants them to be
is pervasive and unquestioning. Second, it is taken for granted that identity is gained from other family members, and these tend to be parents
and grandparents. Affinity to significant family members is a source of
connection and pride and silences any internal scrutiny about identity.
This silencing of introspection operates not just in relation to the self
but also works to quieten the curiosity of others. This is not an aggressive reticence, as people shrug their shoulders in good humour and with
acceptance that they and others are as God made them and/or they are
just like their father/mother/grandmother. The affinities are not always
along patrilineal lines, as matrilineal affiliations are important – even
crucial – for some individuals. Joseph describes in detail an intense and
intimate mother–son relationship (and, while this is an example of a
Lebanese family, this case study is also applicable to many families in
Egypt). This intense involvement between mother and son was accepted
as a normal, mature relationship and was apparently not a cause for
comment (Joseph 1999). We need to be wary of the commonplace
assumption that lines of affiliation are apparent and are patrilineal (the
axes of identification are explored in further detail below).

The dominant viewpoint within psychoanalysis is that a person's
inner world is constituted by their relationship to others. It is the relationship to the other that is internalised and forms selfhood. Laplanche
(1989), a French psychoanalyst, argues that the other is *causal* in the
constitution of subjectivity and, as Frosh (2002b: 399) asserts, is crucially 'right there at the center of psychic life'. In this way, Laplanche
elaborates how the 'shadow of the object falls upon the ego' to draw
upon Freud's (1917) formulation. Freud's theory of the ego is based
on the view that the apparent boundaries of the self are permeable and
that the ego is continually taking in what is outside itself and constantly
assimilating the external world. For Jessica Benjamin (1998: 79), the
ego is not independent and self-constituting, but is actually made up of
the objects it assimilates, with the ego always incorporating the other.
In short, the self is constituted by identification with the other.

The ego constituted through identifications – through an absolute dependence on the other – is particularly vulnerable to the communication of the adult caregiver. For Laplanche, the communication from adult to child is always enigmatic as it is a communication from the unconscious of an adult to the infant or child, the meaning of which is unknown to or hidden from both adult and child (Sullivan 2006: 64). Communication occurs by means of bodily expression – gestures, grimaces, tone of voice – alongside what is spoken or, indeed, silenced. It is through the gamut of unconscious and conscious communications that adults implant messages about the socio-political world that we inhabit. The child cannot fully comprehend the communications received and struggles to understand the messages transmitted. These latter are, nonetheless, absorbed and internalised and form all of us, whatever our heritage and socio-political location. The seduction occurs inexorably as the adult draws the infant into the social world in irresistible fashion, all the while captivating the child and drawing him or her into a socio-political system that neither the adult nor the child fully comprehends, but which is, nonetheless, 'an enigmatic system through which both the parent and the child are ensnared' (Frosh 2002b: 399). It is important to point out that parents are themselves formed through the enigmatic and opaque messages of their own parents who, in turn, had internalised unfathomable but significant messages of the social order. Nobody passes these messages on deliberately or consciously; we are all entrapped within a chain of unconscious socio-political representations. Ngai (2005: 14) speaks of the 'inherently ambiguous affect of affective disorientation in general – a state of feeling unsettled or confused – or, more precisely, a meta-feeling in which one feels confused about *what* one is feeling'.

We gain our subjectivities through other human beings and the external environment. In contemporary British psychoanalytic theory, emphasis is placed on object relations; understandings of gaining selfhood emphasise that we become human through taking in the first and crucial relationship with our primary caretaker. Understandings of subjectivity focus attention on the gaining of identity through taking in and relating to another human being. In short, in this prevalent view, people are objects that are internalised and constitute a person's inner world and their relationships to others. I would like to edge towards adding to this framework a view that we also take in sounds, smells, taste, sights and touch. We internalise the senses which, just like the external world outside, can be inchoate for the child, but these sensations nonetheless form us (Treacher Kabesh 2013b).

While the senses are interlinked and it is difficult to adequately convey the shredded experience of the senses, I focus on sound as a foray into explicating how human beings internalise, inhabit and find ways of being in our environments. Taking sound as a specific aspect of the sensorium, I explore how it is an object that provides many important functions; sounds can provide consolation and support, and enable human beings to give meaning to our environment as we locate ourselves emotionally and physically. Sounds comfort, embrace and throw us into ourselves and outwards into an engagement with others. As Diane Ackerman writes, 'Sounds thicken the sensory stew of our lives, and we depend on them to help us interpret, communicate with, and express the world around us' (1990: 175).

Soundscape – external noises created by people – alongside the words that we speak, form us consciously and unconsciously; we become them and internalise, repeat and recognise ourselves and the external world through them. Sounds from the environment merge with noise made within the self for, as Barthes writes (1977), sound reverberates through the body because, to take in sound, we have to let it reverberate inside the self. Sound cuts through inner and outer space as it resonates and reverberates – it is visceral.

As Sullivan (2006) explores it, the unconscious is, first, a bodily surface that becomes internalised in the formation of the unconscious. As Laplanche asks, 'What is this surface that is projected within us? It is both our own corporeal envelope, and the surface of the other, the corporeal envelope of the human other' (1989: 49). Perception, therefore, involves the positing of oneself as an embodied entity in a meaningful way in relation to the environment and what the environment offers. This view of proprioception is close to Bull and Back's notion of 'voice-bodies' (2003: 70), which draws attention to how the body is critically involved in the production of sound; as we speak and produce different sounds, the noise strokes the skin. We feel sound as it brushes our skin, and it is through skin and sound that 'the world and the body touch, defining their common border. Contingency means mutual touching: world and body meet and caress in the skin … things mingle among themselves [and] … I am no exception to this … I mingle with the world which mingles itself in me' (quoted in Connor 2004: 28). In Cairo, there is no separation between home and the outside, as sounds from the external environment permeate the home – for example, the call for prayer, the sound of car horns, people speaking or indeed shouting; sand and dust, furthermore, easily pervade the home, which means that homes have to be cleaned continually and furniture is eroded by the sand. There is not a private sphere as such, partly due to the pervasion of the environment and because of the interrelationships between people (we know much about people's lives, even those of our neighbours), as everyone's comings and goings are noticed and can be a matter of conversation.

We merge and mingle with that which is external to ourselves, whatever the discourses and narratives to the contrary. Similarly, temporalities are fused and cannot be separated out. How we live in the present is full of the past, which, in turn, is occupied with the future; similarly, subjectivities are never individual but always formed through others. Temporalities are fused in an inextricable web so that it is impossible to know when the past is the past and not the present. Psyches are social spaces, so that it is also impossible to know where one human being stops and another begins. It is our relationships to others, specifically to primary carers, that incorporate us into, and inaugurate the rules of, the social order.

Our fantasies, wishes and complexes are marked by history. We inherit socio-political histories and the values and beliefs embedded in them. The problem with identification is that it can lock human beings into the past and into connections that should be refused if a different socio-political order is to be made. These ghosts of the past whisper and are noisy and insistent, making it nigh-on impossible to listen to one's own thoughts. In his exploration of repudiation, Walcott explains that a disavowal of the past is part of 'an assertion of the self outside of the sins of the fathers' (Walcott 1974), but, as Justin Edwards asserts, such disavowals do not work, for the whispers of history are utterances 'made by disembodied voices that are, like other hauntings, unavoidable and inevitable' (Edwards 2008: 122).

These narratives that haunt are elusive, enigmatic, slippery and intricate, leading to a feeling of being weighed down and full of that 'something' that evades and confounds knowledge and understanding. Narratives, memories, fantasies, emotions and belief systems constitute identities that are formed through the memories of others who 'are themselves suffused with *other* others' memories' (Freeman 2010: 263). These narratives of self and other are not a personal matter, as

culture is introjected through the conscious and unconscious communications of caregivers from the beginning of our lives.

Complex Personhood: Intricate
Identifications

The subtitle above is borrowed in part from Avery Gordon who, in
Ghostly Matters, explores what she describes as 'complex personhood' (1997: 4–5). Complex personhood, writes Gordon, means that
all human beings 'remember and forget, are beset by contradiction, and
recognize and misrecognize themselves and others. Complex personhood means that people suffer graciously and selfishly too, get stuck
in the symptoms of their troubles' (1997: 4). Identification with other
human beings is the mechanism through which we gain our subjectivity
and the very stuff that constitutes being human and our humanity. We
identify with family members (especially in Egypt where the extended
family is crucial, there is no real distinction between primary and other
caretakers) and other important figures. Identification is a way of being
in the world, engaging in the act of recognition of self and others; crucially it is a way of knowing the society we inhabit. Identification is also
contradictory as it can block recognition, knowledge and understanding, and can bind human beings adhesively into that which is familiar
and established. Identification is complex and contradictory, as it can
be adhesive and loving, can facilitate interconnectedness, and hinder,
if not paralyse, connectedness; it can lead to wanting difference and
fearing the 'other' (be that another human being, a mood, an emotion
or a thought). Fuss writes that 'identification has a history' (for Egypt,
a colonial history); she goes on to argue that to understand fully, 'the
notion of identification must be placed squarely within its other historical genealogies, including colonial imperialism' (1995: 141).

In Egypt, as Joseph and Rieker point out, people 'have repeatedly
used the family system to gain security in the face of an increasingly
repressive state, and neoliberal economic dislocations' (2008: 36). Taking the positive characteristics of family life as a given, I want, though,
to open up the problematic aspects of identification more closely. We
become adults through internalising family values, belief systems and
opinions that have been gained from the socio-political spheres. Adult
subjectivities are positioned to reproduce and maintain the social order

and these unconscious pledges are undertaken as human beings attach to certain ideas, emotions, forms of behaviour and other human beings, whether known or not. Identifications are never neutral, as we invest in them frequently with commitment even if they act against our best interests. Gordon points out pertinently that 'forms of dispossession, exploitation, repression and their concrete impacts on the people most affected by them and on our shared conditions of living' (2008: xv).

Both the family and religion are strong institutions in Egypt that are taken for granted and provide important solace and sustenance. They function as ideological state apparatuses to draw on a concept of Althusser (1971) by ensuring that human beings fulfil the expectations, obligations and responsibilities that are placed upon them. We are formed and 'interpellated' as human subjects through the ideological state apparatuses (education, family, religion) and repressive state apparatuses (army, police).

The family and religion are profoundly interlinked in Egypt and the discourses that arise from both institutions cannot be separated (I think this is the case whether the discourses are Christian or Islamic). Discourses arising from the family and religion emphasise loyalty and submission to the family, to God and to the nation. It is incumbent on human beings to fulfil their obligations, be they economic, emotional, action, moral and spiritual. Obligations to, and responsibility for, others are central to notions of maturity and acceptability. The matter of responsibility for selfhood is complex and intricate, as one's identity is partly fate and God's will while, simultaneously, the individual has to struggle against their own appetites, behaviours and thoughts (the original meaning of *ijtihad*). Human beings *must* (this is a strong injunction) fulfil the destiny that has been set out for them and, above all, human beings must *never* go against God's will.

These inescapable discourses are transmitted consciously – through explicit speech from parents, teachers, religious leaders and the peer group – and unconsciously. Language and the words spoken are clearly crucial in expressing sentiments, emotions and the stories that people tell of their own and others' lives. Egyptians are very concerned about their behaviour and how their actions will reflect on the family. About an unknown person, they frequently focus on the question, 'Do they come from a good family?' and, from that foundation, apparent knowledge is gained about the individual. We have internalised this viewpoint profoundly and we become anxious as to how our very 'being' reflects on the family. Narratives are a critical means by which we internalise the social world; what is kept silent is as important as what is spoken. The narratives we tell are formed through our interpretations of what took place and the emotions evoked by the event. As Gordon writes:

> Complex personhood means that the stories people tell about themselves, about their troubles, about their social worlds, and about their society's problems are entangled and weave between what is immediately available as a story and what their imaginations are reaching toward. (1997: 4)

The narratives we tell ourselves and others are shot through with unconscious impulses and phantasies. Transmission of who we should be, what and who we should internalise, and which identifications are obligatory takes place unconsciously, through gestures, tone and inflection of voice and through those subtle and elusive movements of the body that convey loaded messages. Transmission is unconscious both to those who are transmitting and to those who are receiving the messages. Transmission refers to 'the vertical transmission of identities, beliefs, intimacies and hatreds across generations, and the horizontal transmission of messages between and through subjects' (Frosh 2013a: 10).

As I have previously written, these meanings and injunctions are not passed down deliberately or with conscious intent and effect, for parents and/adults have themselves been the recipients of enigmatic messages (Treacher Kabesh 2015). For example, in Al-Nowaihi's exploration of the novel *Ahzan Madina* (A City's Sorrows), she writes that the central protagonist navigates the social world through observing facial expressions, bodily gestures, tones of voice and without fully understanding what is taking place he 'is beginning to note and internalize the demands' (1999: 252). The problem is that it is difficult, if not impossible, to know what has been taken in and to provide robust examples, as what has been internalised is enigmatic and beyond the grasp of conscious thought: I can sense something, feel it and know something is working away within me but I cannot reach it. Our symptoms, as Philips (1994) points out, are never our own. These internalised relationships to history, to the colonised and to the coloniser, are embedded in the unconscious, stubbornly durable and relentlessly pervasive, because they constitute our deepest and most persistent attachments.

Gordon pertinently points out that haunting 'is a frightening experience. It always registers the harm inflicted or the loss sustained by
a social violence done in the past or in the present' (2008: xvi). My
English and Christian mother was ambivalent about her life in Egypt.
She was very proud that she could speak Arabic so well and her life
in Egypt provided her with pleasures and comfort that would not have
been available to her in England. Her need to get away from Cairo does
not contradict what I have written above, but, like all of us, she was a
complex person. My mother learnt (from my paternal grandmother) to
cook in Egypt and her food always had the flavour, texture and aroma
of Egyptian food. But, and this is a big but, she was easily filled with
disgust at the dirt and the smells of the country and, I hazard a guess,
with fear of being engulfed by the other. As Derek Hook argues, postcolonial racism manifests through the body (2012: 46) and, I would add,
through the senses, so that people are disgusted by smells and different
tastes and overwhelmed by unfamiliar sounds. The other is expelled
through the body and the senses. Whether we want to or not, we absorb
these bodily and sensory responses, which are not inevitable or natural
but indeed formed through the resolute socio-political hierarchy. I am
haunted perpetually by what I have absorbed, what may be working
away internally and how this influences my relationships with people
whom I am attached to and love. Double consciousness is key, here, as
that which can be glimpsed and disavowed simultaneously.

Identification, therefore, can lock human beings into the past and into
connections that should be refused if a different socio-political order is
to be made. Identifications and loyalties are, needless to say, overdetermined and ambivalent; they are ambivalent because 'Desire follows
unpredictable directions, its attachment to objects can neither be stabi-
lized nor predetermined. Desire – its perpetual quest and the impossibility of its satisfaction – is a psychic determinant with historical effects'
(Scott 2012: 80). It is frequently unclear – and certainly requires
thought – which story, aspect or feature of a narrative is to be passed
on. Passing a narrative on can both provide a point of necessary reflection and simultaneously be the point where, as Rose writes, thinking
halts and 'out of respect, humility or fear of our own failure, is required
to stop' (2013: 4). However, there is respect embedded in the attempt
not to relentlessly pursue the other and not insist that other human
beings communicate or think in the same ways as the self. This necessary respect arises from a knowledge that the line between opening up

communication and hurting the other through a cruel tenacity is always risky. In Hisham Matar's novel, *Anatomy of a Disappearance*, a son frequently asks his father for stories and information about his father's history and his father deflects the questions. The son understands these deflections as his father honouring the wishes of his mother, who once said to her husband, 'Don't transfer the weight of the past on to your son'. He retorted, 'You can't live outside history. ... We have nothing to be ashamed of. On the contrary'. After a long pause, the mother responded, 'Who said anything about shame? It's longing that I want to spare him. Longing and the burden of your hopes' (Matar 2012: 26).

Identification and Disidentification[5]

Whether we are sons or daughters, fathers are inevitably folded into our most profound psychic investments and desires for reparation. Fathers enable their children to gain subjectivity in particular ways (see Butler 1997) and are, importantly, providers of love, care and sustenance. Via identification, the father is the child's essential route into the socio-political order – children must resemble their fathers (Radstone 2007b: 171) and both identify and distance themselves from their mothers. Relations with the mother as the primary caretaker and relations with the father are critical for socialisation and insertion into a patriarchal society (Hatem 1987). The extended family is important and parenting is not just the sole responsibility of the biological parents as there are other important caregivers who powerfully influence identity. Within Egyptian families there are many influences, various pushes and pulls and countless axes of identification. Children are perceived as extensions of adult members of the family and the attachments formed are intense and provide gratification. Unconscious identification and dis-identification, however, are never straightforward and are frequently intertwined, so that it can be difficult, if not impossible, to trace through the vexed pushes and pulls that do occur across the possible axes of identification.

Colonialism complicates our identifications with our fathers, rendering them more ambivalent in our internal lives. As Lucey et al. (2016: 135) observe, children find an 'intertwinement of strength, love, authority, care, power and vulnerability in their fathers'. This may be more problematic if our fathers, uncles, brothers, husbands and grandfathers have been seduced into colonial rule, with all its contempt and denigrations. I wonder whether what we cannot tolerate is the vulnerability of our Egyptian fathers (this may be a universal question) and the precariousness of their status and power under colonial rule when, indeed, they lacked any authority unless it was borrowed or imitated. We wish to disavow our history and assert we are not like that – we are over it. Above all, perhaps, what we cannot forgive is our fathers' and grandfathers' weaknesses, their inability to stand up to colonialism and overthrow colonial rule.

As Egyptian daughters, we feel protective and loyal towards our fathers. We find it difficult to question them, let alone to distance ourselves from them, as we are bound to them so profoundly. I am writing this as an Egyptian daughter (as I do throughout this book), and I know that one of my tenacious resolutions was to stop my father from dissolving. I grew up knowing, in those subtle and indefinable ways that children have of knowing the world, that my father did not have the same power, status or recognition as the white man. This unthought known has evoked disappointment, along with a simultaneous desire to protect my father from my disillusionment. Alongside this continual disappointment I am deeply enmeshed in Egyptian culture and so do not perceive my desire as such a problem, because what haunts me more is the conscious and 'unconscious terror of the breaking of identifications, of loss of recognition from one's family, where one is no longer the loved father, the loved daughter, may cast a deep shadow' (Lucey et al. 2016: 141).

These important and necessary attachments can lead to a complicity with that which is known, overly settled and stuck. Men and women are as embedded in vexed socio-political structures and discourses, and there is no reason why we should imagine or even speculate that women are immune from aggression, exploitation and cruelty. These deeply troubling aspects of social and psychic life are perpetually transmitted from the past to the present, from one generation to the next and through horizontal circulation. Having said that, we cannot resort to avoiding our responsibilities in perpetuating the socio-political order through the understanding that 'what we call our own belongs to you only in so far as it originally came from, belongs to, somewhere or somebody else' (Rose 1998: 40). At the risk of repetition, we are all, no matter our individual histories, class, gendered and religious positions, formed through and perpetuate social-political structures.

It is critically important to acknowledge our ambivalence, by which I mean those opposing emotions and states of mind that pull in opposing directions. For, alongside our commitment and allegiances to our families, we can also want to repel the emotions and state of mind provoked by another human being. 'I feel choked' is a common Egyptian expression that is frequently declared by men and women and accompanied by a gesture where the throat is held tightly as if to underline the feeling provoked. This lump in the throat is a visceral manifestation of feeling taken over by another human being, perhaps being rendered inarticulate and certainly overwhelmed. The lump arises when a person feels that they are being spoken for and 'more dangerously, in a manner contractually binding him to others without his volition' (Ngai 2005: 92).

We cannot avoid, however, the impact and consequences of inheriting our subjectivities through colonising and postcolonial structures. Fuss (1995) argues that Fanon considers the possibility that colonialism may inflict its greatest violence precisely by attempting to exclude people of colour from the self–other dynamic that makes subjectivity possible. It is this exclusion from the self–other dynamic that is problematic. Fuss writes, 'Fanon proposes that in the system of power-knowledge that upholds colonialism, it is the white man who lays claim to the category of the Other, the white man who monopolizes otherness to secure an illusion of unfettered access to subjectivity' (1995: 142). Due to having been colonised (materially, politically, emotionally), Egyptian subjects are excluded from the self–other dynamic. While this exclusion takes place through the Western imaginary, it has, I argue, been internalised by Egyptian subjects from childhood onwards so that I frequently hear assertions about the superiority of the West. This belief in the superiority of the West and the inferiority of Egypt is termed the '*khwagga* complex'. *Khwagga* means foreigner and is used to indicate that whatever is foreign is inherently superior and that which is Egyptian is intrinsically inferior. As Marylyn Booth writes, in Egypt there is much ambivalence towards the West (*al-gharb*) as it is 'both the focal point of admiration and emulation and the source of social disintegration and decay ... threat and promise' (1997: 832).

Despite stringent assertions that Egyptians are superior to the West and also to other Middle Eastern and Arab societies, the unconscious belief of inferiority persists. This overassertion of superiority and identity cannot bypass the exclusions. To draw on Fuss again, who explores how, in deploying 'the conventional psychoanalytic grammar of "the other" and "the Other" to distinguish between imaginary and symbolic difference, or between primary and secondary identification, Fanon implies that the black man under colonial rule finds himself relegated to a position other than the Other' (1995: 142). The implications of his exclusion are immediate, devastating and persistent. The exclusions endure and have to be endured.

To put it bluntly, this exclusion is violent and leads to what Orlando Patterson termed 'social death' (1982), which affects masculinity and masculine subjects especially. I am going to take a risk here and argue that women are not as affected by social death to the same profound extent as men. Women protect men, are affected by their assertions of patriarchal power and are positioned to sustain and support men, but these effects do not impact as centrally on subjectivities. We are simultaneously close up to, and distant from, the enduring consequences of colonisation. Butler argues that it is the fathers who are subjugated under colonialism and that 'the dehumanization of others under colonialism follows from the erosion of paternal authority' (2015: 175). Stripped of being addressed as a 'you' is to be dehumanised. As Butler goes on to explore the issue, to be addressed as a 'you' establishes human dignity and is crucial, as to be addressed as 'you' establishes the 'condition of becoming a human, one who is constituted within the scene of the address' (2015: 176).

Patterson writes that this relation of domination and, I would add, violence, has three aspects: the first is social and 'involves either the threat or use of violence'; the second is psychological and is the capacity to persuade and influence perceptions – though I feel that it is more unconscious than this and that this psychological capacity involves the formation of subjectivity itself (1982: 1–2). The third relation hinges on gaining cultural authority (1982: 2). These relations of domination and violence permeate everyday life and experience and hinge on matters of misrecognition and power. Symbolic violence, as Pierre Bourdieu argues, is produced, reproduced and legitimated through structures that are embedded and embodied in everybody's habitus (Bourdieu 2001).

These conditions impacted profoundly on our fathers and grandfathers because 'these men were not treated as men, certainly not addressed, directly or otherwise, as men, and so failing that address, they were never fully constituted as human' (Butler 2015: 175). Sons, though, witness their fathers' humiliation and the corrosion of their status, power and right to be in the world as fully human. This knowledge, that can be glimpsed, is disavowed and, alas, continues to haunt. Haunting, as Gordon argues,

> is not the same as being exploited, traumatized, or oppressed, although it usually involves these experiences or is produced by them. What's distinctive about haunting is that it is an animated state in which a repressed or unresolved social violence is making itself known, sometimes very directly, sometimes more obliquely. (2008: xvi)

It is no wonder, then, that Egyptian men can want to take the place of the Western other not so as they are like them but, rather, to gain the power, authority and position of powerful masculinity (Seshardri-Crooks 2000).

These troubling socio-political-affective structures are based on a 'system that is utterly dependent on the repression of a knowledge of *social* injustice' (Radway 2008: ix). Socio-political discourses haunt, along with the family narratives transmitted that lead to 'being weighed down, a palpable reaction' (Stewart 2007: 16). Subjectivities are formed through internalising and identifying with others and, while these complex identifications are essential for subjectivity itself to be gained, identifications can also bind human beings into the past. They can be adhesive and loving simultaneously. Moreover, as Sirman points out, 'This configuration of love that entails unending sacrifice and reason, extends from the love of the other, to the love of the family and the nation creating a singular, easily disciplined form of attachment to these real and imagined entities' (Sirman 2005: 349). The next chapter, chapter 4, concentrates on elucidating the attachments, repetitions and conflicts embedded in Egyptian subjectivities towards the nation. In chapters 4 and 7, I focus on thinking through Fanon's theoretical-political plea to consider the production of a new kind of subject that involves the decolonisation of the mind (Fanon 1986).

Notes

1. Of which the subtitle is a slight reworking of Mbembe's (2006) 'The intimacy of tyranny'.

2. See Elspeth Probyn (1996) for a sustained discussion of belonging, emotion and exclusion.

3. For an excellent edited collection on domestic tensions and national anxieties, see Celello and Khouloussy (2016).

4. See Suad Joseph (1999) in which the author explores the dynamics of connectedness and relationality for people in the Middle East.

5. This section is a development of an article entitled 'Political upheaval in Egypt: disavowing troubling states of mind' (2015). I am grateful to Lynne Layton for her exceptionally careful editing of this article.

Chapter 4

Enduring Repetition

Events, Narratives, Emotions

2011: Many Egyptians took to the streets in huge numbers, protesting against the corruption of the Mubarak regime. They were rallying together against the various aspects of corruption – financial, political, legislative and cultural – and the profound difficulties of living a stable life. The excitement and optimism were palpable, as we all believed profoundly that we were witnessing the birth of a new socio-political order and that the demands for 'freedom, social justice and bread' would be met. Profound schisms between the various factions – liberal, secular, Islamic groups, democrats and conservatives – led, however, to clashing differences that proved impossible to overcome.

1952: A group of army officers overthrew the interlinked triad of the Egyptian government, the monarchy – with its lavish and corrupt court – and British rule, which had been in place since 1882. These were all perceived by many as the source of the socio-economic-political ills of Egypt. This revolution or *coup d'état*, dependent on one's ideological stance, promised a new socio-political order through which social justice would be implemented.

1919: This was an important year for Egyptians, as early that year a national delegation (Wafd) issued revolutionary calls for Egypt's complete independence from the British Protectorate. These demands met with popular approval, and there were massive demonstrations that strongly questioned the legitimacy and authority of the ruling dynasty.

Ideological chasms between liberals, democratic nationalists and conservative monarchists deepened and led to irreconcilable conflict.

All three 'revolutions' promised radical breaks from the past, different beginnings and the institution of a new socio-political order that
would inaugurate equality and social justice. The ills and evils of the
past – exploitation, corruption, oppression, inept rule – were now in the
past and would be overcome. Each period led to confidence and hope
that all that hindered Egypt from developing into a democratic and prosperous society had been removed: corrupt government (all three 'revolutions'), royalty (1952) and, above all, corrupt British rule (1919 and
1952); the 'revolution' in 2011 was also full of the promise that Egypt
would be free of Western imperialism. Decolonisation, in particular,
marked 1919 and 1952, but was implicit in 2011.

The political activity in all three revolutions was based on the belief
and heartfelt wish that a secure future based on social justice would be
delivered; moreover, independence from the past 'portended a blessed
future – a future whereby colonial exploitation would be replaced with
economic "development" and social "progress"' (Go 2013: 5). I hazard
that anger, humiliation, disappointment and optimism were the dominant emotions in all three revolutions. Certainly, my father was filled
with optimism, faith and the conviction that a new Egypt was about to
be built in 1952; my brother and I were also confident that a new Egypt
was on the horizon. My father and I were filled with optimism and hope
in relation to political upheaval but at a different historical period – we
were both profoundly disappointed.

The promise of new beginnings is always fraught, as 'beginnings
always constitute a sort of paradox: a point of departure that – simultaneously – affirms and disavows, acknowledges and displaces, creates
and repeats' (Scott 2009: vii). Revolutions, as Hannah Arendt points
out, 'confront us directly and inevitably with the problem of beginning'
(1973: 21). Embedded in the word 'revolution' are the contradictory
meanings of radical break and rotation. Revolutions, whether a radical
break or a cycle of change and continuity, evoke hope, optimism and
the heartfelt belief that life will improve. Hope, misplaced though it
may be, should always alert us to the precariousness of inhabiting a life.

Memory, phantasy and fantasy,[1] and event and narrative are an interlinked chain that operates within subjectivities and the socio-political
sphere; in this chapter, I attempt to prise apart how these inextricable

loops interweave to form particular subjectivities. Memory, fantasy and emotion profoundly influence the motivation/s towards becoming and sustaining being a political actor (or not) and how the socio-political sphere is conceptualised. As Sally Alexander argues, to write a history

> which takes into account an understanding of memory as contingent, of culture as inimical to the drives, of mental life which is irreducible to consciousness, and of subjectivity which is both forced and irresolute, is in no way an easy one to write. But the problem is that by excluding the unconscious, we lose the concept of psychic instability. We also jettison fantasy, the generative figurative form of psychic life, an integrative moment in all mentalities. (1994: 229)

I focus in this book, as hopefully is clear, on the more problematic aspects of subjectivities, which entails understanding the denial and disavowals of what can appear to be an unyielding refusal to take on that which has been internalised. Freud's understanding of unconscious time is pertinent here, as he understood the unconscious as marked by repetition. A psychoanalytic understanding of subjectivity rests on the view that all human beings are formed through the activity of the unconscious, with its complex and elusive structure. This subjectivity is composed of curious 'multi-layered fragments of memory, odd bits of debris from the past, dream elements, gaping absences, convincing and also unconvincing stories, a history of discontinuities and unresolved questions, of traumas, things unsaid, and memories actively destroyed' (Kennedy 2010: 181). The unconscious does not know and resists time as temporalities co-exist in a kaleidoscope of timelessness. Repetition, phantasy, affect and events constitute psychic life.

Within a psychoanalytic framework, the present is made up of memories, narratives and perceptions from the past (including the gaps and absences in them), as temporalities are fused and no clear distinction exists between the past and the present. The past has a tenacious grip. Egypt's long colonised history is a burden that persists in the present, even if that persistence is disavowed both by the Egyptian state and by ordinary citizens. Socio-political-historical conjunctions trap through explicit discourses and, just as importantly, entrapment takes place in an oppressive atmosphere. While the past is intangible and the effects of events on subjectivities elusive, public secrets (that which is known and disavowed simultaneously) dominate, so that I frequently feel overwhelmed by confusion and at a loss; however, none of these statements undermines our understanding of the various – implicit and explicit – ways in which events, history and prevalent discourses have a material effect on people. The formation of being a citizen, wherever one lives, always involves the act of remembering and forgetting (Alexander 1994), comprehension and repudiation, knowing and disavowal. The formation of being a citizen is especially traumatic if subjectivity itself is founded through the traumatic circumstances caused by colonisation. This leads to a disavowal of the impact of history on personhood, as 'selective amnesia, ignorance and unconscious investments' (Rothberg 2009: 77) can govern narratives spoken or repressed, emotions felt or not felt, and any possibility for a different understanding.

There is an enduring analytic issue of why some narratives are given dominance over others. Much analysis emphasises contradictory narratives, but there is a tendency to treat narratives as if the contradiction exists on just one axis; however, narratives cannot be so easily mapped out – as if they exist on just one alignment. If we take seriously, and I think we should, the notion that we inhabit multiple narratives and memories, then it is incumbent upon us to map out as many narratives as is humanly possible, even if we are at risk of being overwhelmed. There are, however, persistent methodological difficulties: first, the issue of judgement between event, narrative and memory; second, the enduring theoretical and political analytic matter of why some events are remembered or not and, moreover, why we invest in certain narratives and not others.

There are various entanglements at work: entanglement with the past, with other people (whether known or not) and with dominant discourses and narratives. I am in a dilemma here, as I want to respect the connectedness that is embodied in Egyptian subjectivities, yet simultaneously point to the difficulties that can arise from diverse entanglements. I am concerned, however, that my perceptions of entanglement coincide with a Western ideology of possessive individualism (Macpherson 1962) and a prevailing psychoanalytic viewpoint that stresses the necessity of separation and differentiation (see, for example, the work of Jessica Benjamin[2]). Identification which can lead to adhesive states of mind can keep us locked into dominant perceptions, fantasies and narratives whereby there is little socio-political-affective space for something new to take place.

The question of how to write a coherent narrative persists and requires perpetual judgement in relation to which thoughts, ideas, emotions and events to incorporate and which to exclude in order to achieve this coherence – necessary in order to produce a narrative. It is, of course, challenging and impossible to convey the jaggedness and complexity of human beings. Coherence, though, is also a problem, as it can cover over cracks and fault lines and conceal gaps in understanding; furthermore, thinking always involves emotions and fantasies as we can all reach, too fast and too easily, for that which is known and reassuring. The familiar can often be used as an emotional and cognitive resting place, which consoles and reassures, as opposed to reaching towards that which is unfamiliar, surprising and unknown. Resistance to new states of minds is commonplace, unfortunately, and occurs due to fear of the unknown, fear of betrayal, fear that occurs in many places (metaphorical and actual) and through many states of mind. In short, there are ethical responsibilities involved in writing a narrative.

The distinction between a narrative as lived and a narrative as told is crucial due to the gap between our illusions of who we are and our troubling and conflicting fantasies, ghastly emotions and wishes, and how we are riven with various unspeakable and unknowable needs. We are always up against these chasms between the known and the unknown, what can be spoken and what has to be left unsaid, what is known and genuinely not known. We need to tread carefully through the quagmire of citizens, the media, state and government. The 50th anniversary celebrations of the 1952 revolution were full of state discourses about progression, democracy and hope.

The violence, conflict and oppression, however, were completely suppressed and concealed from any official discourse or account. Of especial note is the treatment by the Free Officers of Mohammed Naguib (he was the first president of Egypt following the events in 1952), who was cruelly and deliberately ousted by Nasser and his followers. Internal conflicts that are, after all, inevitable are at times obscured and hidden from public knowledge – a secret that may or may not be glimpsed. We need to be cognisant of the disjunctions between that which is in the public arena and the discourses that are perpetuated by official state discourses.

There may be a gap, however, between what is glimpsed and the official discourses that circulate and these possible openings necessitate elucidation. During the 50th celebrations of the 1952 revolution, I was struck by how often someone (usually men, it has to be said!) declared 'I did not know' in a tone of voice which was frequently bewildered and embodying an atmosphere of feeling lost. I want to stand back and think through the importance of the declaration 'I did not know', which may have validity if knowledge is concealed from the general public, who are in the grip of profound state control. The statement 'I did not know' resonates with Paul Gilroy's depiction of a social state of mind 'in which tragic and disturbing events punctuate quieter periods of apparent forgetting that endure long enough for the inevitable lament of "We did not know" to appear plausible' (Gilroy 2006: 29).

Recurring yearnings

Following the three 'revolutions' (that of 1919 less so, but certainly those of 1952 and 2011), there arose an important socio-political space in which to make a different society based on social justice and equality. Excitement, hope and optimism circulated, leading to a profound belief that Egypt would become a more just and equal society. These periods of buoyancy were short lived but perhaps, following the 1952 revolution – in which a group of army officers (known as the Free Officers and led by Gamal Nasser) ousted the government, Egyptian royalty and, importantly, British colonial rule – an atmosphere of optimism had a longer duration.

While the period of optimism was longer than after the revolution in 2011, both 'revolutions' are marked by the emotions of despondency, despair and profound disappointment felt by Egyptian citizens and by a failure to have made a difference in relation to developing a society based on social justice. Repetition of affect and political failures are striking, and these recurrences cause anxiety and provoke concern. Repetition – emotional, social or political – may be more prevalent than we are willing to acknowledge in the relentless drive to assert our differences from previous generations and our insistence on progress. There are, regrettably, more similarities than we are often willing to recognise and realise. My generation is profoundly disappointed, as was my father's generation, and this distress is full of loss and the absence of hope and promise of a society based on equality of opportunity, where gross poverty is eradicated.

We are in the arena of the 'colonial boomerang', a process elucidated by Arendt (2004/1951) as the bringing of the colonising practices of coercion and domination from the colonies back to home. While Arendt is concerned with the impact of these colonial practices on European nations, I am using the depiction to trace through the process of internalised colonialism in an attempt to elucidate the colonial violence and brutality inflicted on Egypt by Egyptians. It is, therefore, not so much a return but that which has never been absent or indeed defunct; Aimé Césaire describes it as the *choc en retour* (1955), which, as I understand it, refers to the 'backlash' 'of brutality, violence, degradation and dehumisation' (Rothberg 2009: 77). For Fanon and Freud, repetition was a strong and crucial aspect that inhibited thinking and understanding; if catastrophe cannot be thought about as Butler poignantly asserts, we are marked for life, and that mark is 'insuperable, irrevocable' (2003: 472). Repetition takes place within human subjects and as states of historical consciousness and, within every sphere, (socio-political-subjective) repetition is paralysis and leads to petrification.[3] In *Beyond the Pleasure Principle* (1920), Freud argued for the existence of two instincts – life and death – which he conceptualised as being in opposition. As I understand it, Freud used the term 'death drive' to conceptualise the human tendency to reduce tension and to bring about a state of inertia and nothingness. The death drive is destructive towards both the self and the external world.

The necessity of thinking and acting are essential aspects of human life and essential endeavours – here I am beholden to Arendt's arguments in *The Life of the Mind* (1978) and to Mbembe's arguments in 'Consumed by our lust for lost segregation' (2013). I am attempting to explore how repetition as a state of mind, as an action and in narrative leads to inertia and petrification within both individual subjectivities and colonised societies. A cruel and oppressive consequence of colonisation, the violence and exploitation that were wrought on colonised societies are perpetuated relentlessly.

It is extremely tempting to avoid the above analysis and bypass problematic thinking in relation to repetition and to thereby write a narrative of progression that construes analyses as Egyptian society unfolding smoothly from oppression to democracy. These narratives of progression coincide with the discourses arising from the state (the media, education) that also portray the movement from oppression, corruption and inept rule to a more progressive present and future. Previous regimes are wiped out of history – for example, the Nasserite era was dismissed and denigrated along with the era of King Farouk, and, currently, there is a complete, and understandable, dismissal of the Mubarak regime. Since 2011 and still ongoing today – 2016 – there has been a refusal to talk about the

Mubarak regime (indeed, Mubarak's name is barely mentioned); alongside this refusal there is a re-representation of the period of rule of both Nasser and Sadat as a time of material security and emotional certainty.

The production and reproduction of narratives is never straightforward for, as Diane Fuss (1995) argues, narratives reproduce more narratives; moreover, narratives contain multiple condensations and displacements. Narratives shift over time, sometimes slowly and imperceptibly and, at others, so quickly that it can be difficult to glimpse the shifts as they move across fluctuating sands. It is important to render visible these absent narratives, while bearing in mind that they are repeated, so that a particular version of the events becomes fixed as *the* version. There are important shifts in political narratives and discourses: the time of King Farouk is now seen in a more golden light, and Nasser has been resuscitated as a strong and admired leader. Nostalgic representations of the time of the monarchy, especially when King Farouk reigned, are also circulating in the media (*El-malek Farouk* was a popular television series screened in 2012). These representations are perceived by the general population to be a much more accurate portrayal than previous representations, which are perceived as lies.

None of us are immune to the pull of nostalgic yearnings. A daily ritual in my home is listening to an *Umm Kulthum* concert. While listening, I watch the audience delight in the singer's voice, I see the glamorous attire of the women and I am amazed at the differences between then and now. I long for those days of cosmopolitan Egypt when life did seem freer and offered more abundant possibilities. Nostalgia in Egypt circulates among many of the population and the different political groups – from the left, which is insistent that oppression has never been so prevalent, to those of us on the secular left who look backwards, intent on finding inspiration – and these longings are similar to the nostalgia for the monarchy which 'is not so different from the fundamentalists' yearning for the purity for the time of the Prophet and his followers, a wistful desire for a time better than the present when the present is so dismal' (Bradley 2009: 23).

Seeking Political Liberation

Egypt has a long history of colonisation and has been colonised over centuries, and this history is of concern as it influenced many of the events and impacted too closely on Egyptian subjectivities. I concentrate, however, on recent history and events, and this is the focus of the following section. In 1882, Britain decided to occupy Egypt due to its economic desire to control the Suez Canal and thereby secure the trade route to India. Egypt never officially became a colony despite the occupation, and this was not due to any honourable considerations but because the British government could not afford to offend European governments and risk endangering access to the Suez Canal (Osman 2010). Political machinations aside the British still exercised considerable power in Egyptian affairs, and British officials expanded their involvement in the political, social, economic and judicial life of the country. British advisers were installed in key ministries, and all Egyptian ministers, who held inferior positions, were required to obey their British superiors.

During the 1860s and 1870s, British economic and political influence increased considerably and on the whole with little resistance. This rather troubling state of control and domination persisted until 1919. This is a key date in Egyptian history, for, in 1919, a national delegation (Al-Wafd) issued revolutionary proclamations demanding Egypt's complete independence from the British Protectorate. Al-Wafd, as the national party, developed the struggle for independence from occupation by a European power (Osman 2010: 25) and as important it also questioned the authority and legitimacy of the ruling dynasty. Massive demonstrations in March and April of 1919 legitimized the emergent Al-Wafd's claim to represent the national will and to represent the increasing demand by Egyptian subjects for Egypt to rule itself. Al-Wafd was a nationalist movement and involved the demand for the creation of an Egyptian nation state with full representation and equality for all its citizens. Lord Milner headed an inquiry into the causes of the 1919 Revolution and negotiations began to recognise Egypt's independence; while in 1922 the British recognised Egypt's independence, but in reality Britain continued to rule powerfully by proxy until 1945. The constitution of 1923 established the principles of individual civil and political rights (Whidden 2005). During the first sessions of Parliament in 1924, ideological divisions within the various Egyptian parties intensified political conflicts. For example, the Union (Ittihad) Party deepened ideological cleavages by making monarchy and Islam the symbols of the new Egyptian nation state. Needless to say, it is important to point out that the British exploited the ideological cleavages that existed to strengthen their power through divide and rule. James Whidden argues that the British exploited but did not create them (2005: 20) as there was no consensus on what should be Egypt's modern political identity. It is this inability to find a point of consensus or even struggle to understand the various viewpoints that continues to the present day and, I argue, is a major obstacle to Egypt developing a society based on anything close to social justice. From the mid-1920s onwards, the articulation of Egypt's political identity revolved around questions of 'Islamism and secularism, democracy and authoritarianism' (Whidden 2005: 21).

The Al-Wafd formed as stated above to demand self-determination from the Great Powers evolved into a popular party but quickly were perceived as holding onto power as more important than the country. The struggle for independence did not abate, and the slogan 'the Devil take the English' resonated throughout the 1930s and 1940s, and much student activity took place demonstrating for independence. There is a long history of student political activity in Egypt, and all political parties whether of the right or the left drew support from students and communist student leaders. This political fervent was fuelled by the 1936 Anglo-Egyptian Treaty (Britain increased its control over the Suez Canal and sanctioned an enlarged Egyptian military to provide support). During the 1940s, there were increasing popular demonstrations that did not lead to any change in legislation, British domination or the corruption of the monarchy. The British military continued to dominate and to exert power frequently with the collusion of the Egyptian government.

The landed class refused the calls for land reform and resisted any moves towards re-distribution of wealth 'preferring to squander its wealth on the conspicuous consumption of imported luxuries. More dangerously, it undercut local demand in the countryside by reducing wages and increasing rents' (Kandil 2012: 8). The refusal by the landed class along with the capitalists to even consider a fairer economic system fuelled radical tendencies culminating in the Cairo Fire (1952), which destroyed much of central Cairo including western shops and businesses. As stated above, Britain maintained its power over Egypt until 1952 when it was ousted along with the Egyptian Royal Family. The Nasserite era began with the 1952 Revolution, which overthrew the Egyptian monarchy and government and the occupation of the British, and put in place a new government formed by a group of army officers led by Gamal Nasser. The driving forces of that generation were disaffection, disappointment and anger towards the ruling party, the monarchy and the imperial powers. According to Hazem Kandil (2012), the group of army officers were outraged by an incident that occurred in 1942 when the British tanks surrounded the palace and forced King Farouk to replace the existing government. Kandil writes that, witnessing this incident left the

> officers bitter toward the whole political elite: the cowardly king who obeyed foreign dictates, the opportunist majority party that formed a government under foreign tutelage, and of course, the British bullies. In a letter to a school friend, a devastated Nasser bemoaned: 'I am ashamed of our army's powerlessness'. (2012: 10)

Much talk centred on the restoration of Egypt's glorious past, and embedded in these beliefs was the possibility of greatness again. 'Dignity for Egyptians' (the word – dignity – was part of the rallying call in the 2011 revolution so note the repetition of the phrase) and 'Glory be to Egypt' were the rallying calls of the time in 1952.

For the first time in centuries, Gamal Abdel Nasser was the first Egyptian to rule Egypt, and the excitement and hope this raised cannot be overestimated. From 1952, the military took power securely and began to change internal politics, and this project was given an inclusive national appeal with its emphasis on civic notions such as social equality, identification with the poor and Egypt's role as the leader of the Arab world free of an Islamic dimension (Osman 2010: 51). Great emphasis was placed, however, on Egypt's place on the international scene, and the years from 1958 to 1967 saw Nasser attempting to fend off interventions in the Middle East by America and Britain. Much effort was made to establish a coherent Arab region with power and influence, but following the humiliating defeat in 1967 by Israel, Egyptian morale plummeted. It cannot be stated enough that despite the many failures of the Nasser regime – and there were many – Nasser represented hope and optimism.

After Nasser's death in 1970, Anwar Sadat became president until his assassination in 1981. Sadat introduced a more capitalist economic system that is usually described as *Al-infitah* (opening up), and when in 1973 he led Egypt's attack on Israel, he managed, for some of the Egyptians population, to overthrow Nasser's shadow. Despite the introduction of a multiparty system in the 1970s and the holding since then of a number of parliamentary elections, democracy and respect for the rights of the citizen have been diluted. The rule of oppressive law has dominated as is exemplified by the institution of Emergency Law that has sanctioned police repression. The Emergency Law of 1958 has been in force since 1967 (it was lifted for 18 months between 1980 and 1981) and is a permanent fixture despite the occasional promise (that no one really believes) that it will be lifted. The law allows

> for extended detention without trial, denies detainees habeas corpus, bans labor strikes, prohibits demonstrations without police permission, justifies press censorship, 'and sanctions trails of political prisoners by special courts that deliver 'swift justice' and restrict defendants' right to appeal. (Kandil 2012: 199)

Under Mubarak's rule, Egypt has become firmly entrenched as a police state; elections are rigged (bribing people to vote for Mubarak, changing votes that were cast in favour of Mubarak) and the surveillance system is widespread.

The military is admired and respected because of the role it played, specifically in 1952, in overthrowing British colonial rule and the Egyptian monarchy, and the Egyptian monarchy. In short, the military is revered in Egypt. This admiration is felt by many of the population but not all, and one important reason (alongside the role of the military in 1952) is that Egypt still retains national service and so most men have undertaken a spell in the military. This is exemplified at present by Field Marshal Al-Sisi's tight control of Egypt, widely perceived by many as ensuring the safety of Egyptian citizens and by many as necessary and proficient. It is the need for strong leadership that facilitates Al-Sisi's fervent popularity. His popularity was underscored when he told Barak Obama (the then president of the United States) that Egyptians would rule Egypt. This widely perceived anti-colonial stance was greeted with relief, joy and the profound belief that Egypt would finally be independent of foreign interference. When Mubarak also made the same declaration to Obama, it made no impact as it was clear that it was empty rhetoric, but Al-Sisi is perceived as a leader with more authority. A commonplace opinion about Al-Sisi that circulates runs along the following lines: 'He is a difficult man but Egypt needs a dictator and above all he loves Egypt'. I see this declaration about Al-Sisi, as providing consolation, and it acts as a bolster against the profound disappointments that have been suffered for so many generations and for far too long. In short, both Nasser and Al-Sisi are held in especial esteem in the beleaguered psyche of many Egyptian citizens.

Illusion, Triumph, Denial

On the evening before his resignation as president of Egypt, Mubarak made a desperate speech in which he appealed to the Egyptians that he was *the* leader and, importantly, *the* 'Father of the Egyptian Nation', with all the resonances of patriarchal law at the level of the nation and the family. Mubarak called upon the memories of the Nasserite era, when much talk centred on the restoration of Egypt's glorious past; embedded in these narratives is the strongly held belief that Egypt will be a great civilisation again. As I have already mentioned 'Dignity for Egyptians' and 'Glory be to Egypt' were the rallying cries of the time, along with the activity that took place to claim political authority, focused partly on reclaiming the Suez Canal. Mubarak concentrated on how he was an anti-colonialist leader. When the then president of the United States Barak Obama demanded that Mubarak resign, Mubarak reiterated that it was up to the Egyptians to decide – in this way, he was implicitly but powerfully reminding Egyptians of the time of colonisation and the continual threat of the return of oppression and, crucially, of a strong Egyptian desire to return to the Nasserite time of being an anti-imperialist nation.

In 1956, Nasser declared that he would nationalise the Suez Canal; this was greeted with massive popular approval by the Egyptians and sealed Nasser's position as an anti-colonial hero. The Suez Canal is more than just a canal. As the most important trade route linking Europe with Asia, and the crucial reason why England occupied Egypt from the nineteenth century on, it is the site of much symbolic and material machinations. The Suez Canal provokes many emotions, as it was built by Egyptian men, many of whom (an estimated 120,000) died in its construction; as significant is the international debt incurred during the building of the canal.

Much activity took place to claim political authority, focused partly on reclaiming the Suez Canal. Britain and France took centre stage in

Egypt as Britain wanted to assert its influence and France was 'itching to punish Nasser for his support of the Algerian nationalists' (Alexander 2005: 82). Israel quickly joined in the political aggression. The important success of Nasser in 1956 over the Suez Canal and against the aggression mounted by Britain, France and Israel was heralded as a trouncing of imperialist nations and, specifically, the defeat of England. Nasser greatly antagonised the British prime minister, Anthony Eden, who referred to Nasser as 'that colonial upstart'. There followed meetings between the Great Britain, France and Israel in order to mount an attack on Egypt and reclaim the Suez Canal. In early November, the attacks were mounted against a background of international disapproval, in particular American condemnation. Nasser's bold political move was greeted with hope, and the profound belief that this would be the beginning of the Arab region's ascendancy. Nasser declared – and was thoroughly believed – that 'we got rid of colonialism, British occupation, we are not going to accept by any means another sort of colonialism, another sort of collective colonialism, however it is disguised' (quoted in Alexander 2005: 88). The initial success of Nasser, 'laughing in the face of the world powers, reminding them that Egypt too was a nation, Egypt too, had her pride' (Alexander 2005: 87), was crucially important for all countries with a history of colonisation in the Middle East, Africa and beyond. Fidel Castro spoke of how it allowed hope and a belief that life could be different. So, I can provide you with a narrative of triumph, of defeat of imperialism and of honour and courage and we could relish this moment of anti-imperialism – after all, there are precious few incidents of anti-imperialism to celebrate.

The narrative of Egypt taking on imperial powers and winning is the narrative I have inhabited, but politics is never neutral and is always replete with fantasies, emotions and deeply held narratives. While working on this important event, I have begun to realise – uncomfortably and reluctantly – what has been screened out by both Egypt and the Great Britain is that both societies deny the fundamental role of America in the withdrawal from Egypt. It was with visceral shock that, through reading Bill Schwarz's (2011) book *Memories of Empire*, I discovered the extent of American intervention in the Suez crisis. I highlight this to point to our adherence to particular narratives that hold us so strongly despite our best intentions. Egypt at this present moment is full of anti-colonial rhetoric, photos of Fattah Al-Sisi and Nasser dominate posters, banners and front pages of newspapers, and it was with immense pride that Al-Sisi stood up to Obama and told him that Egyptians would do things their way.

I stalled at this point and had difficulty thinking it through, as I was confronted with my parents' own investments which, whether I like it or not, I have internalised. My father's wholehearted commitment to Egypt and his agreement with Nasser's claim to authority over Suez is easier to write about, as here I can provide you – and myself – with a narrative of resistance and triumph, of honour and courage. My English/Christian/conservative mother is another subject altogether, as she profoundly believed in the Tripartite Aggression and was intensely attached to a view of Britain as a country of integrity. I do not know which British newspaper/s she would have read and what propaganda and misinformation it would have contained. My parents, for different reasons, were nationalistic and the irony is that, in their investments of their country as heroic, they bypassed, consciously or unconsciously, the fact that both the Great Britain and Egypt were [are] controlled for different reasons by the United States. My parents and their narratives, beliefs and values haunt me.

Intergenerational transmission is the issue here, but it is difficult to discern, to trace through and to know what is transmitted and passed down, partly because we live it and also because the socio-political-affective narratives we absorb are unfathomable. No one, as Sullivan (2006) points out, sits people down and tells them what to think, believe and/or value, but we internalise these laden narratives through tone and intonation of voice and through bodily gestures; these messages are then handed down and across generations. The unconscious is crowded out with people, ghosts, messages, values, beliefs and emotions. It is surprising, therefore, that we can even hear ourselves think.

The academic is also haunted (no matter the demand and our wish for it to be otherwise). We have our investments in certain narratives, certain versions of the self, and are always motivated to silence and making absent certain aspects of our history and what we have internalised. So, I can wax lyrical about my father's Marxism and anti-imperialism and, through him, present myself as a heroine, but my mother's investment in conservatism and nationalism is another confrontation altogether. I want to make these aspects of my history absent, to deny my shame and, above all, I want strongly to deny that I may have inherited and internalised any of my mother's values and belief systems.

In any case, the above narrative of Egypt taking on imperial powers and winning is *the* narrative. I conceptualise memory, narrative, emotions and events as part of an interlinked and inextricable chain, together with the fundamental role of the unconscious. While working on this important event – the Suez crisis if you are European, the Tripartite Aggression if you are from the Middle East [note the different language] – I have started to realise, uncomfortably and reluctantly, what has been screened out. I was two years old during Suez and living in Cairo with my Egyptian/Muslim father and my English/Christian mother and their different loyalties, identifications and feelings of betrayal. This is one personal story that could be told but there is another one I want to focus on. I have provided this personal example previously (Treacher Kabesh 2013a) and I want to reiterate it in order to deepen the analysis of screen memories. My mother and I went to stay in the countryside. On a few mornings, I struggled to open my eyes. I literally could not open my eyelids, and my eyes had to be wiped clean of a substance secreted from a particular insect, so that I could see again. This literal blindness has not reoccurred, but I have lived it out in just the same way as I, along with so many other Egyptians, have screened out so much of Egyptian history.

Screen memories and narratives are not neutral – anything but – as they obscure any knowledge and/or understanding of other more unpalatable phantasies, affects and memories. Screen narratives and memories that bolster personal and socio-political myths are replete with that which is desired and conceal that which is feared or unwanted. For example, in the 1960 novel *Al-Bab Al-Maftuh* (*The Open Door* 2005), Mahmud (the brother of the central protagonist, Layla) joined the demonstrations against the British (the fictional time is in the mid-1940s, when there was much political agitation against British rule). In the novel, Mahmud becomes active in the nationalist movement and is shot. Layla is convinced that her brother is a hero and that he was shot at by British soldiers because he is a nationalist protestor. In her fantasy, and the story, she tells others that he is a hero. For one wonderful day, she becomes the centre of attention at school as the teachers and pupils alike all want to hear the story of her hero brother and she is exalted. When she returns home after this glorious day, she finds her brother Mahmud lying on his side, barely moving because, he says, 'I feel as if someone hit me hard, really gave me a beating. And I couldn't hit back. I couldn't yell anything' (Al-Zayyat 1960: 12). Desperate, Layla shouts in despair, 'But it was you, you, it was you'. He lies and says, 'Yes, Layla, It was us – we struck the English' (1960: 13).

This fictional narrative of Egyptian bravery resonates with common-place assertions and heartfelt beliefs that reiterate stories about the bravery of Egyptian men. Any other possible narrative is refuted robustly. This narrative of bravery requires careful consideration because it is used to screen out the possible fear and shame that men may experience when they are not quite brave/manly/strong enough. This narrative of the bravery of Egyptian men abuts tightly into official discourses of the strong Egyptian army that conceals the defeats that have occurred; however, as I have been arguing, we internalise and hold these discourses close to our hearts.

There is, nevertheless, one narrative that I could give you which focuses on how 1956 is used to screen out and forget the humiliating failure of the 1967 war against Israel, when Egypt lost the Sinai. There is then another layering, which is that both 1956 and the war of 1973 – also about the Sinai – are used either independently or together to screen out the loss of 1967. So, the memory and narrative of heroic victory functions as consolation. It was with visceral shock that I discovered recently that Egypt did not win because of its brave army but, rather, because of intervention by America, which threatened to withdraw money from Britain, France and Israel – the primary cause of the Tripartite withdrawal (Schwarz 2011). We are in the arena of pushes and pulls: to push away from Britain and France, Egypt pulled itself towards America, which, incidentally, Nasser admired for its restraint in the Middle East and never believed would attempt to dominate and exploit the region.

There are other screenings, which the narrative of Egyptian defiance obscures and represses, and that is the appalling aggression that Egypt inflicted on other nations. So alongside Nasser leading the Pan-Arab Union and being an icon of anti-imperialist struggle, what is repressed out of sight is Egypt's inexcusable aggression in the Yemen, for example. Nasser, and he is certainly not alone, unconsciously perpetuated, mimicked – and I mean this in the most profound way possible – and internalised the aggressions of the coloniser.

Repeating Recognition/Misrecognition

Repetition is disturbing and distressing. The initial impulse that propelled me to start this endeavour of understanding political authority, or the absence of it, was ignited when I witnessed my father weeping copiously over the failures of the 1952 revolution. Having never seen my father crying, I was startled and puzzled by his tears and the way in which he was torn apart by his overwhelming feelings of responsibility and disappointment. I discovered that my father was not the only person in distress, as I heard of many men of a similar age, profession, class and status who were equally upset. There is an irony in that I now find myself in a similar emotional and political place and space as my father, as my generation is perturbed and angry by the persistent lack of social justice and perpetual inequality.

The persistence of socio-political structures, cultural formations and subjectivities is a puzzle, as Orlando Patterson (2010) argues. The persistence of exploitation, cruelty and violence is entrenched in all societies and *embedded introjection* – to draw on Patterson's apt description – is a dominant characteristic whatever society we inhabit (Patterson 2010: 147, italics in the original). It is essential that the embeddedness of subordination, domination and exploitation is traced through and understood for, as Mbembe (2013) stringently argues, 'Hard questions have to be asked. They have to be asked if, in an infernal cycle of repetition but no difference, one form of damaged life is not simply to be replaced by another' (2013: 29). The insistence that all has changed, and that colonialism has been overcome, stalls the capacity to think about the subtle but various ways in which colonialism endures in the violence and exploitations that are wrought on other human beings. These assertions get us absolutely nowhere, as we have not only absorbed colonial structures with their laden brutality, contempt and denigration because, and more problematically, we perpetuate violence on other human beings.

There is, as Fuss points out (1995), violence at the heart of identification. Identification is never straightforward, as we identify with those who have exploited and denigrated us and treated us with contempt. In the case of Egypt, identification has taken place not just with those who have been colonised (an axis of identification with those who are in a similar structural position); another problematic axis of identification with the coloniser has occurred, so that the subject 'becomes a veritable cemetery of lost, abandoned, and discarded objects' (Fuss 1995: 38). Crucially we become human subjects through identifications that 'form the most intimate and yet the most elusive part of our unconscious lives' (1995: 2). To formulate identification as just a matter of intimacy is to miss the crucial point that identification does not 'travel outside history and culture. Identification names the entry of history and culture into the subject, a subject that must bear the traces of each and every encounter with the external world' (Fuss 1995: 3).

Identification is a means of gaining control in a socio-political context in which there was little control, power or authority to be had. One aspect of the atmosphere of colonisation in Egypt was that Egyptians were represented, perceived and positioned as without history (except for the relentless fascination with the time of the Pharaohs). Identification with the British coloniser is a repudiation of these perceptions and representations; this is understandable, but the problem is that this imagined hierarchy of superiority and inferiority is perpetuated on other human beings. Imagined inferiority can be expressed in an assertion of superiority and in mimicry of the coloniser. These internalised relationships to history, to the colonised and coloniser, are embedded in the unconscious and are stubbornly durable and relentlessly pervasive as they constitute our deepest and most stubborn attachments. Political and emotional imperialism colonises our imagination, our thinking and our action, which paralyses our capacity to make and experience different relationships – as the colonial past is internalised and absorbed, and hierarchies of superiority and inferiority are replicated.

What happens out there, what occurs between people and becomes transmitted and absorbed into selfhood, is, in part, the hierarchies of superiority and inferiority; in short, who can take up his or her place as a full human being. Oppression and inferiority are absorbed for, as Fanon writes, the black man is not a man until he is liberated from himself. Fanon poignantly describes his desire and need 'to help the black man to free himself of the arsenal of complexes that has been developed by the colonial environment' (quoted in Hall 2002: 14). As Catherine Hall puts it:

> Colonisers assumed that black men had no culture, no civilisation, no long historical past. In learning their masters' language, black men took on a world and a culture – a culture which fixed them as essentially inferior. Meanings of blackness were taken inside the self by the colonised, both inscribed on the skin and internalised in the psyche. Lack of self-esteem, deep inner insecurity, obsessive feelings of exclusion, no sense of place, 'I am the other' characterised what it is to be black. (Hall 2002: 14)

These troubling and troublesome aspects of subjectivity cannot be located in the past as they have been absorbed and transmitted into present-day subjectivity.

The issue of being positioned as inferior is crucial here, as this has been transmitted and has become 'embedded introjections' (to draw on Patterson's 2010 phrase again), leading to the inevitable and understandable need to disavow certain aspects of the selfhood. Colonial imaginings and thinking represented Egyptian men as lazy and irrational; this legacy persists in the depiction of Muslim men as 'dangerous brown men' (Bhattacharyya 2008) and, I would add, the problematic representation of Middle Eastern men as dominant patriarchs. There are two understandable reactions (minimum) to these representations. The first is to deny vehemently any sign or knowledge of human vulnerability and fragility. We cannot here draw on resistance to colonial representations as pertinent to explain the attempts to overthrow normal aspects of subjectivity such as vulnerability, frailty and insecurity, as these characteristics of being human continue to persist within the self and indeed to haunt the self. Second, and as problematic, is the projection of vulnerability, insecurity and 'failed' subjectivity into the other.

I am asserting that the attempt to overthrow and disavow vulnerability and insecurity is a prevalent secret in Egypt that is simultaneously both known and frequently dismissed. This known and disavowed secret is a crucial aspect of the unthought known (Bollas 1987). Frosh describes the unthought known as a memory – though I would add narrative – that cannot be recalled 'yet is never lost, keeps finding its way through into consciousness only to be rejected by the subject. Something speaks, but even as we hear it we pretend that we do not know what it is' (2013a: 39). Frosh poignantly explores the 'secret' as that which cannot be tolerated but which also serves a protective function because the 'secret' is transmitted *from* the other but is also *a part of* the other who is frequently known and loved. Frosh writes that 'there is a *protective* factor at work. Something is being preserved, some precious idealisation or maintenance of a bond, or a lost object that cannot be let go of by allowing grief to come to an end' (2013a: 39, italics in original). A protective secret is one which focuses on protecting our fathers, uncles or grandfathers from our contempt and disappointment that they were (are) not powerful enough, phallic enough, brave enough, strong enough. In short, and I do think this, whether I like it or not (and I do not) they were (are) not manly enough. Disappointment, anger and sadness circulates and becomes an abject aspect of the self that has to be denied and repressed, as these emotions cannot be assimilated and I cannot stress enough that to even glimpse at these emotional states of mind is risky.

Secrets, other human beings, representations and 'embedded introjections' – the stuff of living a life – are embodied, persist and have to be tolerated. As Schwarz points out, 'Men's bodies are never far away', as masculinity and personhood acquire meaning in relation to those who are perceived as having lesser claims or rights to personhood. In short, white masculinity – which I insist is relentlessly represented as superior and innately better than masculinity, which is deemed as 'other' – and masculine subjectivity have less to do with empirical beings 'than with an entire, fantasized, discourse complex which underwrites its creation' (Schwarz 2011: 20). The shaping of the subjective and socio-political spheres of the colonised and coloniser are profoundly interlinked and cannot be separated out, as both spheres impact on and form the other but always within unequal power relations.

There is a difference between denying and hating the vulnerable self and the situation in which doubt, uncertainty and self-interrogation are perceived and experienced as weaknesses that must be expelled from the mind. I have mentioned this idiom previously but it is worth repeating here, as it is such a powerful injunction: 'A person in two minds is a liar'. Ambivalent and ambiguous thinking has to be expelled due to a need for safety, security and, above all, the desire to be seen as strong, independent and rational. Egyptian men are fearful that they will be positioned and represented as feminine, and the phrase 'Just like a woman' is redolent with contempt and aggression. As Maud Ellman (2005) points out, we find it easier to say murder, mourning or melancholia than to utter the word 'mother'. While mothers are idealised in Egypt, the injunction that parents (mothers especially) are not to be criticised is taken very seriously. In seeming contradiction to this idealisation, denigrating and humiliating the other, particularly women, is commonplace. Women are humiliated and positioned as inferior for two different reasons. First, it is a powerful means to bolster the powerless self and as a powerful process that represses that which is perceived as 'irrational', 'feminine', 'soft and therefore weak'; all that which is perceived as powerless has to be repudiated, as these are aspects of the self which are hated. This cannot just be located with men, who do humiliate and degrade women, for women also denigrate other women (this point is taken up more fully in chapter 6).

Second, humiliating women is another route through to shaming and humiliating other men – their husbands, fathers and brothers. One powerful means of humiliating women is through sexual harassment. Despite the amount of coverage in the Western media (in the United Kingdom at least), it is unclear whether the sexual harassment of women is on the increase or not. As Nadje Al-Ali writes, the 'focus on harassment itself evokes a mixed picture as the widespread mobilisation, campaigning and advocacy against harassment is unprecedented, and has allowed for a previously sensitive issue to be addressed publicly by Egyptian women, and I should stress, many men' (2014: 123). Whether it has increased or not (the figures are shocking: 98 per cent of women report being sexually abused), various points need to be made. First, that denigration is always written across women's bodies and women bear the marks of socio-political-emotional vilification; second, that women are used for humiliating men and this is felt keenly; third, that power relations exist between and among men and this is never neutral.

One way in which both colonised and colonising societies are shaped is through the adamant representations and profoundly felt beliefs that the Western man is superior due to his 'natural ability' to inhabit democracy, to be free and independent and, of course, not to be controlled or, indeed, be the domineering patriarch. These may be illusions (and I would argue that they are) but they are powerful and sustaining fictions that serve to bolster significant beliefs in Western masculinity. One way to boost these projections is to place the colonised other as incapable of these attributes and/or values – an enduring aspect of colonial thinking. Problematically these values, belief systems and value systems are internalised and embedded within Egyptian subjectivities.

In different ways, Egyptian men are placed as having either too little or, indeed, too much agency. In the description of the events of 2013 as a *coup*, the Egyptians – but let us stay with men here – are placed as passive, powerless and without agency. In the same way, representations of the Muslim Brotherhood as victims of the army have a similar function. No man in this account can be agentic but rather is passive to controlling forces. A psychosocial positioning of masculinities across a hierarchy of superiority and inferiority is relentless. In seeming contradiction, though they are interlinked, the representations of and beliefs in relation to the military serve to reinforce the discourse of all Egyptian men as the embodiment of oppressive patriarchs who do not allow freedom, movement and thought. Egypt apparently cannot be a democracy, and this stubborn view rests on a notion that Egyptian men cannot and do not understand liberalism or democracy and further reinforces persistent values from a colonised past. This viewpoint that Egyptians are 'not ready for democracy' is a prevalent opinion that is repeated endlessly and is difficult to counteract. The feeling that Egyptians cannot handle democracy and need a strong and firm leader – as if they are wayward and irrational children – circulates and forecloses any nuanced discussion as to what would be a suitable democracy for Egypt and why a democratic system has not been instituted. Through these ubiquitous beliefs, the oppressive rules of Nasser and Al-Sisi remain unquestioned; more problematically, repressive dictatorship is heralded as necessary and desirable (Treacher Kabesh 2015). It is almost impossible to question a country's dominant belief system, as its values are reinforced by vertical and horizontal transmission. By horizontal transmission, I am referring here to the role of the peer group in perpetuating a refusal to think creatively and effectively. Fear is a key component in repetition and should never be underestimated – our fear of alienation, of losing the love of friends and family and of not knowing to whom or where we belong. To deny fear, as Rose asserts, is 'as ineffective as it is absolute. Nothing, we might say, is more dangerous that the repudiation of fear – at which men (often) and nations (regularly) excel' (2014: 10).

There are strong attempts to repudiate inferiority alongside doubt and uncertainty, as Christopher Bollas writes: 'Ideological certainty, then, in spite of its binding of the self through simplification and the exile of other views, is threatened by a sudden breakthrough of the pushed-aside thoughts, which now must be dynamically ordered by an over-decisiveness' (2011: 84). The role of the state in Egypt is, at this present time, profoundly entrenched and referred to as the 'Deep State'. It has become commonplace to declare that it is now more oppressive than ever, but I genuinely do not know if this assertion is true, as Nasser repressed cruelly and harshly any dissent, imprisoning members of the Communist Party. As is also well known, membership of the Muslim Brotherhood, even in the 1950s, was declared illegal. The Muslim Brotherhood is again illegal and perceived as a terrorist organisation: Egypt Against Terrorism was the tag line in Egypt during the summer of 2013. Members of left-wing parties, journalists and some political agitators are to this day subject to torture and/or imprisoned. Cultural commentators are continually at risk of being gagged. A state of mind in which all opposition or different views and values are not tolerated dominates. Other ways of thinking, doubt and ambiguity are pushed aside and repressed. Both sides of this divide – the military and the Muslim Brotherhood – brook no opposition. Both institutions denigrate and ridicule the views of the other; both assert their superiority and state that their way is the only way; these modes of thinking have entered Egyptian civil society so that it is difficult, if not nigh-on impossible, to have as open a conversation as is humanely possible. This does not bode well for the future in relation to making an effective and open society.

The assertion of superiority is undertaken by linking to other sociopolitical categories of class, sexuality and race: the other who is positioned as inferior. The other troubles partly because he/she/it functions as a material reminder of the precariousness of living. The other human being provokes and evokes anxiety about who the self may have been or may, in this precarious life, become. This identification can lead to compassion and a wish to reach out to others who are less fortunate, or to a cruel dismissal. Christopher Bollas warns us that the dehumanisation of the other 'has the function of squeezing out humanity and preventing human understanding from modifying the cruelty' (2011: 82). One way through to recovering humanity is to elucidate our complicities, to begin to uncover the secrets that we keep absent and out of sight and to find a way through to more effective thought.

Resistance, in the psychoanalytic meaning of resisting the new, the unknown and the surprising, is frequently a response to the intolerable. As Rose writes, for Freud 'resistance was a psychic reality that blocked the passage of the psyche into freedom. One of the mind's best defences, it cuts subjects off from the pain and mess of the inner life' (2013: 5). I am not convinced that any of us have psychic freedom, as I do think that all human beings struggle, no matter their colonial heritage, with the 'pain and mess of inner life'. As Schwarz (2011) points out, there is no way of imagining the means by which the imperial past might ever infiltrate the present. He emphasises the possible wish to forget and, to this, I would add the possible contradictory wish to remember, to capture and for the present to be the same as the past. Rose (2013) writes that remembrance hovers in the space between social and psychic history and hovering in those spaces is the unconscious and temporality.

What is it about the past that may come back to haunt us, or the future threatening us with what we might become? Fear is usually directed towards what might happen; after all, as Frosh puts it, 'The fear that one may discover something about the past that will put the future in jeopardy is surely enough, a haunting fear' (2013: 25).

Notes

1. The different spellings of 'fantasy' and 'phantasy' require clarification. Melanie Klein deliberately spelt phantasy with a 'ph' to indicate the unconscious nature of phantasies and to distinguish them from the more everyday understanding of fantasy. Within a Kleinian framework, phantasies are woven through all thought and emotion.

2. The work of Jessica Benjamin is invaluable and generative, leading to rich insights – see *The Bonds of Love* (1990), *Like Subjects, Love Objects* (1995) or *In the Shadow of the Other* (1998).

3. I am grateful to Derek Hook for his excellent article 'Indefinite delay: on (post)apartheid temporality (2015) and for his pertinent use of the word 'petrification'.

Chapter 5

Female Agency

Struggling against Constraint

It is my usual pedagogic practice, at the beginning of teaching a module, to ask students to think of a topic that they want to explore and understand. Over the past four or five years or so, female students inevitably declare, with wholehearted sincerity, that they want to learn more about women in the Middle East. Something odd then takes place as, when I attempt to open up the matter of gender in the Middle East, specifically in Egypt, I am met with incredulity and frequently told that I am wrong (a female colleague who teaches on modern slavery is met with similar responses). There is a similar reaction when female friends – older and liberal feminists formed within a particular feminism of the late 1960s – ask me relentlessly about the position of women in Egypt.

The questions tend to focus on why women are absent from political protests and silent on socio-political matters; alongside the assertions of women's absence from the political sphere is another commonplace preoccupation – sexual harassment. These women cut across generations and diverse socio-political formation but their rejoinders are surprisingly similar. Their responses are full of concern and pity for women who are apparently hapless and helpless and require urgent rescue. I persist in my attempt to talk about the complexity of femininity and gender relations but am told, in the subtlest yet firmest of ways, that I do not really know what I am talking about. I witnessed a friend of mine being interviewed on the BBC programme *Hard Talk* shortly following her election as the leader of the Egyptian Constitution Party (a broad centre–left alliance) in early 2014. Hala Shukrallah was the first female to head a major political party in Egypt and is a Christian. The dominant theme in that interview was the refusal by the female journalist to take seriously Hala Shukrallah's opinion that she was not on the receiving end of prejudice as a female *and* a Christian; the journalist was adamant that Hala Shukrallah had been subject to profound discrimination.

In none of these examples – and I could, unfortunately, give countless others that take place far too frequently – does recognition of self–other relations and/or a dialogue take place. As Lila Abu-Lughod (2013) trenchantly points out, none of us who speak out against stereotyping are quiet on the issue of women's suffering, but we are treated as if we are silent and our understanding is wiped out. This mirrors the attitudes and values of nineteenth-century missionaries; however, this cannot be pointed out, nor can a robust engagement take place. To be honest, I am not sure why this dynamic is so entrenched, but I do know that it is depleting. These commonplace responses ignore the hard work that local Middle Eastern feminists have been putting in for a long time and the importance of these interventions. Furthermore, these reactions dismiss the viewpoints of those who disagree or simply have a different viewpoint to that of their white and international sisters (Abu-Lughod 2013: 11). Žarkov argues stringently that within Western thought women who are deemed as other are reduced to the same ontological category (2016). Diminished to the category of victim and positioned resolutely as passive, without any real capacity to think and above all confined to the domestic sphere. Importantly, as Žarkov points out, Western representations take 'radical feminist arguments about sexual violence to tell non-western men and women what they are today, and liberal feminist arguments about equality to teach them what they should become' (2016: 120). I have said this before, and it is worth repeating: I will know that there is some hope of proper recognition when a Western feminist expresses her indifference, fury, contempt and perhaps even envy of the woman who is deemed as other, as opposed to persistent pity and concern.

Nadje Al-Ali, a feminist theorist who works on Iraq, has written recently (2014: 122) that she finds that people's attention drifts when she tries to answer their questions more fully, as her perception is that what is required are sound bites. So, what is going on when other women and I from the Middle East find ourselves relentlessly in a place where we are positioned as knowing little and understanding even less?

This is not personal; it is too ongoing and stubbornly pervasive for that, but, needless to say, it is felt as personal when one's knowledge, judgement and understanding are dismissed and misplaced belief and value systems take precedence as the source of knowledge.

An important matter of communication then arises that focuses on how to adequately respond. I find my responses limited as I assert Egyptian women's agency, autonomy and political participation going back to the nineteenth century and/or I can verge on the absurd as I refute that any patriarchy exists in Egypt. I am especially prone to that response when I am told categorically that it is 'patriarchy', as if declaring the word – patriarchy – delivers the answer and as important as if it is straightforward to discern and understand how power functions. There is, however, a difference between asserting a narrative of resistance that obscures the intricacies of complex subjectivities and providing an understanding that corrects (I use that word unashamedly) misperceptions and misunderstandings.

Inevitably, when starting to write a chapter, there are many directions that open up, and I could provide you with numerous examples of powerful and agentic Egyptian women; we could all breathe a sigh of relief that patriarchy does not have such a hold on Egyptian women and thus becomes one thing to cross off our worry list. Or, I could provide you with numerous examples of women's oppression in Egypt, so that the focus becomes on the violence wrought against women, female unemployment, education and health; however, then all I would be doing is reinforcing already deeply held views based on strongly held beliefs which have little, if any, foundation in knowledge.

I want to be clear that, in this chapter, I am in dialogue with the discourses embedded within Western and Egyptian feminisms. These discourses share similarities while simultaneously having crucial differences and these focus, for example, on questions of religion and nationalism. We need to engage with addressing the real material and psychic differences that divide us and, from that basis, we can then move towards constituting a somewhat different understanding of recognition. Recognition, I argue, is different if we allow the other to make a difference to the self. I am reliant on Elisabeth Young-Bruehl's exploration of empathy, and that entails allowing the other *into* the self (1998). It is certainly a different ethics if we attempt to trace through, and understand, the intricate spectrum of similarities and differences as opposed to using another human being (whatever their gender, class, religion or sexuality) to bolster the fragile self. This involves the crucial matter of judgement, and I am becoming increasingly firm in my belief that judgement cannot be avoided.

The vexed matter of women, agency, choice and autonomy is at the forefront of many debates within feminist postcolonial theory. The tendency is for many Western feminists to position women from the Middle East, sub-Saharan Africa and South Asia as victims solely of patriarchal and familial structures that are firmly embedded within oppressive socio-political configurations. From this vantage point of superiority, 'brown' women are perceived and represented as in need of rescuing from 'dangerous brown men' (Bhattacharyya 2008) and are securely positioned within a myth of rescue. Moreover, a commonplace assertion in the West is that women from the Middle East are oppressed, passive and have little control or freedom over their lives. More problematically, Middle Eastern women are perceived as lacking the 'enlightened consciousness of their "Western sisters", and hence doomed to lives of servile submission to men' (Mahmood 2005: 15).

In an attempt to counteract this dominant narrative, some feminist theorists working on the Middle East think through the pressures for women of living in patriarchal societies, taking full account of the nuanced pressures on women (a classic example is Deniz Kandiyoti's 1988 essay 'Bargaining with patriarchy'), while other feminists working on the Middle East and within postcolonial theory (Abu-Lughod, for example) tend to assert the opposite – that women from the Middle East have agency, control and the capacity to resist the oppressive conditions in their lives. Making heroines of women and of the oppressed, however, can obscure the web of local relations which provide the context for and often the limits of resistance. A common theme that exists between Middle Eastern and Western feminism is the emphasis on the absolute difference between these geopolitical societies. The assertion of difference occludes knowledge of the socio-political conditions for all women and paradoxically obscures the divergences that exist between them.

Female subjectivities are complex, contradictory and dense, as women are also replete with emotions, phantasies and belief systems that push and pull in different directions. Women can be rendered invisible by 'classic' postcolonial theory (Fanon and Said, for example) that can take masculinity as the norm. In this chapter, I attempt to convey the complexities of Egyptian female subjectivities and the socio-politico-emotional structures that produce and restrict women's lives. It is important to take full account of historical trajectories, specific contexts and location. I assert that it is crucial to understand location, through its various aspects, in terms of history and temporality, place, class, religion and sexuality, as the basis for understanding female subjectivities, whether it be the women who are being thought about or the female reader/observer/scholar.

This conceptualisation hinges on the matter of judgement; this cannot be avoided by asserting that 'It is all so complex' or 'It's their culture' so that these assertions foreclose explorations and perhaps troubling thought. Paradoxically, the statement 'It's their culture' can mean that the cultural and socio-political conditions are not thought through or understood. Many feminist scholars working on the Middle East, for example, Al-Ali (2014) and Abu-Lughod (2013), refuse cultural explanations, as they perceive resorting to 'It's their culture' not as a means to understanding complex formations of culture but as a covert way of asserting innate differences and inferiority. In short, culture becomes fixed, as if cultural characteristics are ahistorical and unchanging. Nadje Al-Ali writes that, for a long time, she has felt compelled to write about political economies, authoritarian dictatorships and conservative patriarchal interpretations and practices as a way of resisting the vexed statement 'It's their culture' (2014). Importantly, Al-Ali explores her previous theoretical and political stance to determine how her previous position sometimes provided a

> gloss over forms of gender-based violence, the political marginalisation of women and extremely socially conservative attitudes towards women and gender relations that do of course need to be analysed by reference to foreign interventions and authoritarian regimes, but surely cannot be reduced to them. (2014: 123)

While the assertion 'It's their culture' is resisted with good reason, there remains the question what do we obliterate or obfuscate by not thinking about culture differently? Suad Joseph puts this theoretical dilemma thus:

> How can the question of culture be addressed with more nuanced constructs to study Arab culture as operating on, between, among, by, for, against, and with Arab women as subjects without essentializing or

> dissolving culture, so that 'Arab culture' informs rather than obstructs
> analysis of Arab women. (Joseph 2012: 13)

There is a wealth and range of postcolonial theoretical frameworks that
draw on various disciplines (history, economics, feminism, philosophy,
political theory, psychoanalysis), but many theorists draw on more
than one discipline, as postcolonial theory tends to be interdisciplinary.
It is almost impossible to provide a succinct overview of the different
conceptual, methodological and political positions taken up by postcolonial theorists. Therefore, as an inadequate way though, I indicate here
the theoretical frameworks that influence and form my thinking and
understandings: feminist theory, especially a psychoanalytic framework
(gender, 'race', ethnicity); feminist theory in general; postcolonial and
political theories that focus on the Middle East; and theories of subjectivity (which focus on certain strands of ethics). I have begun many
times to write a list of specific theorists but the list always came up
short; so, I have abandoned the inadequate attempt. The links that join
those of us engaged in feminist-postcolonial-political theory are, first,
the endeavour to challenge that which is taken for granted socially,
politically and emotionally; second, the serious attempts to understand
subjectivities in all their complexities and contradictions; and third, the
political desire, implicit or explicit, to live otherwise.

Whatever the various positions taken by the theorists mentioned
above, a common thread that unites them is the view that, as Nadje Al-
Ali (2014: 122) points out, it is 'challenging to get across the complex
and contradictory ways in which the (counter) revolutionary processes
and political transformations have affected women, men and gender
norms and relations over the past years'. In this chapter, I am opening up the importance of thinking through location, judgement and
the effects for women of inhabiting the ideology of neo-liberalism and
neo-liberal subjectivity.

Neo-Liberal Subjectivity:
Struggling with Constraint

A recent collection of edited essays, *Gender, Agency and Coercion*
(Madhok et al. 2013), explores the intricate matter of women, agency
and autonomy. The authors do so from a range of geopolitical regions

but are all intent on drawing out the complexities in theorising gender and agency. In the book, Clare Hemmings and I explore the ambivalence embedded within feminist theory in relation to women and agency and how feminists advocate that women should pursue freedom from oppression and strive to realise their own ability to act and influence the society that we inhabit. This bold injunction can frequently slide into a discourse about the individual subject. Simultaneously, feminist theory is engaged with tracing through the various ways in which women are oppressed (through different socio-cultural-political structures) and, for some feminist academics, emphasis is placed on the internalisation and perpetuation of these repressive structures (2013).[1] Whatever the differences in understanding and conceptualising agency, theorising it is central for much feminist theorising and activism. The crux of my argument is that the three terms – judgement, location and neo-liberalism – are profoundly interlinked and form the web of complexity through which, I am asserting, we need to think through matters of agency.

The insistence that Middle Eastern women are agentic and possess autonomy and power is problematic because these responses remain locked within neo-liberal values of subjectivity. The ideology of neo-liberalism is that of freedom, untrammelled choice and autonomy. The independent self is valued and desired above all else, and this is a self that is free of history and the demands of the other and is able to live a life without constraint. The difficulties of thinking through, and being bound by, discourses of freedom and choice can entail wiping out the intricacies involved in any analysis of female subjectivity so that we (that is, feminists, whether from the West or the Middle East) only perceive agency as that which is 'against custom, tradition, transcendental will, or other obstacles – whether individual or collective' (Mahmood 2005: 8). We need to be vigilant in ensuring that feminism is not complicit with neo-liberal notions and values of freedom, autonomy and choice. As I am arguing that all subjectivities are formed within, even if in part, the discourses of neo-liberalism, then there is an inexorable inevitability to this complicity. Our identity itself, along with the values and belief systems through which we make judgements, must always be questioned no matter the risk to the phantasies of ontological security and certainty.

One dominant value that pervades Western feminism is the 'stubborn conviction that women's rights should be defined by the values of choice and freedom' (Abu-Lughod 2013: 17). As Mahmood asserts, we 'cannot treat as natural and imitable only those desires that ensure the emergence of feminist politics' (2005: 15) because we cannot avoid confronting the question of how to think about choice and what it means to assert freedom as the ultimate value. After all, we are all born into families and inhabit their values, beliefs and ways of being; 'We all find ourselves in particular social worlds. We are placed in certain social classes and communities, in specific countries at distinct historical moments. Our desires are forged in these conditions and our choices limited by them' (Abu-Lughod 2013: 18). In short, we need to reflect on our experiences, limitations and challenges to being in the world, no matter our geo-politico-temporal location.

I have been attempting to draw out in this book how we are all bound to the socio-political conditions for our very existence, as subjectivity is always embedded within socio-political and affective structures. The formation of gendered subjectivity does not take place prior to its imbrication in socio-political structures but, rather, is formed *within* these structures. Mahmood, drawing on Foucault, writes that 'the paradox of *subjectivation*: the very processes and conditions that secure a subject's subordination are also the means by which she becomes a self-conscious identity and agent' (2005: 17, emphasis in the original). To elaborate this point further, subjection is the making of a subject and '*acts on a* given individual as a form of domination, but also *activates* or forms the subject' (Butler 1997a: 84, emphasis in the original).

As our subjectivity is formed, inhabited and perpetuated within the structures we live in, our capacity to live a life free of controls and constraints is impossible. This argument can only become stronger once we consider the unconscious to be that which acts against resistance and agency. Taking the unconscious seriously necessitates recognising that it can act against agency because taking on a psychoanalytic framework requires accepting that the subject cannot be conceptualised as the source and repository of psychic life due to the continual decentring activity of the unconscious. The unconscious always skews what we think, what we believe we know and the very notion of a secure knowledge about our identity. We are never free from either the unconscious or the social, as both are at work and influence profoundly what we can grasp and comprehend. Unconscious and conscious lives are at odds, and we ignore this tension at our peril, destined instead, as we are, to repeat the misrecognition of self and other over and over again. The unconscious pulses through everything we do, think and feel.

The unconscious is the most mischievous aspect of the self as it is always in hiding; however, it is always making itself felt and continually does its best to ensure that we do not remember our promises to ourselves. Whatever the various concepts of the unconscious and its workings, psychoanalytic theorists agree that it is forever disruptive and continually pervasive. Moreover, as all human beings we are constituted through the subjectivities of others, we internalise and inhabit other people (primarily the family), so that it becomes difficult, if not impossible, to recognise the boundary between self and other. Inhabited by others, it can be difficult to find the space to even hear oneself think.

Suad Joseph (1999, 2012) argues persistently for the importance of connection, bonds and relations with other people which are crucial for Middle Eastern people. While Joseph rejects psychoanalysis as being reductionist and ahistorical, Jessica Benjamin (1998) is reliant on psychoanalysis – and specifically object relations[2] – to theorise intersubjectivity as the 'shadow of the object'. As Benjamin writes, 'The ego is not really independent and self-constituting, but is actually made up of the objects it assimilates; the ego cannot leave the other to be an independent outside entity, separate from itself, because it is always incorporating the other' (1998: 79). In the novels *The Open Door* (Al-Zayyat 2005) and *Butterfly Wings* (Salmawy 2014), however, the central female protagonists – Layla and Doha, respectively – are depicted as autonomous individuals free of dependencies and obligations, possessing the capacities required to transform their lives. In this way, the representations of these female characters coincide with the neo-liberal discourse that individuals are autonomous entities, separate from relationships and independent of social strictures.

Before engaging with a discussion about the problems embedded in these novels, I briefly summarise them. *The Open Door* explores the complex dynamics of family life through one central protagonist – Layla. The novel begins with her adolescence and ends in her early to mid-adulthood and tackles issues of sexuality, love and the social expectations that are brought to bear on young women. It explores the internal and external conflicts of this young protagonist in her quest for freedom and to break free from socio-cultural-emotional constraints. It also depicts the pressures on parents to sustain a particular social order through what Layla describes as the 'fundamentals'. The 'fundamentals' relate to marriage, maintaining an outward persona, security, material possessions and, above all, status. The book explores the conflicts within the family and within Layla, together with the political conflicts that are rife (the novel starts in 1946 and ends at some point in the 1950s; it is not clear to me quite when the novel ends).

The Open Door 'is woven through the daily conversation of its characters, the "small" as well as the "large" events of mundane existence' and, as Marilyn Booth goes on to point out, 'More often than not, these conversations take place among women without any men around, or with one man, always a family member present' (Booth 2005: xxv). Even though women had been writing and publishing fiction since the turn of the nineteenth to the twentieth century, this novel influenced a later generation of women writers. It confronts issues 'of personal freedom and sexuality in the context of received social expectations and the constraints of political inertia, economic travail, and class – and to do so as a women writing about female experience – was new and shocking' (Booth 2005: x).

This is an important and influential book, and the novel *Butterfly Wings* (Salmawy 2014) reverberates with many of the same themes: freedom, sexuality and marriage interwoven through imagined political upheaval. *Butterfly Wings* was initially published in Arabic in 2011 and is set in the present. There are important overlaps and differences: Doha is older than Layla and is unhappily married to an important politician. While *The Open Door* is intent on being modern and describing Layla as wanting to leave the 'imprisoning' past behind her, *Butterfly Wings* is more intent on reclaiming the past – which is represented as authentic and, importantly, as a point of difference from the West.

Both novels are preoccupied with freedom; however, while the yearning for freedom is apparent, it is never really clear what freedom would mean for any of the protagonists. How to achieve freedom is never discussed and so the call for it reads rather like a repetitive mantra which obscures more than it reveals. Freedom is represented as if it is a state of being that we would all recognise, desire and reach towards. These novels, therefore, coincide with a view and an assumption that 'all human beings have an innate desire for freedom, that we all somehow seek to assert our autonomy when allowed to do so, that human agency primarily consists of acts that challenge social norms and not those that uphold them' (Mahmood 2005: 5). This viewpoint corresponds with the construction of the neo-liberal subject and has become an aspect of the ego-ideal. The ego-ideal, for Lacan (1998), is that which installs and maintains the subject within cultural intelligibility (Butler 1997a: 86).

Ironically, the quest for freedom becomes that which overlaps profoundly with the contemporary cultural ideal of freedom, autonomy and self-governance.

Freedom is frequently conceived as freedom from constraint and control, especially the demands from other human beings. The demand for freedom and autonomy are problematic in my view for at least two different reasons. First, autonomy is frequently conceived as a freedom from relationships with others, as if sovereignty of the self is achievable or even desirable. The complexities and dynamics involved in communicating and being in relationships with others are impediments to be avoided, if not shunned. Second, the yearning to be free from the demands of other human beings is a longing that can be in contradiction with the pleasures and securities that others provide. Although whatever pleasures, joys, love or satisfaction that other human beings provide, there are also the irritations, frustrations, disappointments, regrets and disillusionments that inevitably arise and which have to be tolerated.

In Egypt, a dominant discourse and narrative is an idealisation of parents. This idealisation is based on religious injunctions that demand that parents be obeyed without question, that children, even as adults, be loyal, loving and grateful. In a hierarchy of love and obedience, God is first, mothers a very close second and fathers third. Spouses, siblings and children come further down the register. *Butterfly Wings* and *The Open Door* explore the underbelly of the mother–daughter dyad as they both represent the mother as controlling, fearful of breaking social rules and demands, and overly concerned with social status and financial considerations. Fiction can explore the pushes and pulls and the intricacies of familial relationships without risk of accusations of betrayal or disloyalty. Dalya Abudi writes that, in Arab women's literature,

> the mother–daughter relationship is largely depicted as oscillating between a variety of opposite poles: love and hate, blame and guilt, tenderness and anger, intimacy and estrangement, solidarity and animosity, harmony and conflict, bonding and separation, devotion and betrayal, oppression and empowerment. (2011: 7)

In the two novels that I am exploring in this chapter, the maternal characters are represented differently. In *Butterfly Wings*, Doha's mother is described as ruthless, cold and formidable and whose word was law, while in *The Open Door* the mother is represented as concerned, anxious and compliant. The fathers in both novels are rather distant and absent from the mess of domesticity. The central parental figure in the family is the mother, and the daughters, Doha (*Butterfly Wings*) and Layla (*The Open Door*), confident that their lives were different to those of their mothers, are portrayed as wanting to be free of maternal demands and to be liberated from the social demands that have been wrought on their mothers:

> The whole mentality has changed. ... There's no doubt about that. For our mothers, marriage was a fate written on their foreheads from the day they were born. No one could change it in the slightest or escape it. You had to accept it as it was. For us the situation is so different. ... Today's girl doesn't accept what her mother took as a given (so says Sanaa – a female friend of Layla's in the novel *The Open Door*). (Al-Zayyat 2005: 78)

While in chapter 3 I described the adhesive identifications between parents and their children, here I want to open up the desire to be 'what she is not'. There is a determination in both novels to live a life different to that of the previous generation and, alongside this resolute purpose, there is unquestioning confidence that a new and better life is available for the younger generation. The cost of living a life limited by social restrictions and obligations is poignantly represented by both the mothers and the aunts in these novels (especially in *The Open Door*), though, needless to say, I find these representations affecting due to my socio-political location. The older generation is represented as fearful, in particular, for the loss of connections, bonds and social security. The women are compliant not due to an inherent timidity but, rather, due to the possible losses of that which is known and that which provides material, emotional and social security. The peer group also pulls human beings into line and can act as a constraint to, at the very least, the imagining of a different way of being. For example, Adila in *The Open Door* (she is a close friend of Layla's) persistently reminds the latter of social rules and conventions, thereby foreclosing any discussion or rumination on how to live otherwise. In short, vertical and horizontal relationships constrain and foreclose discussion and possible imaginings.

Aspects of the unconscious reveal intent, desire and hopes for a different way of being; simultaneously, the unconscious can, and does, resist what it so hopes for. In both these novels, the mothers *and* the daughters are complicit with the social order: the mothers through their compliance with and acceptance of the conditions of submission and exploitation and the daughters by accepting without question the ideologies of freedom and autonomy and the belief that transformation can be achieved with ease.

The Necessity of Struggle

In this section, I briefly summarise Egyptian women's activism in order to provide some knowledge of the socio-political activities that have been undertaken by individual Egyptian women, feminist organisations and NGOs. Egyptian female activists can and do take up a range of political positions – secular, Islamic, liberal or pious – though the latter does not necessarily require a belief in feminism. The inheritance of this political past, which stretches back to the nineteenth century, is clearly important for contemporary Egyptian political activists, as the political activities of the past provide inspiration and hope. The term 'feminism' is ambiguous for Egyptian activists and is not a word widely used in Egypt; nevertheless, this is not to say that women's rights are not at the forefront of much political activity in the country. Arenfeldt and Al-Hassan Golley (2012) point out that the lack of a single and unambiguous Arabic word for feminism has been and is used by opponents in an attempt to argue that feminism is a Western import. Due to this relentless criticism by opponents of feminism, women may be reluctant to call themselves feminists, even though they may have feminist beliefs. In short, there can be a difference between what women believe and how women name themselves.

In any case, there has been much feminist political activity from the mid-nineteenth century onwards, both in civic endeavours and in women's extensive efforts to advance their well-being, educational opportunities and civic engagement. Egyptian female activists, whether secular or Islamic and whether they stand by the label feminist or not, are the beneficiaries of a long history of political activism stretching back to the mid-nineteenth century. Early female activists who focused particularly on educational opportunities for women include Nabawiyya Musa and Malak Hifni Nasif. Much feminist activity also focused on philanthropy, seen from a wide range of perspectives. Importantly, Beth Baron has documented that there were 30 Arabic women's periodicals in the period before the 1919 struggle for independence; these journals, along with the establishment of literary salons, were central to the awakening of, in particular, middle-class women (Baron 1994).

The early part of the twentieth century witnessed Egyptian women partaking in nationalist and anti-colonial movements and the liberal projects of reform. In 1911, Malak Hifni Nasif makes the first set of feminist demands to the Nationalist Congress: the right of women to a full education and, importantly, their inclusion in mosques. Women played a significant role in the independence movement and, alongside this nationalist project, they demanded women's suffrage and greater civic involvement. Unsurprisingly, as Leslie Lewis points out, these were concerns of the upper-middle classes, as 'poor women had long been in the "public", working to keep their families afloat, and had little time to spare over concern for these issues. The concern of most poorer and working-class women was not to gain the vote, but to be able to feed and clothe their children' (Lewis 2012: 49). In 1923, Huda Sha'rawi and Saiza Nabarawi formed the Egyptian Feminist Union (EFU), which focused on education, employment and reform of the Personal Status Law. Over a decade later, after the establishment of the EFU, Zainab Al-Ghazali founded the Muslim Women's Association in 1936; this movement was profoundly influenced by the Muslim Brotherhood and argued for women's role as mothers, tutors and guides to future generations (Lewis 2012: 50). In this view there is no 'woman question'.

During the 1920s and 1930s, the EFU saw the social problems of Egypt – health, education, money – as caused by the neglect of the state. Leaping unashamedly ahead, from 1945 onwards the women's movement shifted from being orientated towards welfare to a more politicised movement which linked women's full participation in politics to the nationalist movement and class struggle. Since the end of the Second World War, a new public discourse about women centred on their attaining full political and legal rights. According to Cynthia Nelson (1991: 330), the EFU had three main objectives: first, the establishment of constitutional and parliamentary rights for Egyptian women, in order to defend the laws guaranteeing those rights; second, the institution and organisation of cultural, health and social services for poor Egyptian families, including the promotion of literacy programmes; third, the calling of attention to mothers and children to guarantee their protection. These demands for political rights were interlinked securely with the call for social reform.

Doria Shafik is perhaps best known nationally and internationally for her feminist activities which she undertook primarily during the 1940s and 1950s. She fought with admirable conviction for women's full political equality and persistently challenged male authority, for example, she went on hunger strike at the Press Syndicate in 1954. In 1957, she went to the Indian Embassy and started another hunger strike as a protest against the occupation of Egyptian and Palestinian territories by military forces. But it was perhaps her robust critique of the Nasser regime and her unrelenting demands for democracy in Egypt which placed Shafik under house arrest in 1957. She spent the remaining 18 years in virtual seclusion and committed suicide in September 1975. In 1950, the feminist organisation Bint-al Nil (Daughters of the Nile) became the National Council of Women in Egypt and gathered momentum over the issue of full political rights for women (women gained the right to vote in 1956). It is important to point out, however, that a theme across the different periods of history is the linking together of women's political rights with social reforms such as health education, literacy and improved social services.

There has been recently a reassessment of Nasser's regime in relation to women (Al-Ali 2000). This reassessment argues that the 1952 revolution 'inaugurated a new age for women by altering the class structure and by the ideological, legal and practical inclusion of women in the new state' (Al-Ali 2000: 67). Needless to say this is a complex picture, which has continued, in that the Nasser regime's commitment to women's welfare lies alongside the prohibition of all forms of political activism. It is the Personal Status Law (legislation that covers marriage, divorce, child custody) that most fuels many feminists' anger in Egypt. This law is regarded as profoundly restrictive and as a barrier against women gaining full citizenship. Under Sadat's rule, many commitments to gender equality were abandoned and yet paradoxically the personal status laws were reformed in favour of women's rights. Known as 'Jehan's Law' (Jehan was Sadat's wife) the Personal Status Law of 1979 granted women legal rights in marriage, divorce and child custody that granted a woman the right to divorce, the right to travel without her husband's permission and raised the legal age of marriage to 18.

Under the presidency of Hosni Mubarak and the increasing pressures of the ever-growing Islamic movement, the Personal Status Law was amended, and many of the rights that women had attained were revised; but soon after these amendments were instituted, the law was changed yet again which restored some of the benefits. Feminist organisations and NGOs have become more prevalent since the mid-1980s, and alongside this proliferation there is increasing state control (for example, who can sit on the board of these organisations, insistence on seeing minutes and reports) and there are more divergences among women and feminist organisations.

Perhaps the biggest division rests on the matter of religion, specifically the Islamic Revival. The Islamic Revival is a dominant sensibility that has been growing and taking hold since the 1980s and onwards. It is apparent in the growing amount of mosques, attendance at mosques, religious programmes on the TV, cheap books that are easily available and religious icons in homes. Women are a major presence in this movement, and many have embraced the rules for proper conduct (for example, being shy is seen as a positive attribute), being modest (for both men and women) in dress and above all living what is perceived as an Islamic life. Living an Islamic life encompasses all aspects of social life including what can be thought and felt. Those women who are part of this movement are deeply committed to living a life according to Islam and to perfecting their thoughts and actions towards a pious ideal (Lewis 2012), and many, if not all involved in this movement, spend much of their time and efforts towards improving the health and well-being of other women. Feminists, according to pious women, and perhaps those who are members of the Muslim Brotherhood, have lost all proper connection to religion and to the duties involved in being a wife and mother. The prevailing discourse in Islam about gender equality is that men and women are equal but different and from that belief it flows that men and women have different responsibilities, duties and obligations. Within Islamic movements there is a strong belief that women's spiritual equality to men should be honoured. Alongside this belief in spiritual equality, there exist other values: that women should be given their rights according to Islam, that all women should be supported, valued and cared for in marriage emotionally and materially and that if divorce occurs then women and children should be properly supported financially.

One common assumption in the West, as Leslie Lewis points out, is that Muslim women and, in particular, those who embrace strict interpretations and practices of Islam are 'by definition passive observers of their own lives, oppressed in turn by fathers, husbands' social norms and legal institutions' (2012: 43). But as Abu-Lughod points out, many

Muslim women are shocked that anyone can believe that it is Islam as a religion that oppresses women, as for many women their identity 'as a Muslim is deeply meaningful to her, and her faith in God is integral to her sense of self and community' (2013: 1).

To state the necessary but obvious, we (that is, women who are secular whatever our inheritance) have to accept that some women might want different things from what Western feminists want for them. The differences are products of 'different histories, expressions of different circumstances, and manifestations of differently structured desires' (Abu-Lughod 2013: 43). For example, living in a family, inhabiting that honour is the litmus paper of a moral life in which service is perceived as the value, of how to live a life and/or living in a godly way. There are different ideas about justice, equality, liberation and what makes for a good life. To echo an important question raised by Abu-Lughod: Are emancipation, equality and rights part of a universal language or just a particular dialect? (2013: 45). Mahmood argues that the 'desire for freedom and liberation is a historically situated desire whose motivational force cannot be assumed a priori, but needs to be reconsidered in light of other desires, aspirations, and capacities that inhere in a culturally and historically located subject' (2005: 16). However, the stubborn conviction persists that women's rights should be defined by the values of choice and freedom but beyond that 'we have to ask ourselves what we think about those for whom choice may not be the only litmus test of a worthy life' (Abu-Lughod 2013: 48).

We (that is, Western feminists) need to be wary that we do not reinforce the matter of choice without considering power and without reinforcing every ideological stereotype that reinforces the view that it is Western women who know best, have choice, have freedom and are free from domination. We also need to be careful that we do not ignore that secularism is also an ideology as it was set up by landed property owners against the Church. A power struggle took place between the Church and landowners for the right to own property, and from its beginning it was a conflict that focused on access to material wealth, that is, who possessed rationality and reason, above all, it was a clash of interests in relation to a new moral order (Calhoun 2011).

Whether Islam is the source of liberation or oppression is a fracture line for many Egyptian feminists, but the two sides of the debate agree that it is patriarchal men's interpretation of Islam that is oppressive and not Islam as a religion as such. For those who are secular or indeed religious but not members of an Islamic movement, Islam reinforces women's oppression and subordination. And for those women who are more reliant on an Islamic framework, Islam is the only route through to liberation. Their argument runs along the following lines: patriarchal culture is oppressive to women, but it is only a return to pure Islamic practices and beliefs that liberation for women will be achieved. The arguments run on and perhaps the divisions, values and belief system are too big for any hope of a resolution at present.

Problematising Resistance

Taking at face value the narratives provided by Egyptian women leads to theoretical problems, as the total acceptance of what is spoken conceals the way in which the unconscious always intervenes in our representations of our selves – which tend (in the West) towards representing ourselves as heroines and/or victims and the unconscious intervenes profoundly in our perceptions, values and phantasies of the other. In any case, in all the work that I have read on women and agency, there is a profound tendency to not investigate the narratives spoken; rather, the insistence is that the narratives prove that Egyptian women are agentic and self-possessed. Frequently, they are represented as heroines of their own narratives. Self-possession becomes *the* litmus paper of maturity and agency. Nevertheless, as Abu-Lughod (2013: 5) points out, we all live complicated cultural, emotional and moral lives that are replete with the nuances of social relations and values, and full of dreams, desires, anger, joy and disappointment – wherever and whoever we are.

The understandable motivation to represent Middle Eastern women in general and Egyptian women specifically as active and energetic hinders the complexities involved in inhabiting a complex life. Nabawiyya Musa (an influential Egyptian feminist mentioned above) wrote explicitly about her anxiety in relation to writing; I provide, here, a few details about her life before entering into a discussion about speech, power and anxiety. Musa was an Egyptian feminist and educationalist (1886–1951), who struggled against her family's stipulations that she should neither be educated at home nor attend school. At the age of 13 she applied to a girls' school by forging her mother's signature, sat for the entrance exam and was accepted. She graduated from the teacher-training section of the Saniyya School and became one of the first Egyptian women to teach in a state school system and also the first to become the principal of a school (Civantos 2013).[3] Musa then went on to hold a position in the Ministry of Education from 1923 to 1926, founded a weekly magazine, was briefly involved in the EFU and lectured at events organised by and for women. In addition to all of this, Musa published extensively. Besides poetry, a novel, pedagogical materials and essays calling for social reform, Musa wrote directly about herself in *Ta'Rikhi Bi-Qalami'* (Civantos 2013: 6), which translates as, 'My History, By My Pen'. Musa was outspoken and committed to women's education and participation in the workplace and she argued persistently for women to be educated; for her, literacy should not be the end point.

Civantos explores Musa's difficulties in holding and controlling the pen and argues that difficulties in writing arise from the power wielded over Egyptian subjects by the British and from that exerted by Egyptian men over Egyptian women. The power dynamics of the pen reveal literate control as well as authorial anxiety (Civantos 2013: 10). Expressing oneself, whatever one's gender or class position, is always riven with anxieties. The acts of writing and speaking are those of assertion of the self. Simultaneously, we can never know what we will say or write as, at risk of repetition, the unconscious always intervenes – placing us within the symbolic of the socio-political order – and disrupts any sense of written and spoken coherence. As Judith Butler explores in *Excitable Speech* (1997b), speech is always at risk of being out of control and unstable. The knowledge that speech and writing can be unstable and incoherent lies alongside a contradiction – that no expression 'can take place in isolation from dominant norms and pre-given ideological forms. For a narrative to be meaningful and to acquire a degree of social authority it must draw to some extent on cultural dominant discourses of truth-telling' (McNay 1999: 180).

Musa's anxieties are not without foundation, as the pen is laden with symbolic significance in the Middle East, within Islam and Arabic language. In Arabic, *qalam* means pen and it is interpreted that the pen is divine, as it was used by God to inscribe destiny. In this way, as Civantos points out, 'The *qalam* is associated with the greatest of all powers, the divine power to establish destiny. Likewise, writing, in the hands of mortals is a sacred gift, one of which the user must be worthy to enjoy legitimately' (2013: 13). The risk for Egyptian women and men is in asserting certain values and opinions that are counter to religious ideology and parameters. There is, moreover, a semantic link between pen and penis in Arabic and writing is conceived as 'a means by which power is created and enacted' (Civantos 2013: 13).

In the political sphere, Musa was robust in her criticisms of the prevailing regimes, which included the Egyptian government as well as British authorities (this led to her schools being closed and her magazine shut down in the early 1940s). I want, though, to focus on the implicit bid for patriarchal censorship that Sa'd Zaghlul attempted when he was at the Ministry of Education. Zaghlul requested that Musa submit her writings to him so that he could correct her grammar, but she refused.

Many middle-class women during the late-nineteenth and the twentieth centuries believed profoundly in the power of the word to transform the restrictions imposed on women. Clare Hemmings advocates that feminists should be wary of narratives of progression, as these narratives, she argues, obscure the persistent conditions of exploitation and provide too-simplistic segues from oppression to freedom (Hemmings 2011). The belief that the power of the pen would lead to transformation led to an underestimation of the need for control and censure by patriarchal men and those in authority. Civantos draws on Pierre Bourdieu's understandings of language and symbolic power (1991) to illustrate that correcting grammar is not just about clarity of meaning but, frequently, is a ruse for exerting power; simultaneously, the function of narrative is to render that which is incoherent and irrational into the illusion of a meaningful and rational account.

Deniz Kandiyoti's (1988) article 'Bargaining with patriarchy' provides a broad-brush yet textured approach to understanding women's strategies towards patriarchy. Kandiyoti argues that some women in certain patriarchal conditions can optimise their life options 'with varying potential for active or passive resistance in the face of oppression' (1988: 274). Women's strategies, she argues, are always played out in the context of 'patriarchal bargains' and these arrangements (conscious and unconscious) act as implicit scripts that define, limit and inflect options (1988: 275). It is important to point out that defining patriarchy is not straightforward and cannot be wrapped up as if we all know what patriarchy means and how it functions, as it is not trouble free 'to put one's finger on how power works' (Abu-Lughod 2013: 6). There is always acceptance, accommodation, adaptation and collision of interests alongside conflicts over resources, rights and responsibilities (Kandiyoti 1988: 285).

Patriarchy is subtle and, needless to say, changes over time as it adapts to fluctuating socio-economic conditions. Currently, due to the dire economic conditions in Egypt, more women are working and, simultaneously, more men are forced to stay at home. More men are required to undertake childcare while the women go out to work. This changing landscape in the domains of men and women effects the experiences and perceptions of young people as they witness the shifts in economic power. While this, at one level, can be seen as positive, it can, of course, lead to an entrenchment of patriarchy, as men fear the possible loss of status, power and control. We need to be vigilant in ensuring that we do not circumvent an understanding that men are also positioned within and caught up in patriarchal structures due to their age, class or profession. Nor should we bypass this understanding when it is men who protect women by providing them with an education and prevent female circumcision and/or by stepping in to refuse a marriage arrangement that is in the process of being organised.

Men are, of course, embedded within patriarchal structures and are the main beneficiaries and are therefore profoundly invested in them. Men, however, do not always support other men unquestioningly and here I want to give two examples. Zaghlul wanted to control Musa's writing and this can be taken as a clear example of patriarchal control – which, needless to say, it is. However, he publicly supports Musa when she criticises her male colleagues' teaching methods. In more detail, the events leading to this criticism unfolded thus. The Ministry of Education decided to replace all male teachers in girls' schools with women. A leading Islamic scholar disagreed with this decision and male teachers anxious about their livelihood also opposed this announcement. In response to this opposition, Musa wrote a robust essay criticising male teachers' emphasis on the importance of grammar rather than of meaning and writing skills. Zaghlul had the report printed and distributed widely to all Egyptian girls' schools (Civantos 2013: 19). The other example is from fiction; I could provide many similar instances from my personal experiences, but the people involved are too easily identified. In the novel *Butterfly Wings*, Doha, after many years in a very unhappy marriage, is thinking through whether or not to divorce her husband. When she is talking with her brother about her dilemma,

he responds with unconditional support and says, 'I'm your brother.
I can't abandon you or let you down', and then he continues:

> We only live once, so we have to enjoy it. There's no reason to put up
> with unhappiness as long as we can still change it. This might seem
> strange, but in all honesty I tell you that you must ask for a divorce.
> I promise you I'll back you up all the way. (Salmawy 2014: 115)

Although we can celebrate Musa as a feminist role model and applaud
her resistance, where does this then leave the troubling matter of those
women who desire and need patriarchal control. To be honest, they are
the majority of us, but this does not mean that we should abandon our
desire and need for social conventions, though we should avoid con-
stricting political norms because, as Mahmood writes, it is important
'to interrogate the practical and conceptual conditions under which
different forms of desire emerge, including desire for submission to
recognised authority' (2005: 16). We cannot only recognise and priori-
tise activity when it arises from social protest, nor perceive the need for
submission and control as the 'phantom imaginings of the hegemon-
ized' (Mahmood 2005: 16). As Lynne Layton points out, despite all the
evidence of gender multiplicity and fluidity,

> each of us, no matter what our race, class, or sexuality, contends in some
> way psychically with dominant gender, race, class and sexual categories,
> because the dominant categories hold the power to define what a proper
> race class, gender and sexuality is. (2002: 202)

We cannot and should not assume that women desire liberation and
freedom from male domination. There endures the obsession with the
constraint in which Muslim women who wear the *hijab* are assumed to
be coerced into doing so or capitulating to male pressure but it is not
so straightforward; I am Muslim and I do not wear the *hijab* but it is
always assumed that I do this out of my free choice. I grew up, however,
in socio-political conditions when not wearing a veil was a resistance
and a necessary sign of being modern and these socio-political perceptions have affected me profoundly. As always it is also more personal,
as my father, as well as my husband, vehemently opposes the wearing
of the *hijab*. Ironically, then, my 'choice' not to wear it is my way of
obeying the law of the father and of being complicit with patriarchy.
Layton (2002) uses the term 'normative unconscious' to describe the

range of practices that replicate and perpetuate dominant cultural categories, and these cultural injunctions cannot be avoided or disavowed
as our need for love, approval and acceptance frequently leads to
compliance and complicity. To thwart the injunction or indeed to think
about the injunction to be docile, submissive, loyal and so on is not the
same as 'changing the terms of subject constitution'. What do we make
of our unconscious attachments to subjection? As Butler (1997a) points
out, the unconscious is no more free of normalising discourses than any
other aspect of the subject. Moreover, subjection is installed in the very
formation of the subject and to become a subject is inevitably to be
complicit with socio-political structures.

Part of the politics of recognition must consist of perceiving and
understanding when it is women who oppress other women through the
quest for power and status. Spivak (1998) is clear that it is important
to be attentive to the particular balances of power and power between
women. Women can and do sustain patriarchy. Within psychoanalytic theories that account for both the unconscious and the conscious
aspects of our lives, relationships with others are filled with aggression
and hostility. This is never unidirectional – from the privileged to the
marginal – but circulates within and across all self–other relations.
Thinking through political identities throws us up against our unconscious and conscious investments in power, which are frequently gained
through a subordination of 'the other'. We are always divided against
ourselves and others – full of conflicts, pushes and pulls – as we want
to move towards and against 'the other' and our experiences do not
necessarily lead to emotional generosity. Older women can control and
exert authority over younger women (sisters, daughters, daughters-in-
law) and, in this way, the internalisation of power circulates inexorably.

A confrontation with vulnerability and precariousness will evoke
not only care and generosity but also hatred and disavowal. We are
reminded of what we prefer to forget or deny: that it is sheer luck
that some human beings are privileged and that the majority are not.
Everyday behaviour may take the form of creating or perpetuating the
continued subjugation of other women and men – for example, the
exploitation of those who provide domestic services such as the porters,
the women who clean and the young children who shop for small items.
The exploitation takes various forms such as underpayment, rudeness
that can, on occasion, verge on verbal abuse, and the persistent suspicion of theft. As Jessica Benjamin astutely points out, other human

beings can thus 'threaten to evoke in us what we have repudiated in order to protect the self: weakness, vulnerability, decay or perhaps sexual otherness, transgression instability – the excluded abject' (Benjamin 1998: 95). While Benjamin argues that recognition is required to maintain the boundary between self and other, indeed is essential so that the self is not incorporated into 'the other', Judith Butler sees recognition as a problematic social and psychic illusion (2004) as she pertinently asserts that we all 'wish ourselves to be wholly perspicacious beings. But that would eradicate all the active and structuring traces of our psychological formations and to dwell in the pretence of being fully knowing, self-possessed adults' (2005: 102).

This is not to suggest that we are not responsible for our actions – both morally and politically – but the idea of the intact, rational, decision-making subject is a myth that we all live by, a necessary but contradictory illusion that enables us to imagine ourselves 'at home'. To take the unconscious seriously, then, challenges simple notions of recognition, choice and agency, because these fail to grasp the complexity of who the subject is and what she might need or desire in others. The unconscious challenges both the assumption that we can know ourselves fully and act accordingly and the fallacy that what we want from others is always benign. We can at least begin to think through the conditions of our existence, conditions that are not exploitative or dependent on the other, that bolster the self and are a different, albeit, powerful exploitation.

Notes

1. This chapter draws in part on this essay. However, more importantly, I am influenced by the ongoing conversations with Clare Hemmings that have taken place over many years. I thank her for her unflagging energy and commitment to feminist theory and her invaluable friendship.

2. Object relations are usually associated with British psychoanalysis, specifically psychoanalysts such as Fairbairn, Klein and Winnicott. It emphasises pre-oedipal relationships and the internalisation of 'objects' (aspects of people) that are internalised to form the self.

3. I am grateful to Christina Civantos for her (2013) exceptionally thoughtful analysis of Nabawiyya Musa.

Chapter 6

Power, Domination, Struggle

As I attempt to write this chapter, I realise the depth of my reluctance to engage with the events that have taken place since 2011. I am hesitant – to be more truthful, 'unwilling' is a more accurate word – to engage in the task of tracing through the profound shift from the short period of optimism to the atmosphere of apathetic resignation that prevails at present (2016). I keep staring out of the window; household chores have more appeal than thinking, and I am delaying endlessly. The challenging question as to why I am so dominated by this negative state of mind refuses to go away. The refusal to engage is not just a personal matter as it is part of an atmosphere of resignation and withdrawal that seems to characterise Egypt at this time.

Atmospheres are ambiguous, for, as Ben Anderson writes, they are 'real phenomena. They "envelop" and thus press on a society "from all sides" with a certain force. On the other hand, they are not necessarily sensible phenomena' (2009: 78). Atmospheres are indistinct and simultaneously equivocal as they shift 'between presence and absence, between subject and object/subject and between the definite and indefinite – that enable us to reflect on affective experience as occurring beyond, around, and alongside the formation of subjectivity' (Anderson 2009: 77). The tone and atmospheres of a society can be enigmatic, elusive and yet have material effects on subjectivities and subjective experience. There are many socio-political discourses that circulate and that obscure more than they reveal and function as public secrets;

simultaneously, many states of mind that are elusive with one emotion concealing another feeling and a seemingly rational action hiding another action.

Apathy is one aspect of subjective experience that is a complex state of mind. It is complex because as Freud, perhaps rather acerbically, pointed out, it takes a lot of energy to achieve being passive (1915), and in any case apathy corrodes and is corrosive as two states of mind take place simultaneously. One state of mind is that of impassive resignation (staring out of the window) where little, if any, thinking takes place. Alongside this seeming apathy, there is another state of mind which is that of a rather odd turbulence and where too much – affect, confusion, turmoil – is taking place. If this is not convoluted enough, it is further complicated by the difficulty of pinpointing apathy. Apathy is elusive because it is a state of mind that we all want to deny is a part of our self, as being active, knowing, rational are all crucial aspects of neo-liberal subjectivity. Being and feeling apathetic, therefore, leads to shame because apathy is about absence, and how can any of us 'fully disclose something whose chief property is deficiency, to be in some sense absent from history and missing to yourself' (Rose 2003a: 218). The difficulty of knowing negative emotions is that a feeling provokes another feeling, and so we can shun emotions that we find tough to comprehend. Emotions can produce, as Ngai points out, 'an unpleasurable feeling *about* the feeling (a reflexive response taking the form of "I feel ashamed about feeling envious" or "I feel anxious about my enviousness")' (2005: 10). It can be tough to know about one's apathy, shame and envy without feeling that one should not be feeling a negative emotion, and ironically the negativity of the emotion is reinforced. Perhaps, above all, apathy reveals that which cannot be thought about is an inevitable protection and defence against that which is unbearable.

I am at risk of rendering absent the unbearable torture and oppression that takes place in Egypt (it is not by any stretch of the imagination, alas, the only country that engages in systematic torture of its citizens), but as this book is about Egypt the necessary focus is on the oppressive practises that take place there. To read about the torture is unbearable due to the repetitive nature of the violence, and it taints because to read about the violence is bludgeoning and implicates us all no matter whether we are engaged in violent acts or not. Witnessing the violence is numbing, and leads to a feeling of shame that I have not done more and that some Egyptians perpetuate violence and do not resist the appeal of hatred and brutality. Above all, it is the need to avoid such brutality that means most of us want (need?) to live under the radar and to declare that 'nothing much' is taking place, but as Ben Highmore points out, the phrase 'nothing much' reveals that there is too much going on (2010: 3).

The summer of 2013 was dominated by an odd disjunction, which is that as much as many emotions were flying around simultaneously 'nothing much' seemed to be taking place. A quick reminder during: the summer of 2013 the Muslim Brotherhood occupied major squares in Cairo and elsewhere in Egypt and tensions were running high. We spent all our time talking about what should be done and when the squares would be 'cleared', and people declared with confidence they knew when the military and the police would act. We were dominated completely by the events and we adapted our everyday lives to take safety into consideration. Alongside too much going on, that is, too much talk, too much adaptation and watching too much TV to get any hint that something was about to change, there was also this atmosphere of a relentless and numbing 'nothing much'. As Highmore points out, 'nothing much' reveals that there is 'too much' taking place (2010). It is difficult to find the tone to describe that summer as there are delicate lines to be negotiated, which focus on how to represent the activities, how to talk about the events, the bitter conflicts that arose within families and friendship groups and the emotions that were evoked.

There was far 'too much' going on, and it cannot be easily put into words, and so my concern is how to represent the events and the atmosphere without somehow missing something significant, to accurately depict everyday life without dismissing or exaggerating the sense of danger. There is a delicate fault line between being overemotional or indeed dismissing the emotions and thereby providing an overly rational account. I remember the overwhelming sense of fear: standing on our balcony scanning the horizon so that I could make a decision about whether to go shopping (I frequently needed to move) and the continual noise of all of us talking but really with nothing to say. Under normal circumstances, we live our lives, if we are fortunate, where the ordinary can be taken for granted and the habitual provides a certain if fragile security. During that particular summer, the everyday was foregrounded and usual habitual ways of living and getting through the day could not be taken for granted as everything was over-foregrounded. The usual patterns of the everyday and the ordinary, which are elusive and complex, became freighted with emotions, insecure activity and fantasies. For example, scrutinising the environment before going out shopping for signs of danger and ensuring that the shopping list is tight and that all that is on the list is bought because it was unclear quite as to when we would be able to venture out again in the near future. The political events taking place have impacted profoundly on self-hoods and the experience of everyday living.

Since experiencing the recent political upheaval, I now have more respect and tolerance for the ordinary and everyday 'stuff' of life as I realise how everyday routines hold human beings together, facilitate engagement, enable ordinary satisfactions and are an important means of 'establishing a kind of reliability ... and reflect a concern for coherence' (de Certeau 1984: xxii/xxiii). The extraordinary with all its apparent excitement and allure dulls the senses, emotions and thought. In addition, the atmosphere is marked by a mood of waiting for life to progress, waiting for material conditions to improve, waiting to feel more secure and waiting for Egyptian society to recover from corrosiveness suffered under Mubarak. Waiting, as Hook poignantly points out (2015), involves banality that is, paradoxically, embroiled in the sense of being overwhelmed.

The interlinked web of 'emotions and memories, sense and sensitivity, energy and affect, congregate and congeal in complexly singular ways' (Highmore 2010: 140). Since towards the end of 2011, energy is not much in evidence, instead irritability, anxiety, indifference and a pathos dominate the atmosphere and mood in Cairo. By using the word 'pathos', I am not implying the commonplace meaning of 'pathetic', but rather I am trying to point to the bleakness and despair that is prevalent and a shutting down due to too much anxiety and fear.

The following sections of this chapter will focus on elucidating the socio-political conditions that have led inexorably to oppression and repression in all aspects of Egyptian society from political activism to the entrenchment of the Deep State.

Oppression, Repression, Domination

I want to provide a quick snapshot of the pervasive atmosphere in Cairo during early 2015: the current dominant mood focuses on the hope that Fattah Al-Sisi will deliver a new future based on economic opportunity and security, and this hope lies alongside a widespread fear that an economic recovery will not take place. There is heartfelt irritation at the bombings that are happening regularly, anger at the activity of radical groups in the Sinai and relief that the military is taking strong action. There is widespread relief that the rule of the Muslim Brotherhood is over and for many that the military is in power once again. This is of profound concern to political activists, but the majority of the population are more concerned with feeling secure and wanting stability (especially economic) and care little that the Deep State exists. Indeed, the opposite is frequently the case as people welcome the presence of the Deep State and rarely comment on the existence of the machinery of the state on the streets – for example, soldiers in tanks, which are now a feature of everyday life. It has become commonplace among activists and those on the centre–left of the political spectrum to declare that the Deep State in Egypt has never been as entrenched and political opposition subsequently so oppressed. While the existence of the Deep State and the extent of the oppressive activities is the cause of profound worry, the difficulty with the perception that oppression is on the increase is that it bypasses the history of oppression in Egypt. The Deep State has always existed in Egypt and has always been oppressive and that in my view is the tragedy. The degree of oppression and repression is, of course, worrying and should cause profound concern, but the acceptance, if not resignation, of most Egyptians is based on an internalisation of the need for security. This explanation, however, does not go far enough, as there is much refusal to know about the oppression of the state and any opening up of the conversation is strongly rebutted with claims of possible attacks from various enemies.

Before opening up an exploration as to the myriad reasons as to why so many Egyptian citizens accept the activities of the state, albeit reluctantly, I will provide an account of the many activities of the Deep State in Egypt. The alliances between the various dominant institutions – military, police, security forces – are complex and the machinations that take place are convoluted, as a union that maybe strong can be fractured with hasty speed. As Kandil illustrates, it is too simplistic to place the military as the lynchpin of the political scheming that has occurred in Egypt (2012), but to understand this should not lead to an underestimation of the central place that the military holds in the political sphere. As Kandil writes, the

armed forces and the security establishment are full partners in any
country's ruling block. They work *with* rather than *for* the political apparatus. ... And while the interests of the three partners usually coincide
(projecting an image of unity), they are never identical. (2012: 2)

Importantly, on the whole, Egyptians are grateful to the military, and
this gratitude has a long history stretching back to the nineteenth century; they are proud that their military is highly esteemed in the Arab
Region, and most want a 'fair and strong dictator'.

The entrenchment of the Deep State is a vexed and worrying feature
of Egyptian society, and it has become commonplace to declare that
the Egyptian population has never been so oppressed. They point to
the continuing torture and imprisonment of those who oppose the present military regime. Activists, they claim, are too fearful to persist in
political activity, and those who have the resources apparently have left
the country as they are fearful that if they stay, they will be harassed,
tortured or imprisoned by the security forces. These fears are grounded
in reality as the security forces are everywhere: tanks remain on the
streets, police and the army continually stop drivers to check ID cards
and to search the cars, and Egypt remains in a 'state of emergency',
which grants the government and the state limitless powers to control
the Egyptian population.

Needless to say, the presence of a powerful state and the dominance
of the security forces have a long history and a determined presence in
Egyptian society. This history reaches back to the time of occupation
from the nineteenth and early to mid-twentieth century. The activities
of the state have been built and consolidated from that firm foundation that was entrenched during the era of colonialism. We should not
conflate the interests of the armed forces, government, police and security forces as if they always coincide and reinforce their institutional
power. As Kandil argues, following the revolution in 1952 (he terms it
a 'coup'), the Free Officers instituted a strong division between those
who ran the government and the security forces for the 'political leadership needed military and/or security support to preserve its power
should the masses refuse to obey, but played them off against each
other to increase its autonomy and avoid falling hostage to any of them'
(Kandil 2012: 3).

While the various institutions – military, police, security forces –
were, and remain, motivated by the drive for power, competition and

different interest, the balance as to who held power was precarious, but by the early 1980s Egypt had become a police state. The various wars (1967 and 1973) along with the exceptionally precarious economic situation tilted the balance of power firmly towards the security apparatus, even though Nasser vowed to dismantle the power and apparatuses of the security forces in 1967. This dismantling did not occur, and prior to that declaration Nasser was heavily reliant on the security forces to dominate the Egyptians. The Nasser regime imprisoned many of its opponents and strictly curtailed freedom of expression and the right to organise. During the 1960s, prisons contained an average of 20,000 political detainees at any one time (political dissidents ranged from communists, liberal intellectuals, members of the Muslim Brotherhood). Twenty thousand political detainees is a staggering figure that indicates the level of political oppression (the Egyptian population was about 28 million during the 1960s), and the consequence of this level of oppression meant that to live in Egypt was to be 'constantly under the purview of a pervasive surveillance structure' (Kandil 2012: 44). The security forces held sway as phones were bugged; mail was regularly checked and confiscated; conversations could not take place easily with acquaintances. Taxi drivers were frequently in the pay of the security forces and were paid to report any untoward conversation. Once, following a discussion with a taxi driver, I relayed the conversation to my father, who visibly paled and asked in some despair, 'What were you thinking?' Clearly, I was not thinking as I had allowed myself to be lured into a conversation. I have never made the same error again.

It is common to know people who have been arrested at dawn and homes that have been searched for evidence of political activity in the middle of the night along with learning of many anecdotes about phone calls made by security officers who relay the precise movements of a member of the family. It is common knowledge to be able to identify the places where torture occurs. While we may not be at the personal end of various investigations and/or assaults on personal liberties, they nonetheless have profound effects on the sense of political freedom/s. The shrinking of the possible space for socio-political freedoms is a direct consequence of living under a robust police state and underneath the rubric of powerful security forces.

The uprisings in 1919, 1952 and 2011 are all marked by the attempt to free Egyptian society from the control of the state (whether British control, as in 1919 and 1952, or the police state, as in 2011). The uprising on 25 January 2011 was not the beginning of protests as the police state under Mubarak's rule had become increasingly powerful and progressively more unpopular with the Egyptians. It also has to be mentioned that most people were appalled at the dynastic manoeuvres that would have instituted Gamal Mubarak as the next president. Mubarak centralised the power structures and concentrated power to an unprecedented extent. The eruption of political protest on 25 January 2011 focused on legal and political grievances, police brutality (it is of no coincidence that 25 January used to be a day to celebrate the police), emergency laws, lack of free elections and free speech. Alongside these political grievances, there was much fury at the level of financial corruption, the rising rates of unemployment especially for men under the age of 30 and also the cost of living. Egypt has been under Emergency Law since 1967, more or less continually (the laws were suspended in 1980 until 1981 and then reinstituted), and these laws are hated as they sanction police repression and police brutality. Emergency Law is a permanent fixture of the Egyptian political system and allows for extended detention without trial, the prohibition of demonstrations without police permission and the banning of labour strikes, and enables press censorship and trials that can deliver 'swift justice' and restrict the right to appeal. The law also limits non-governmental activity and enables close scrutiny of those involved with NGOs.

Despite the Emergency Laws, there had been much political activity, labour strikes and small demonstrations before the explosion of protestors (political activists and ordinary citizens alike) on the streets of cities across Egypt. The political groups included the 6 April Youth Movement, 'We are all Khaled Saeed' (a Facebook group set up to protest against the murder of a young man in Alexandria in 2010), the Revolutionary Socialists and perhaps the best known outside of Egypt – Tamarrod. Tamarrod (meaning revolt, rebellion) lifted off from the political movement *Kifaya*! (meaning 'enough'), which had petered out in 2006. Despite the amount of overwhelming popular support, the fervent activities on the streets and the numbers of people demonstrating, this important popular uprising lost the initiative. What happened in February 2011 is well known, but to recap: the demonstrations increased, and 28 January came to be called as the Day of Rage due to the number of people on the streets; this was followed by The March of the Millions (1 February), when people marched from Tahrir Midan to the presidential palace in Heliopolis. On 2 February, the infamous

Battle of the Camels took place when pro-Mubarak supporters violently attacked the demonstrators, army tanks flooded Tahrir Midan and both live shots and rubber bullets were fired at the protestors, which outraged many Egyptians even if they had not been supportive of the demonstrations previously. Protests and demonstrations took place throughout February until Mubarak was forced to resign; the Supreme Council of Armed Forces took over the running of the country promising that it would be an interim governing body and that it would institute and oversee free elections and a new constitution.

The chanting of 'one hand' in relation to the army and the protestors, the declarations of unity, albeit moving, between Muslims and Christians and the coming together of men and women from different classes and professions was (and perhaps remains) crucially significant and should not be underestimated. The following is not meant to undermine the courage of the protestors, anything but, and it is intended to provide an account of why any hope of a different society slipped away so quickly. As Hugh Roberts, writing about the events that took place in January and February 2011, points out, neither a coup nor a revolution took place because it

> was a popular uprising that lost the initiative because it had not positive agenda or demand. 'Bread, freedom, social justice' aren't political demands, just aspirations and slogans. A social movement might have made these slogans into demands by pressuring the government to take specific steps. But a movement that wants these desiderata provided by government, and, at the same time, wants the government to clear off has a coherence problem. The only demand that mattered politically was 'Mubarak, irhal!' (2013: 5)

The slogan 'Mubarak, irhal' (meaning, 'Mubarak, go') could not deliver a revolution, and the lack of robust political demands led to a fundamental fault line as, frankly, mantras delivered little and the lack of political experience revealed itself inexorably. The demand – Mubarak, go – fatally coincided with the military's own objective that required Mubarak to resign so that they return to a central position of power. The excitement, hope and optimism that arose during those two (rather wonderful) months were palpable, and we wholeheartedly believed that the future was there for the taking. It is, perhaps, when a belief that the future is there for the taking that we should be most alert to our illusions and resistances to making a society anew leading to the description of 'The Stolen Revolution'.

The events that have taken place since those exhilarating months are depressing, depleting and worrying as what took place reinstated the military as the central political plank. When the protestors destroyed the headquarters of the National Democratic Party (the officially sanctioned political party), they damaged the building but not the power structure, which remains unscathed. Very quickly any alliances that were forged between the protestors and the Supreme Council of Armed Forces (SCAF) did not last, and increasing demonstrations against SCAF illustrate the increasing anger and disappointment. Protestors were killed during various demonstrations: the crushing of a demonstration by Copts in October 2011 when many were injured and 28 demonstrators killed (the Christian community had been increasingly marginalised from political power); 45 demonstrators were killed during demonstrations in November 2011 while protesting against military rule, and again 17 demonstrators were killed during protests in December 2011.

The sexual and physical attacks by the military on women have been a worrying aspect of the responses by the military. Women made clear their intent to participate fully in the political activity taking place, and many attended the demonstrations and protests with the purpose of declaring that they were active members of society. Very quickly women were targeted and subjected to humiliating virginity tests that were carried out by army doctors in the presence of male soldiers. Despite the courage of Samira Ibrahim, who filed a legal action against the government in order to bring this matter to public attention, women have continued to be harassed and targeted. On 20 December 2011, thousands of women demonstrated against these abuses; the army seemed to relent, and a court declared the virginity tests illegal. The head of the judicial military authority, few were surprised, declared that the ruling could not be implemented. Humiliating women is one powerful attempt to silence us, force us back into the domestic sphere and stop our potentially unruly demand that social equality is impossible without gender equality. Controlling women's bodies is also another technique to humiliate men as women's bodies are the site of control, domination and shame.

The repressive state apparatuses – military, police, security forces – are characterised by their oppressive measures and techniques and, above all, the state is a 'machine of repression' (Althusser 1971: 137) which ensures the continuing power relations and the status quo. In our daily lives, we are continually reminded of the role of the state, as in many residential areas, there are armed police and soldiers stationed on the streets. Also many areas are littered with road checks, and drivers are regularly stopped and their ID cards and licences checked. In the area where I live, there are tanks near the police station and tanks that are permanently on various streets. There are different responses to the presence of armed soldiers and police: many people find it necessary and indeed reassuring, whereas for others it is a persistent reminder of the presence of oppression. The material actuality, there is nothing metaphorical about the presence of the military in residential areas, is a perpetual reminder of power, control and domination. It is an actual physical manifestation of the risks of stepping over the boundaries of authority.

Most of us are reluctant to engage with the police and so we do not report crimes, because, as John Bradley points out, we are fearful of getting on 'the wrong side of a surly officer, or worse, are found to be filing a complaint against someone who has "connections" and who can make the claimants' life hell by placing a few calls to influential individuals in power' (2009: 125). The poor are frequently at the end of police cruelty for a variety of reasons: they often do not have licences for their vehicles, whether it be a motorcycle or a car; they do not have the resources to employ a lawyer to defend them; and perhaps, above all, they are beleaguered by constant threats and bullying; they have little, if any, faith in a just system.

Bradley describes in horrific detail the torture methods deployed by the police: beatings, electric shocks, suspension by wrists and ankles, threats that members of the victims' family will be tortured, abused or killed (2009). We all know about the scale of the torture, and, as mentioned above, we also tend to know where the torture takes place. I write this to convey the widespread knowledge of the torture practices. According to Bradley, the Egyptian national budget for internal security in 2006 was $1.5 billion, which is more than the entire national budget for health care (2009: 139).

The threat of terrorism is used as the rationale for this expenditure, and this is reinforced by the continual conflict that is taking place in the Sinai. The bloody and continuing conflict in the Sinai ensures that an area of Egypt is frankly a war zone that Egyptian citizens and tourists are not allowed to enter. The media emphasises the attacks on the military and the necessity of killing those who are represented as a threat. Most of the Egyptian population accepts the government's view that these killings and torture are necessary in order to ensure the safety of the nation and its people. A significant slippage takes place as ordinary Egyptian activists are represented as if they pose the same 'threat' as members of groups such as Al-Qaeda. This perceived threat of invasion and occupation resonates with the long history of colonisation that Egypt has suffered. These occupations go back over centuries from the time of the Mamelukes to the Ottoman Empire and finally to British occupation and rule. These colonising occupations were in the past, but the fear of the aggression persists in the present even if this disquiet is unexpressed and unconscious.

There are also subtle ways of reinforcing who is in power and control: for example, the sound of circling helicopters overhead at night, the relentless threat of detention and imprisonment that is in the atmosphere implicitly and, as mentioned above, the reports from the media that reinforce the need for security and that emphasise the apparent threats from various groupings. While the soundscape is full of the sounds of domination, there is also a curious absence of noise when it comes to football matches. Since the dreadful clashes at a football match in Port Said (February 2012) when 74 people died and 400 were injured, spectators are not allowed into football games. Watching a football match without spectators, shorn of the sound whether of excitement or despair and completely lacking the general visceral presence that accompanies watching any sport is a surreal experience. It is also a weekly reminder of the consequences of conflict and the impact on daily life of the aftermath of challenging authority.

The Allure of Power

Repressive state apparatuses gain their power also through ideological mechanisms as they reinforce fear, conflict between people and complicity. As Jacqueline Rose points out:

> Inhuman political structures depend, for as long as they last, not just on the power of the oppressors and the silent complicity of the beneficiaries, but also on numbers of the oppressed being struck with an inability to connect, or give themselves, to their own cause, as well as on those beneficiaries who may have hated the system. (2003: 217)

And, I would like to add to this number those of us who did not do enough. We are in the arena of a troubling question: Why do we give ourselves over to authoritarian and oppressive power structures? In part, all societies (whatever the history of colonisation as coloniser or colonised) depend for their smooth functioning on a 'continuous interplay of subtle social incentives – not least, threats of social exclusion' (Frankel 2015: 362). The threat of social exclusion is omnipresent and powerful especially in a society in which social bonds, alliances and affiliations are of marked significance. James Ferguson (2013) explores pertinently the topic of subjection and subordination and argues that it is the reward of social membership that is a crucial reason as to why people are subservient. The reward of social membership is an important element that is intertwined with the desire to possess authority, power and dominate others. It is a psychoanalytic assertion 'that we are far more often complicit in the coming to pass of our own nightmares than we imagine' (Hook 2015: 63), or, indeed, that anyone of us would wish to acknowledge. Desire and dread, as Hook points out, are often intertwined (2015: 54); moreover, as human beings we frequently sacrifice 'reality' to 'psychic need' in the attempt to overcome our anxieties (Hook 2015: 63). There is an overwhelming fear of annihilation and this prevalent fear is leading to inexorable effects. The majority of Egyptians are relieved, and more pertinently, feel safer, more secure along with an overwhelming relief that 'life' can go on as usual when the military is in power. For the majority of the population, security is welcome and works to allay anxiety and fears in relation to 'terrorists', the activities of the Muslim Brotherhood and so on.

Fears about being robbed and/or assaulted are prevalent and many stories abound of kidnap, robbery and killings, and these rumours effect how the organisation of daily life: people are careful about how much money they take out of cash machines, have copies of their ID cards and passports in their homes in case bags and wallets are stolen and are more conscious of locking up their homes. The anxieties about safety especially affects women as most women do not take a taxi after nightfall as too many stories abound of women being robbed or sexually assaulted by taxi drivers (I am always relieved if I can get in a taxi driven by my favourite taxi driver – Mohammed or his son Ali – as I know I am safe). The difficulty is that fear works to attach itself to persons that cannot be identified easily and places that are somehow deemed as dangerous.

Fear should never be underestimated, as it is a key component in repetition due to our fear of alienation, fear of losing the love of friends and family and the fear of not knowing to who or where we belong. The need to belong fends off many fears: the fear of annihilation, the fear that frequently we do not quite know to whom and where we belong alongside the profound fear that we need the protection of significant others to whom we are attached and love. Fear, as Ahmed points out, 'is all the more frightening given the potential loss that it anticipates' (2004: 69). Fear is problematic because frequently we do not quite know what is that we fear and thus it is a free-floating affect that does not really attach to an object. The discourses of threat, danger and menace work to produce fear and to persistently position those who are 'other' as precisely the dehumanised other. These discourses produce a defensiveness and justify repressive state apparatuses as essential requirements for survival, thus *'the policies of continual surveillance of emergent forms is sustained as an ongoing project of survival'* (Ahmed 2004: 79, italics in original).

Fear can, therefore, function as one powerful explanation as to why so many Egyptians align themselves with the discourses of repression and the necessity of security. I could leave the matter rest there and leave stranded the more challenging aspects of subjectivity that require attention to our unconscious identification and compliance with authority. Subjection and subjugation involve attachment, fantasy and identification to other human beings, both those who are known and those who are unknown. Subjection, alas, involves the process of 'becoming subordinated by power as well as the process of becoming a subject' (Butler 1997a: 2). There is no subjectivity without power relations, no subjectivity without an intensive involvement in power relations, but, and this is crucial, power relations and subjection involve attachment and love. In short, subjectivity is developed and forged from power relations. Identification, fantasy, power come together to form subjectivity and the structure upon which our very subjectivities are gained. To ensure our very existence, we have to submit, and give ourselves over, to power relations. Judith Butler explores throughout her essays in *The Psychic Life of Power* that the human being is embroiled and embedded in power for to 'persist in one's own being means to be given over from the start to social terms that are never fully one's own' (1997a: 28).

Power relations operate within sedimented conditions, and these conditions of power form complex subjectivities and relations to power. Whatever our gender, we seek power as we are all vulnerable to subordination and susceptible to exploitation. Exploitative power relations persist due to what Butler terms 'passionate attachments'. These passionate attachments occur in relation to other human beings as well as our attachment to our existence. We attach to power and its various forms of 'regulation, prohibition, suppression' precisely to survive. In the novel *In the Eye of the Sun* (Soueif 1992), there is a description of a public event that is taking place in Cairo. The president has arrived and even surrounded by others, 'He was the still centre, he stood out ... the heart leapt in his presence ... the audience leapt to its feet in an ecstasy of applause' (1999: 62). Rereading this extraordinary novel recently, I was struck with the thought that while Soueif is talking about Cairo in the 1960s and the then president, Gamal Abdul Nasser, this description is applicable to present-day Egypt. The name Al-Sisi could easily replace that of Nasser. The responses are the same: the adoration, the excitement and the belief in his leadership. It is an example of the narcissism of bewitchment and of being beholden to and seduced by authority.

Said points out pertinently that we 'should always assume that officials representing a position, administrators, people who have authority and power over others, et cetera, are all involved in keeping their places and their authority intact' (in Viswanathan 2004: 420). Those in power have conscious and unconscious investments in retaining their authority and domination, and, simultaneously, 'complex personhood means that even those who haunt our dominant institutions and their systems of value are haunted too by things they sometimes have names for and sometimes do not' (Gordon 1997: 6). To recognise that as human beings we are vulnerable to and complicit with the workings of power does not necessitate understanding human beings as agents of our own destruction but is rather to posit the inextricable workings of power (Treacher Kabesh 2013a). Power is troublesome and troubling because it involves violence and socio-political relations entail and require the operations of power.

Arendt in her essay *On Violence* (2004) argues that the terms 'power', 'strength', 'force', 'authority' and 'violence' should be separated out as they refer to distinct phenomena. Power is perpetuated by the state and through symbolic and actual means by ordinary citizens, who are not immune to the allure of power. Violence, as Gill, Heathcote and Williamson write, 'is a key factor in the production, maintenance and legitimisation of domination and subordination. People often experience multiple forms of violence that are interrelated, co-constitutive and mutually reinforcing' (2016: 1). Domination and violence is reproduced in everyday life through symbolic violence that is internal to everyday life and engrained in 'everyone's habitus' (Bourdieu 2001: 33). Thapar-Björkert, Samelius and Sanghera explain symbolic violence as 'imperceptible, insidious and invisible. Invisibility constitutes an effective tool of silent domination and silencing the dominated. Dominant discourses often work to silence all other peripheral or subaltern discourses' (2016: 148). Furthermore, Thapar-Björkert et al. go on to argue:

Domination that arises from symbolic violence is less a product of direct coercion, and more a product of when those who are dominated stop questioning existing power relations, as they perceive the world and the state of affairs in a social activity as natural, a given and unchangeable. (2016: 148)

Symbolic violence embroils us all as it is embedded within psychic lives and is engrained within and through society. Symbolic violence is elusive, subtle and persists as 'something-in-the-air', but it has material effects nonetheless. Symbolic violence is intricate as it involves profoundly our attachments, identifications and insertion in the law.

In her exploration of identification, Diana Fuss considers Freud's essay on *Totem and Taboo* (1989) as a story of 'jealousy and love, hatred and admiration, violence and commemoration (that) once again revives the question of a parental identification' (1995: 32). The identification is with masculine authority, paternal identification and the affective ties of sons to fathers. The sons are fearful and envious and as a way of overcoming that fear are driven to become identical to their fathers. This story is not straightforward by any stretch of the imagination because the sons are ambivalent and, in turn, identification is replete with ambivalence that is full of love and hate. Subjectivity is always full of 'multiple and contradictory identifications coexisting in the subject at the same time' (Fuss 1995: 34). Subjectivity is always conflicted and the conflicts exist both within and across human beings. The conflict, according to Freud, led the sons to murder their father, but once murder was committed, ambivalence is to the fore again. As Fuss puts it:

The criminal deed is accomplished in vain, for as soon as the sons' hatred for the father is satisfied, an unconscious pull of affection takes over and produces in the brothers an overpowering remorse. The dead father becomes much stronger than the living father had ever been, for now the sons, under the pressure of internalised guilt, attempt to revoke the crime by subjecting themselves to their own social and sexual prohibitions. (1995: 34)

Within a Freudian psychoanalytic frame, this is the story of the origin of the law that orients all subjects to obey and submit to the law. Critically, as Fuss points out, it is the dead father who has such a psychic hold and is impossible to shake off. The weight of the dead and symbolic father weighs heavy and remains alive within subjectivity.

There are two important symbolic paternal figures who are para-mount within Egyptian subjectivities: the symbolic father of the presi-dent and the symbolic father of the coloniser. All the presidents, Nasser, Sadat, Mubarak, Al-Sisi, position themselves, and are positioned, as fathers of the nation. So, as much as most of the Egyptian population wanted Mubarak to resign as president (Mubarak, *irhal* – 'Mubarak go' was after all one of the fervent demands of the protests in 2011), there was also guilt and profound disquiet about his resignation. I heard many people express guilt and remorse when he appeared in court. It is not that they did not want him to stand trial, but the footage of him lying on a stretcher provoked guilt and remorse. One state of mind does not replace the other as they co-exist simultaneously.

It is this profound loyalty to the symbolic father that exists inescap-ably in Egypt that can lead to a difficulty in challenging authority, a fearfulness in demanding change and not quite being able to engage in the present. These difficulties that are paramount can lead to a 'pet-rification' (Hook 2015: 53) that is needless to say problematic as it produces a stalling of thought and action. The complexity though is that there is a tenderness and a loving commitment to what has been (Hook 2015). Hook writes tenderly about the conflicts that can and do arise:

If, psychically, one option is unpalatable and frightening, then one will likely experience a 'spontaneous' affinity or likeness, indeed a love, for an option to which to some degree screens out the threatening scenario. … What was a resistance to change can now be more favourably framed as a fidelity to the past. (2015: 52)

This fidelity to the past can be illustrated through the character of the father in the novel *The Open Door* (2005). On 23 July 1952 (the day the 1952 Revolution took place), Muhammed Effendi Sulayman was listening to the radio, and felt pride at being an Egyptian and what Egyptians can do, but quickly following this emotion of pride, a different reaction followed and an

> 'agonizing fear throbbed through his body as he heard that the revolution had moved into a new stage, and it mounted as he heard that they wanted to dethrone the king'. How could those revolutionaries change the course of destiny? And he ponders as 'Tears collected in his eyes, reflecting the blend of alarm and pride he felt as the paramount icon of the old Egypt was demolished before his eyes. (Al-Zayyat 2005: 159–160)

Problematic identification with authority, previous states of mind such as fear and being beholden to authoritative and patriarchal fathers can lead to being complicit with a problematic socio-political order. Compliance can lead to psychic compensations and these may be imagined, but that does not take away their power. The compensations, I hazard a guess, are of imagining that authority can be possessed, that power and status are there for the taking and that being on the 'right side' entails security (material, social, psychic). It is also as I have been attempting to prise apart about the need to attach and the yearning to belong. Complex identifications are always acts of repetition *and* remembrance, are never straightforward or linear and always entail 'interiors and exteriors, boundaries and permutations, transgressions and resistances' (Fuss 1995: 52). Identifications lead to the wish to redeem, the wish to disavow our history and, simultaneously, also to the assertion that we are not like our ancestors. This disavowal of the inheritance of history is problematic as it can and does lead to further repetition. The desire to get rid of the shame and humiliation of colonialism leads, and this is a profound irony, into repetition of colonialism itself with its denigration, exclusions and humiliations. This understandable and inevitable desire leads to persistent problematic identifications and further repetition.

Julian Go argues persuasively that decolonisation did not bring about the end of colonisation as violence, global inequality and domination continued (2013). Go argues that decolonisation in the political sphere did not bring about a decolonization of consciousness or culture. Racialized forms of thought persisted among ex-colonizers and ex-colonized alike; as did self-negation, cultural annihilation, and feelings of marginalization among postcolonial peoples. The 'West' was no longer the center of traditional colonial power but it surely retained its cultural power, beckoning the ex-colonized to be like it. (Go 2013: 5)

The persistent representation of stripping people (specifically men) from the Middle East of history and political context divests any possibility of understanding. The difficulty is that being divested of history is replicated within subjectivities and through the socio-political context. It is this disavowal of the impact of colonisation that causes, in part, psychic violence. As Dominic LaCapra argues, violence always returns as the repressed and remains a core aspect of subjectivities (2001).

Pointing towards prevalent discourses should not lead to an analysis that denies the impact of the wounds and how human beings can be riven with injuries. Rose elucidates how unconscious histories repeat themselves and raises the following pertinent matter: How can we remedy injustice and what can be done about the 'non-rational, unconscious, almost pathological dimension of political power?' (2004: 426). There is a profound silence in relation to a fear that there may be more congruence between the coloniser and colonised than is seemingly apparent. The fear of recognising this resemblance is complicated because it would be based on an acknowledgement that identification has occurred through the biological father and symbolic authority. Identifications are overdetermined, are multiple and never occur just along a biological axis, and an analysis of identifications cannot rest along the following line of real 'black fathers and "symbolic" white ones' (Hall 1996a: 30); we cannot assume that identifying with the white symbolic father leads away from identifying with the biological parent, or indeed the other way round. Subjectivities are complex precisely because they are forged through multiple identifications that can, and frequently do, bring about conflict and cause divisions and splits within the self.

Identification is a means of gaining control over the objects outside of oneself, and importantly identification is always a turning towards away from something/someone that is unwanted and unbidden and a turning towards something/someone that has more psychic appeal. Identifying with the coloniser is based on a repudiation of inferiority, and an assertion that those from Egypt are also rational, strong and civilised is

based on the desire to be just like the coloniser. These precarious assertions of superiority are based on identification with the coloniser's own
haughty and confident self-image. These impulses are never rational
as they arise 'unmediated from the unconscious and hence (have) not
been worked over by the secondary processes of thought' (Frosh 2013b:
144). Alienation is always an aspect of all subjectivities, whatever our
inheritance and socio-political locations are, but there is a massive difference in the effect of alienation. As Frosh writes for the colonised
subject, 'The reflection is not of the image as seen by the subject her or
himself (and directed by the gaze of the mother); it is a reflection of the
colonizer's gaze, and as such is doubly alienating' (2013b: 147).

The colonised subject is excluded from the very self–other dynamic
that makes subjectivity possible (Fuss 1995: 142). In short, colonised
subjects are not even in the place of the other and are excluded from
'full cultural signification', and the 'implications of his exclusion from
the cultural field of symbolization are immediate and devastating'
(Fuss 1995: 143). No wonder then that the responses to these multiple
and various exclusions lead to troubling, albeit unconscious, dynamics. Kalpana Seshadri-Crooks in her book *Desiring Whiteness* (2000)
argues through a Lacanian lens that people of colour, or indeed those
who have been colonised, wish to have access to power and status and
to, I would add, be a part of history.

This powerful desire to be in a place of authority threatens the
unspoken and often unconscious knowledge that the white person is the
measure of humanity and possesses a privileged place. For Seshadri-
Crooks, this desire coincides with a fear that the privilege of being a
white subject is natural and deserved. For Seshadri-Crooks, the desire
to take up the position of white subjectivity is not based on a wish to
be Caucasian but rather on an anxiety of being 'the lack of a lack'
(2000: 37). I am not so convinced as Seshadri-Crooks that those who
have been colonised or indeed people of colour do not wish to take up
the place of whiteness for a number of diverse and possibly overlapping
reasons. First, there is too easy an elision of race and power, and this
is underlined persistently. By this I mean that power is associated with
whiteness (with good reason) and there are the relentless troublesome
psycho-social-political investments in power and authority. Racial difference and colonising differences elicit investment because race promises access to being itself – not just power, status, belonging – but *being*.
Being here is completeness, no matter how illusory and the certainty

again a powerful illusion – and as Seshadri-Crooks puts it, 'The jouis-sance of Oneness' (2000: 7). Second, whiteness is still perceived in Egypt as that which should be desired. Every pharmacy in Cairo is full of skin bleaching products that are cheap, and many adverts abound that reinforce the desire for whiteness. Whiteness remains a master signifier and maybe a floating signifier, but it retains, alas, a signifier with pow-erful and material effect.

Being Muslim and Egyptian is a double rejection from valued sub-jectivity, and one illusory means of overcoming this exclusion is to mimic the coloniser. Mimicry is problematic for a number of reasons not least of which is that mimicry is forged on the illusion that power and recognition are equal between the 'white' person and the person who is othered. For example, my father was proud to be Egyptian, loved Egypt and gave much to improving the intellectual climate in Egypt and wanted desperately for Egypt to become a society based on social justice. Alongside his pride of being an Egyptian, and especially of being a Muslim, he also mimicked being English, and as a family we frequently teased him by saying he was 100 per cent English. My father was caught between pride, longing and ontological vulnerability, and he knew that he could never be perceived as European despite his frantic efforts and his pride 'at being more English than the English' (Treacher Kabesh 2013a).

Identification is often based on overcoming loss, lack and, more posi-tively, an investment in the future. Identification also, I suspect, gains its power from feelings and experiences of powerlessness as one of the burdens for all men is that they cannot, and will never, be powerful enough (all men have to inhabit the gap between the phallus and the penis). The fallacy of power has to be sustained and the knowledge that flesh and blood men know and experience that they cannot 'man up' has to be disavowed stringently and perpetually.

Having been incorporated in the psyche of the white man and exploited to bolster the coloniser's fragile sense of self, a paradox takes place, which is that the colonised attempt unsuccessfully a project of ambivalent assimilation. As Goffman (1952) points out, mimicry always evokes humiliation when people know they are not the right thing and feel the madness of pretence as well as the emptiness and hideous familiar feeling of fraudulence, of 'loss of face'. Goffman asks, 'At what points in the structures of our social life are persons likely to compromise themselves or find themselves compromised?' In the lives of the colonised, or those who have inherited a history of colonisation, compromise and mimicry are, in fact, ongoing. Witnessing the mimicry of previous generations and knowing in that incoherent way that we sense intra-and inter-relationship is never successful. Indeed it reveals the undoing of subjectivity. Witnessing the attempts by previous generations to assimilate and knowing it has failed, I think leads to a wish to redeem the humiliation, the wish not to be in that place – who after all wants to be humiliated? An understandable desire is to be *someone* and to *have a place in history*. Having witnessed violent indifference, there is the understandable wish not to be in that place and to be stripped of humanity and of being human. As I have previously argued, and I am repeating the assertion here, that while subjection is always problematic it is always preferable to abjection (Ferguson 2013). Abjection coincides fatally with social death (a laden phrase from Patterson 1982) and the inexorably state of shrivelling up inside, for as Ferguson rather pithily expresses it, 'For those thus abjected, subjection can only appear as a step up' (2013: 231). Power is alluring and seductive because it provides a hope and an optimistic illusion, a refusal to be in the same place as that which has taken place previously.

Attempting to Make a Difference

The refusal to endure the socio-political conditions in Egypt takes many forms from official opposition parties to demonstrations to strikes. I provide a partial list of political parties to indicate the range of political positions that exist in Egypt, and these include Arabic Popular Movement (set up by former Tamarood members), Youth for Egypt (constituted by former members of the Muslim Brotherhood), the Constitution Party (its slogans are bread, freedom and social justice, and it was set up by Mohammed ElBaradi and others), Justice Party (created by the April 6 movement and Kefiya), the Popular Current movement (formed by the Nasserite – Hamdeen Sabahi), the Egypt Reform Party (founded by young members of the Salafi religious movement) and, finally, the banned Freedom and Justice Party (the political wing of the Muslim Brotherhood).

Worker militancy escalated throughout the last decade of Mubarak's rule as 'the longest and strongest wave of worker protest since the late 1940s rolled through Egypt' (Beinin 2012: 92). Beinin provides the following figures: over three million workers (textile industry workers, bus drivers, rubbish collectors, blue-collar and white-collar workers) participated in 3,500–4,000 strikes and demonstrations (2012: 92). The strikes and protests were successful in relation to gaining higher wages and better working conditions. Alongside these demonstrations for more materially secure living conditions, there were also protests against the Mubarak regime and its governance. These protests were crushed by the use of Emergency Laws, police brutality, arrests and trials. From 2004, a coalition of political opposition forces including Nasserists, socialists, Islamists and liberal democrats organised a series of demonstrations – *Kifaya* (enough). While the protests were small (maybe a few thousand attended), the consequence was much more important as '[T]aboos were broken with the call for the end of Mubarak's rule, the explicit demand for putting police generals on trial for torture and illegal arrests. The exposure of the corruption of the ruling family and top state officials resonated strongly with a much wider audience' (Naguib 2012: 9). These protests have historical resonance with the Cairo Fire of 1952, which destroyed many buildings in Cairo and, more importantly, expressed the indignation and fury of many Egyptians that was directed towards foreign occupation, the government and the monarchy. More recently, the Bread Riots in 1977 were demonstrations against the demand from the International Monetary Fund that food subsidy should be reduced, and there was widespread outrage at the cutting of basic food subsidies. Sadat agreed due to the double pressure from his own government and the Egyptians. These political demonstrations, the Cairo Fire, the Bread Riots, labour strikes and increasing political demands from movements such as *Kifaya*, illustrate the strength of discontent and also the importance of overcoming fear. As Mahmud (Layla's brother in the novel *The Open Door*) writes in a letter in which he relates

> sensing some strength grander than yourself, greater than your fear, a force that pushes you on and makes you do what you have to do it keeps you steady and precise all of the time. ... You feel like you are one in a collective, that your life is significant as long as you are serving this collective. (Al-Zayyat 2005: 110)

The importance of political belonging is also illustrated in the demonstrations and protests in support of the Palestinians. The wars of

1967 and 1973 are deeply embedded in the Egyptian imagination, and memories of these wars are a constant source of humiliation and rancour. Israel is a constant point of suspicion, as is America, who is seen as wholehearted supporter of Israel (it must be pointed out that Egyptians separate out governments and citizens). Ironically, one reason that Mohammed Morsi was so vehemently disliked was due to his perceived support of Israel. Ever since Egypt's peace treaty with Israel in 1979, the US-Egyptian alliance 'has been one of the main pillars of US strategic hegemony in the region' (Naguib 2012: 6). The Egyptian regimes have supported US interventions, and the Mubarak regime played a central role in facilitating the US programme of 'extraordinary renditions'. This strategic role was not welcomed, and there were many protests against the US strategy in the region: the invasion of Iraq and in support of the Palestinian people. Israel and America are two nation states that are perceived as Egypt's arch enemies, which are continually plotting to break Egypt up because they are threatened by Egypt.

The above account is a very truncated summary of the political activities that have taken place and the attempts to overcome the impediments to social justice and equality. I want to now turn to focus in more depth on the current political campaigns against sexual harassment that illustrate two issues. First, the complexity of sexual difference, identification and the wish to repair a troubling socio-political dynamic. Second, and as important the political campaigns reveal the 'impossibility and inadequacy of thinking and making revolution first and gender second' and furthermore 'no challenge to the nation-state can succeed without a broader shift in values' (Andrijasevic et al. 2014: 3).

As Shereen Abouelnaga writes, the experiences of women under the rule of the Islamists show how the body became the marker of identity as 'women's subjectivity was reduced to the corporeal body, which was used in turn to augment sexual difference' (Abouelnaga 2016: 93). Soon after the Freedom and Justice Party took power, groups of men took to the streets verbally and/or physically attacking women, both those who wore the *hijab* and those who did not (these groups became so virulent that I seriously considered whether or not to wear the *hijab* when outside the home). Alongside these, unfortunately, commonplace attacks, there was an increase in sexual harassment against women. Sexual harassment has always been a persistent problem for women in Egypt (98 per cent of women report having been sexually assaulted), and certainly since the Revolution of 2011 it has been even more widespread. Towards the end of 2012, a march took place protesting against sexual harassment, but hundreds of men assaulted the women who were taking part in this march. These men groped and molested several of the women who were protesting, leading to several members of Parliament asking for legislation to make sexual harassment illegal.

Azza Al-Garf (a female member of Parliament and a member of the Muslim Brotherhood) argued that passing such legislation was unacceptable as it is the woman's responsibility to ensure that sexual harassment does not take place. Blaming women for sexual harassment, domestic violence and abuse was commonplace in Egypt, but I hazard that this is less widespread as many families have a female member who is now speaking more openly about the experiences of being in public. The Islamic movements accused women of inviting sexual harassment and condemned female bodies that did not conform to their notion of appropriate femininity in relation to dress, conduct, inhabiting in public spaces. As Abouelnaga writes, it is hardly surprising 'that one of the very early efforts of the Islamists was to organize medical convoys to villages to circumcise girls' (2016: 96).

Women's rights organisations have been resolute in the struggle against sexual harassment – for example, Harassmap and other organisations, such as El-Nadeem Centre for Rehabilitation of Victims of Violence and Torture, Narzra for Feminist Studies and the New Women's Research Centre, all are actively addressing the widespread phenomena of sexual abuse. These activities have increased since gender-based violence became a feature of demonstrations. Groups such as Tahrir Bodyguards and Operation Anti-Sexual Harassment (OpAnti-SH) protect female demonstrators against assault; some women welcome this protection, while others perceive it as another form of control. There is, therefore, much political activity in relation to women and the various forms inflicted. This activity ranges from providing legal support and representation, to physical protection, to mapping the areas where harassment is most likely to take place.

This, needless to say, is about patriarchal control and domination, but a new form of patriarchy maybe emerging in Egypt as much of importance has taken place: much political activity that was there for all to witness, much political debate and arguments either within the home or in the public sphere alongside open disobedience undertaken by women by attending the demonstrations. Patriarchy maybe taking a new form in Egypt as socio-political conditions do not change smoothly or easily (patriarchal domination as well as capitalism always finds new ways of retaining power) but socio-political-emotional conditions for Egyptian women cannot be the same as before 2011. It remains to be seen how sexual difference, gender relations and sexuality will be changed, or not, by the socio-political events that have taken place since 2011.

Chapter 7

The Essential Endeavour

Being Accountable

I am preoccupied with the following question: Why do we act against our best interests? This is a theme with universal resonances, but needless to say the enquiry has to be located within the specifics of time and place with a focus on what kind of society (as in form and as in compassion) could facilitate full political participation. Judgement though, in my view, is central to any investigation and I am influenced profoundly by Arendt's conceptualisation of judgement (2003). Arendt argues that judgement, more than any of the other mental abilities, is exercised in relationship with others, and, importantly, judgement forms the basis of what Kant termed 'enlarged mentality' and enables the possibility of engaged citizenship. It is the precise difficulties involved in inhabiting an 'enlarged mentality' that has been a central, albeit implicit, theme of this book.

The enduring matter focuses on how to think through, and accept, the responsibilities of being accountable in the Egyptian socio-political context, which is complex and troubling. It is troubling and troublesome as attempting to think this through necessitates being cognisant of the inextricable connections of internal and global politics, the impact of history on the present, the vexed power dynamics and shifting alliances that undermine the possibility of a secure foundation. There is a risk of posing too many questions in this chapter and yet a pertinent enquiry remains unanswered: What were and remain the obstacles to Egypt becoming a society based on social justice? We can reach for many reasons: the role and obdurate exploitations of the West, the various machinations of the superpowers and their profound impact on Egypt, the complicities of the Egyptian political elite and the resultant compliance of the Egyptian state with the hegemony of the superpowers alongside the grip of the Egyptian Deep State. All these rationales are embedded in truth and resonate powerfully, and yet there is a dimension to these interpretations and I am at risk here of returning responsibility to the individual and of avoiding the power of the state.

It is not my intent to place responsibility on individual human beings in pointing to Fanon's insight that none of us are immune from socio-political structures (1986). We are all embedded and formed within these relentless structures that transmit socio-political structures unremittingly. The confrontation, as always, focuses on our subjection that forms our compliance, if not complicity, in perpetuating aggression, indifference and cruelty. We cannot avoid this confrontation by asserting resistance, innocence or victimhood. There is the persistent matter of knowing our responsibilities while being cognisant, paradoxically, of the limits of our accountability. A full account needs to pay due attention to the constraints on citizens in relation to public participation. This account cannot pass over the matters of accountability and responsibility as if these are burning objects that must be bypassed so that blame is shunted and we can all breathe a sigh of welcome relief and reside in thoughtlessness.

I want to think through the issues of guilt, accountability and responsibility of ordinary citizens, specifically my middle-aged, Egyptian generation, and what we could have done and thought differently and engaged in more effective judgements in order to forge and secure a society based on social justice and equality. I am preoccupied with the impact of inhabiting a society and political system that is profoundly authoritarian, deeply oppressive and repressive and marked by devastating corruption. There is no sign, despite the impressive political activity and engagement of younger generations in Egypt, of the repression and oppression easing and weakening. Indeed, the destruction of human bonds along with the destruction of public spaces is deepening (Young-Bruehl 2006: 52). We are without words and are dominated by a state of mind, accurately described by Arendt as 'wordlessness' alongside profound sadness, disappointment and anger. We, and I am unashamedly using the pronoun 'we', are bewildered at the endless repetition of disappointment and anger (if not fury), and we struggle to find coherence and meaning. The struggle to find words may be the only truthful place to be as reaching out too quickly for language may obscure more than it reveals and grasping too fast for words may take us away from that which is unbearable.

Many feminists have persisted in nuanced analysis that links the personal and the political without depoliticising the socio-political spheres. Here, I am pointing to the analysis of Sara Ahmed, Wendy Brown, Judith Butler and Jacqueline Rose. From their diverse positions, they explore the following: how emotions bind (Ahmed 2004), power, subjection and psychic life (Butler 1997), the endurance of emotional and political attachments (Brown 1995) and tracing through and comprehending fantasy and its workings in the political sphere (Rose 1998). In Jacqueline Rose's book of essays, *States of Fantasy*, she argues that fantasy should be at the heart of our political vocabulary for 'Like blood, fantasy is thicker than water, all too solid – *contra* another of fantasy's more familiar glosses as ungrounded supposition, lacking in foundation, not solid *enough*' (Rose 1998: 5, emphasis in original). The issue for Rose is not that of recognising fantasy, as if all can be read off from that acknowledgement, but rather the point is to grasp how fantasy fuels politics and of course, politics fuel fantasy. There is though a troublesome question which focuses on how we take proper account of the emotions and their work in the political without allowing the emotional and that which may be conceptualised as belonging to the private to override political, historical and social considerations.

My generation, like my father's generation, is responsible and accountable for the persistent inability to make a future replete with effective possibilities. We too easily reached out for the following explanations: it is the West, it is Israel, it is the past and we have done our best; and we shrugged our shoulders and declared rather insistently, 'What else could we have done'. I cannot, and should not, continually return responsibility to previous generations as I am disappointed in the left's incapacity to make a difference (and I consider myself a member of the broad left and I am disappointed in myself as well as others for our failure to make a difference). The matter of persistent thought and judgement is crucial and psychoanalysis is an important framework for thinking through the continuing issue of resistance. By resistance I am pointing to a particular defiance of thinking, acting and judging differently. For psychoanalysis, resistance 'is the mind at war with itself, blocking the path to its own freedom and with it, its ability to make the world a better, less tyrannical, place' (Rose 2013: 21). Facing up to the past, to present responsibilities, to how one is formed is never easy, nor straightforward. The more laden the past, the more painful is the process of remembering. Here I am at risk of romanticising remembering as if the very act of memory will deliver a different future. In an ironic twist, to remember, as Luisa Passerini points out, the self has to know that something is absent, forgotten indeed (2003). In short, 'To forget you have to forget that you have even forgotten' (Rose 2003a: 7). There are endless twists and turns for, as Freud argues, remembering and forgetting are closely intertwined. Within this Freudian viewpoint, we use memories and narratives to conceal and obscure other memories and other narratives. There is a responsibility that focuses, however, on resisting the compulsion to repeat. As Ashis Nandy argues, colonisation is internalised and the external coloniser is blamed, but the external coloniser is also exploited to legitimise the perpetual internal divisions, corruption, social and political failures (Nandy 1983; Treacher Kabesh 2013a).

Remorse haunts and should not be sloughed off through banal clichés such as 'we had no choice', 'we did not know' and/or 'what else could we have done'. Responsibility depends on many aspects: thought and judgement primarily and importantly involves judgement about one's actions or indeed lack of action and intervention. As I have already pointed out, as Rose reminds us, it takes a great deal of energy and activity to achieve passivity (2003a: 218). I would add that thinking and judgement require energy, time, reflection and troublesome confrontations, but it also takes effort not to think and to avoid judgement. My generation, I insist, is accountable, and the younger generation is understandably indignant and angry that we did not do more. It is not enough to resort to resigned helplessness as if that will get us out of our moral quagmire and our helplessness. Regret and remorse cannot, and should not, be avoided, no matter how painful (Treacher Kabesh 2011). There is a value in regret (Olick 2007).

As Olick argues, the politics of regret focuses attention on individual responsibility, the power of the state and the socio-political context in a specific place at a particular time. Olick points to the vital difference between the politics of conviction which is driven by assertion, lack of thought and fervour and the politics of responsibility, which is marked by consideration and the knowledge of the complexity of socio-political conditions and events (2007: 15). Egypt, I argue, has been driven, whether in power or in opposition, by the politics of conviction. Paradoxically, for all the rhetoric, noise and affect, the politics of conviction has led to resistance to thinking anew; for, as Olick points out, the distinction is 'between quiescence, which is cheap and temporary, and peace, which is expensive but durable' (2007: 15). This is neither to undermine or cheapen those revolutionaries who gave up their lives in January 2011 and beyond nor to underestimate the amount of political activity in the shape of strikes or the valuable efforts of many NGOs; the issue here is how these diverse and important activities have impacted little on socio-political institutions or 'structures of feeling'. I am preoccupied, however, with another angle, which is to understand the underbelly of repetition and resistance in order to move towards more effective engagement. Necessary regret is one way through to understanding the impact of the past on the present, which is that colonialism persists in the dynamic of internalised colonialism and in problematic identifications that I persistently argue paralyse effective engagement and action. Ross Poole asks pertinently as to how can we respond to the injustices of the past and make reparation and attempt to repair the claims for recognition, love and nurture (2009). Responsibility involves the ethical drive to repair, to be repaired, to redeem oneself and to know that one is guilty of indifference, lack of thought and absence of judgement, or the opposite, that is, being too quick to judge, which is equally an avoidance of thought.

I am proposing that political authority is gained through persistent thought and judgement, and that it is only through a stringent exploration of public life that a polity based on social justice can be created and sustained. Judgement, action, will and thought are essential requirements for a different social order to be made and sustained. Persistent thought is key as it is thoughtlessness, blind obedience and complicity, lack of regret for the suffering we have passed on that leads to corrupt socio-political societies. Political activity, in its diverse forms, is taking place in Egypt, important cross-faith and cross-gender and class alliances are taking place, and alongside the importance of hope we need to think responsibly and persistently, even if it causes pain and offence, about our actions and judgements.

The profoundly precarious and vexed endeavour to have a political life of the mind to draw on Arendt, and to 'learn to live without consoling fictions and consoling memories' does not occur, and as Rose expresses it, learning to live without consoling fictions is essential, for it is 'in the death of such numbing and dangerous fantasies lies our only hope' (Rose 2003b: 68). Fantasy is both essential for action and for making something anew, and is dangerous in its capacity to trap all of us in thoughtlessness and to forget our ethical and political obligations. As Arendt reminds us, we are nothing without our promise to the other, without our obligations and without giving ourselves over to an idea, an ideal, to the body politic. The first consideration of politics is that human beings co-exist together and are interdependent on each other. Cavarero positions interdependency at the hub of social and political life (2000). We are utterly dependent on other human beings fulfilling their promises and commitments; more crucially, we are utterly depleted and emptied out when we do not fulfil our obligations to other human beings. Part of fulfilling our socio-political commitment is to recognise our responsibilities, and to think about the political past anew one has to focus on what has occurred and, as Avery Gordon writes, on that which eludes, the 'hauntings, ghosts, and gaps, seething absences, and muted presences' (Gordon 1997: 21). This requires stringent and careful thought, and a continual revisiting of what has been, and what is in the present. Resignation of thought and passive complicities are perhaps two states of mind (individual and collective) which lead to stagnation, perpetuation and, above all, hinder, if not paralyse, any movement towards a creative body politic.

Reaching out towards remembering may provide an easy solution, but it is not so clear to me that we learn very much from the past; indeed, memory is an intricate aspect of subjectivities as it is riddled with fantasies (conscious and unconscious) and is replete with the desire to forget. Edward Said describes human identity as elusive, inconsistent and unstable and while that is a valuable position, indeed it is difficult to disagree, but that stance does leave stranded identities that are fragmented, struggling to fend off uncertainties and subjectivities that are too burdened with the past. So, while Said argues persuasively that we need 'to reach out beyond identity to something else, whatever that is ... it may be an altered state of consciousness that puts you in touch with others more than one normally is. It may be just a state of forgetfulness which, at some point, I think is what we all need – to forget' (2004b: 431).

Cruel Indifference

How do emotions hinder or foster a society that should be based on social justice? For example, how do the emotions of fear, vulnerability, anger, hope and betrayal impede at best and paralyse at worst the making of a different and better society? What kind of society (I am using kind here in two different ways: kind as in form and kind as an emotion that reaches out to others) would facilitate social justice? I will use Martha Nussbaum's careful discussion of compassion as a basis for discussion of this particular point (2008). Nussbaum argues that a society pursuing justice might legitimately rely on compassion, and an effective socio-political formation can facilitate the thought required to confront effectively the impediments to justice such as shame, resentment, envy and disgust. Critically, compassion for Nussbaum is not sentimentality which, as Winnicott pointed out, frequently is disguised hate (1965), but rather compassion is based on a knowledge that our very identity is constituted in part by its relations to the outside world. In short, we do not just have an internal or solipsistic relation to the self but are always dependent on the other for our very selfhood. Recognising our very dependency on other human beings for our selfhood leads to the ethical matter that focuses on how to relate to another human being or another community without the need to triumph or annihilate the other. To echo Jessica Benjamin's apposite questions: 'Can a subject relate to the other without assimilating the other to the self through identification? – corresponds to the political question, Can a community admit the Other without her/him having to already be or become the same?' (1998: 94).

To be compassionate, however, is easier said than done as it is a painful emotion, and, as Nussbaum carefully traces through, it is an emotion that causes emotional, cognitive and ethical upheaval. Moreover, compassion is based on a world view and needless to say requires judgement. For Hannah Arendt, being in the world is a crucial endeavour which citizens have to undertake in order for a full political engagement with societies inhabited; she persists with her view that being in the world should involve activity, judging and thinking (I am deliberately using verbs) are vital for political citizenship (1958). For Arendt, thoughtlessness is the major problem as it hinders at best and paralyses at worst political participation. Moreover, thoughtlessness impedes understanding of being in the world and the political judgement required to understand and to know the meanings that 'being in the world' necessitates. Furthermore, Arendt writes in her book *Men in Dark Times* (1968) that evil deeds are not what constitutes the darkness, but rather the 'darkness is what comes when the open, light spaces between people, the public spaces where people can reveal themselves, are shunned or avoided; the darkness is a hateful attitude toward the public realm, toward politics' (Young-Bruehl 2006: 6).

As Nussbaum asserts, compassion is based on one's world view in relation to what is perceived as important, valuable and worthwhile and is centrally embroiled in the fantasy of who one wants to be and who one wants to reach towards. As implicit in the emotion – compassion – is a conception of human flourishing and the major predicaments of human life. This all necessitates judgement and we make these judgements unthinkingly in relation to our perceptions of the size of pain, suffering and injury. But judgements may be skewed either by the onlooker or by the sufferer, and at risk of being tautological compassion is felt, or not, based on the judgement in relation to size of suffering and whether it is appropriate or not and whether the event or suffering impedes human flourishing. Whether we like it or not, we base our judgement on fault and blame with all the resonances of who is deserving and/or undeserving of our compassion. Those who are perceived as good are perceived as not deserving their misfortune, and this judgement is based on issues of culpability as we are much more likely to feel compassion if we feel that the person is without agency as the difficulties have come from outside of the person. For example, people tend to feel compassion for my autistic nephew and our family as his autism is perceived as a misfortune for which no one in my family is responsible. In short, whether compassion is felt or not requires, and hinges on, notions of responsibility and culpability.

Compassion is also frequently based on the knowledge that one's place in the world is precarious and fragile (Butler 2004) and so to be able to place oneself and others in a shared community is vital for compassion otherwise violence or indifference is most likely to occur. The profound difficulty is, how should we treat other people? It is too easy to reach out and declare with well-meaning intent words such as respect, tolerance and acceptance but these can carry the tone of mantras that though well intentioned can also silence. The Christian injunction 'to love thy neighbour as thyself' is, as Adam Phillips point out, ironic – 'because actually, of course, people hate themselves. Or you could say that, given the way people treat one another, perhaps they had always loved their neighbours in the way they loved themselves: that is with a good deal of cruelty and disregard' (2015). There is, perhaps, no other place to be than to recognise our cruelty, aggression and wish to rid ourselves of the other.

As I have already described, during the summer of 2013 the Egyptians were in a state of high alert and dominated by the political events that occurred following the ousting of President Morsi and the imprisonment of many leading, and ordinary, members of the Muslim Brotherhood. People were dominated by overwhelming anxiety as everyday life became impossible and freighted with affect – primarily anxiety, fear and a state of mind that can only be described as mindless waiting. We were on super-alert to any sign – not necessarily of change – of something, and, to be honest, I am not quite sure what would have constituted that 'something'. Caution and hyper-vigilance meant that nothing could be taken for granted, and paranoia dominated. During that particular summer, I, along with many Egyptians, had internalised profoundly a sense of danger that was all too pervasive and overwhelming. This particular state of mind was commonplace, and it was partly formed through endless conversations with others and reinforced profoundly by the media – especially the television that was full of emotive footage.

The same footage of violence was shown over and over, and was overlaid with emotional music that was intended to and certainly did provoke intense feeling. The nationalistic mythscape of Egypt during that summer and still dominant is that of a united nation that is automatically against the Muslim Brotherhood; and additionally in a problematic slide, if you are against the Muslim Brotherhood, you are automatically on the side of, and committed to, Egypt as a nation. These discourses have a history that stretch back to Nasser's regime when Muslim Brotherhood members were frequently imprisoned and the leaders assassinated; these discourses of denigrating the Muslim Brotherhood persist unremittingly in the present. My generation was formed through these discourses, and for those of us who do not support the Muslim Brotherhood, we perpetuate a cruel indifference.

I want to turn towards considering indifference. Indifference can have different meanings that are attached to different states of mind. Indifference can be healthy as it can allow self and the other to exist as distinct human beings but linked in a shared humanity. Indifference can also allow the other to exist in an ordinary way and to just walk down the road without scrutiny or the projections and emotions of the other. In these ways, indifference can be valuable as it can enable another human being to exist without loading them up with projections, fantasies and affect. Indifference, however, can also be ruthless, aggressive and oddly devoid of emotion marked by an emptiness and coldness. Indifference, paradoxically, can lead to hate and overloaded affect and, in a complicated mechanism, it can work in an opposite way as hatred can unleash indifference.

Indifference can be empty as it empties out the self and empties out the other human being as nothing happens, and there is an indifference to that empty space within the self and between self and other. I want to open up the possibility that some states of mind have no emotions, and I think indifference can operate precisely as a void that is devoid of emotion. The problem with perceiving indifference as violence, as hate, as contempt or whatever it is that is loaded and in a way it reassures us that we are still human and while we may feel hate, rather, paradoxically, it proves that we still have a humanness. While all of these emotions of hatred, fear and contempt were evoked specifically in the summer of 2013, there was also a ruthless coldness – a deadness of feeling – which was vacant alongside fear and hatred.

As Sara Ahmed writes, hatred creates and enforces boundaries between self and other and between communities – the other is always a threat to survival or rather is represented as a threat to our very existence even if in phantasy. Ahmed writes:

> Fantasies construct the other as a danger not only to one's self as self, but to one's very life, to one's very existence as a separate being with a life of its own. Such fantasies of the other hence work to justify violence against others. (2004: 64)

These powerful phantasies of threat and possible annihilation have profound purchase as they tie into an already-existing feeling of vulnerability and/or precariousness. Hatred is intense, visceral and a negative attachment to others as it creates the 'I' and the 'we', the 'them' in problematic alignments (Ahmed 2004). Through forms of identification that align, subjects through imagined likeness become loved while the 'them' become hated. Identification frequently involves disidentification, which is an active giving up of other possible identifications. Conflict, identification and disidentification are such that some families are divided to the point of fracture and friends have fallen out irrevocably, and it is difficult to know at present if these breaks can ever be healed as these ruptures are too deep and with far too many consequences. A state of mind (hopeless, helpless, fearful) has left little room for thought while simultaneously there was (is?) far too much space for projections, phantasies and affect to dominate and overwhelm.

Persistently, there has been a dehumanisation of the other and here we are into a web of emotion, narrative, discourses of the state that are circular, reinforcing and perpetuate each aspect of the chain. An atmosphere of cruelty dominated through conversation, media reports and representations, and 'the practice of cruelty' had the function of squeezing out humanity and preventing human understanding from modifying the cruelty' (Bollas 2011: 82). There was an attack on complexity, different values and belief systems. A particular way of maintaining certainty occurred through eliminating doubt and uncertainty. Opposition was through mental processes that rejected the other, and any questioning of self and other became equivalent to weakness and had to be expelled (Bollas 2011). One cruel way that the other human being was dismissed was to turn the views, especially of the Muslim Brotherhood, into the absurd and thereby rendering them less intelligible but more importantly as ridiculous. This is worrying, and should be so, as while the dominant discourses had the appearance of the moral, underpinning them was a false unity which attempted to suppress the difficulties inherent in the prevalent and governing positions.

The issue here, as it always is, focuses on thinking and how to understand the position of the other that is not laden with cruelty and hatred. This is what we could not do as we could not imagine the state of the camps; we refused to engage in that act of the imagination as we refused to listen or understand why they had set up camps and, so, must have lived in intolerable conditions for over seven weeks. We turned our identification and aligned ourselves to people like us as we wanted to identify with them and too easily understood the absolute disruption to their daily life. Empathy did not take place, and by empathy, following Elisabeth Young-Bruehl, I mean allowing the other into the self to enable other human to make a difference to the self (1998).

I am arguing that in different ways we were all perpetrators of violence either through not doing anything or, if you are a member of the Muslim Brotherhood and the military, through enacting violence. The violence enacted by ordinary citizens, in the attempt to save our illusion of humanity we want some things to remain unseen (Bollas 2011). There are many ways to be violent, and while we did not take to arms, we were violent in our contempt and dismissal and in our relentless projection that it is only members of the Muslim Brotherhood that are violent.

I found it difficult – to be more honest, I found it impossible – to use the word 'massacre' when talking about what happened when the military and the police cleared the camps. I still find it hard because in using the word 'massacre' it confronts me with what I was complicit with, confronts me with what I witnessed and my own cruel and thoughtless indifference, and I numbed the experience by 'refusing to name the act of killing, finding instead many alternative words' (Bollas 2011: 83).

Indifference is loaded with motivation – we did/do not want to know, but as Bollas points out violence is never more deadly than when it believes itself justified (2011: 146). One way that we justify violence and cruelty is to blame the other in the following way: 'If *they* were not like that, *I* would not hate *them*'. Another way that we reassured ourselves was through turning hate into love – so it become love for the nation and love for our families, friends and community. This is a commonplace manoeuvre, as Ahmed points out, through which we persuade ourselves that we act in this way or feel negative emotions not because we hate but because we love our nation, our community, our family (2004). Love becomes the justification for hatred and violence.

Compassion requires the human being to be disturbed as it does cause upheaval, and we have to make a judgement, conscious or unconscious, that the event and/or people are worth it and that it/they are sufficiently worthwhile to cause all this upheaval. As Nussbaum points out, however, suffering, deprivation and inequality are not necessarily ennobling because these states of mind can interfere with judgement as they can brutalise perception or indeed corrupt it. Compassion pushes boundaries and is complex. To feel compassion, you have to make a judgement about what is worthwhile and know that it could easily be oneself that is in that place of suffering or deprivation. That in turn is complex because, simultaneously, you have to know you are not the sufferer and retain the knowledge that it is not happening to the self. As Proust (1932) rather pithily, and worryingly, asserts, a real person poses 'a dead weight that our sensitivity cannot remove'. Compassion and empathy are inextricably linked. As Young-Bruehl writes, and it is worth quoting her in full:

> Empathizing involves, rather, putting another *in yourself*, becoming another person's habitat as it were, but without dissolving the person, without digesting the person. You are mentally pregnant, not with a potential life but with a person, indeed, a whole life – a person with her

history. So the subject lives on in you, and you can, as it where, hear her in this intimacy. But this, as I said, depends upon your ability to tell the difference between the subject and yourself, which means to appreciate the role that she plays in your psychic life. (1998: 22)

Being at a Loss

It is a difficult confrontation to recognise how our identity, our very being itself, is forged from power relations, and, moreover, to know fully how we are all seduced, embroiled and complicit in corrosive socio-political conditions. As Butler argues persuasively, we are dependent on these complex identifications for our very existence and so at the risk of asking an impossible question: Should we feel guilty and/ or ashamed of our wish for our existence? Perhaps a more effective starting place is the recognition that our being is made from inexorable socio-political structures that we inherit and, unfortunately, perpetuate. We need to start with the reluctant awareness and understanding of our complicities and compliances with the inexorable material, emotional, social and political structures that corrode us all. It is from that starting place that we can begin to trace through the consequences of these complicities on the interrelationships between self and others and the effects of inhabiting destructive socio-political conditions. The difficulty here is that we are confronted by the persistent obdurate power of the state that is enacted by some human beings. The state after all is both an abstract entity and simultaneously material in its effects. It is human beings who perhaps have no choice, who act on aggression and hostility and who perpetuate divisions.

We can retreat into imagining it is other human beings who are embedded and complicit with the dominant social and political orders, but this is to bypass a central, if uncomfortable, insight, which is that we are all embedded within these structures. Judith Butler explores throughout her book *Giving an Account of Oneself* (2005) that it is our ethical responsibility to know how we are embedded within language, social customs, dominant values and certain world views. As Butler argues, the force of socio-political morality in the production of the subjectivity is crucial; but, and this is a crucial but, while our identity is produced by morality, we must find our relation to morality. Therefore, 'Even if morality supplies a set of norms that produce a subject in his or her intelligibility, it also remains a set of norms and rules that a subject must negotiate in a living and reflective way' (2005: 19). In short, we have to take responsibility for how we have internalised dominant beliefs and values.

My next step, brave if not foolish, would be to think through my accountability to members of the Muslim Brotherhood and my internalisation of them as the enemy. This internalisation occurred through inherited family narratives and the dominant discourses of a particular historical time. These discourses from the time of Nasser, which have continued to the present, are powerful as they captivate and are persuasive. So, I could leave the matter at rest there and open up a discussion of the power of these discourses, but the point is that *I* internalised them, *I* perpetuated them and *I* live through these discourses. I am not alone in grasping these discourses as truth because the power and seductive appeal of these discourses – it is they who are cruel, violent, backward – link into the need to belong, to be the right thing and to be acceptable. It is important to state that in opening up this discussion I would only be morally accountable if I undertake this, not through the fear and of other's opinions and/or anxieties of my place in the affections of others, but rather this troubling exploration has to be based, following Butler, on 'a desire to know and understand that is not fuelled by the desire to punish, and a desire to explain and narrate that is not prompted by a terror of punishment' (2005: 11). It is also crucial that the 'you' is central to this undertaking and does not become another endeavour to insert the 'I' back into a solipsistic relation to the self and to others.

We have to endure our aggressions, indifferences and capacity for cruelty that the need to belong can provoke. Belonging, I am arguing, pushes and pulls in different directions. It can pull us into identification with others. As Kirsten Campbell explores it, identification can mediate the relation between self and other as identifying and recognising the other can provoke 'listening to, the other in intersubjective dialogue' (2004: 104). Identification is based on a recognition of emotional bonds and alliances, and it is 'the process by which the subject constitutes and establishes a relation between its inner and outer worlds. Identification constructs an "I" and an "other" by constituting the subject in relation to *another*' (Campbell 2004: 94). Identification can, therefore, be a crucial means through to a more effective politics.

Belonging though can push us away from others as the pull towards that which and who is known can be a powerful stronghold. This is illustrated in the novel *The Open Door*, when the central protagonist is told in no uncertain terms that if you follow through on the family's plans for you, she found herself thinking, you

> enjoy the love, affection, and accord of the family. But if you do not, thought Layla, if you contravene that design and violate the family's principles, the family will strike you down, as her father had done when she joined that demonstration. The family would withhold its love. (2005: 125)

People can belong in many different ways and to many different objects of attachment, and it always involves identification. Belonging can lead to effective political attachments and the attempt to live differently. This can only occur if ethical risks are undertaken and, centrally, this involves placing the 'you' at the centre of moral, social and political life. The need to belong can, frequently, however, involve and is embroiled in exclusion. Elspeth Probyn articulates the question thus: 'What to do with all the various longings for belonging?' (1996: 19). This political and theoretical puzzle resonates as it focuses attention on 'the ways in which individuals and groups are caught within wanting to belong, wanting to become, a process that is fuelled by yearning' (Probyn 1996: 19). The various yearnings to belong must be taken seriously as long as belonging does not becomes destiny that justifies the exploitative and corrosive structures that currently exist.

The need to belong can produce effective identification and can pull human beings away from recognising the other. Belonging can produce a resistance to the new and can also evoke ethical responses to the other and a resistance to the exploitations that have previously occurred. Hallward describes Caygill's quest to explore what he calls an 'affirmative capacity to resist', which Caygill (2013) 'understands as an ability or "energy" that links traditional virtues like courage and fortitude with a readiness to hold one's ground, whatever the cost and for however long it takes' (Hallward 2014: 21). This affirmative life energy is crucial for living a life, and through this monograph I have been preoccupied with that which hinders this vital capability. I have been exploring how repetition of previous states of mind such as fear, being beholden to authority and authoritative figures such as fathers, being complicit with a problematic socio-political order/s obstructs movement towards effective thought and impedes what Howard Caygill describes as an affirmative life energy.

It is partly through being caught in the hold of the past that impedes our capacity for resistance and for a lively life energy. It is this close attention to temporalities that may produce a more effective future. Close theoretical consideration needs to be given to a series of paradoxes that are outlined by Butler as

> the past is irrecoverable and the past is not past; the past is the resource for the future and the future is the redemption of the past; loss must be marked and it cannot be represented; loss fractures representation itself and loss precipitates its own modes of expression. (2003: 467)

These paradoxes along with loss have to be endured, the disappointments known and tolerated. Above all, for endurance to be accepted, mourning has to take place, and mourning here involves the loss of an ideal object, idea and country. Identification is one important means of surviving loss, disappointment and trauma. Trauma, however, can block mourning from taking place as melancholia is the only response to that which cannot be assimilated. Egypt can be marked by an atmosphere of melancholia (alongside an energy to living that abounds), but it is melancholia that I want to bring into relief. Fathers are crucial for mourning to take place as they need to facilitate the next generation to make a future that can be there for the taking. Much of what has to be mourned is enigmatic, but it is deeply felt nonetheless. Mourning needs to occur in relation to what has been and as importantly what never was, never has been and possibly never will be until the more life-affirming energy is claimed. We cannot rush to claiming resistance as if that is the solution as we need to be still so as to be able to trace through that which is elusive and challenging. Or, as Frosh puts it, the importance of claiming the 'virtues of endurance' (Frosh 2015: 157).

It is impossible to know how Egypt will develop and how it can become a society based on 'social justice, bread and equality' (reaching out for democracy as a rhetorical device may not be the answer). It is sobering. It is difficult to avoid feeling despondent at best and defeated at worst. I desperately wanted to find a different and hopeful conclusion, but optimism is not available at present. Drawing on Hannah Arendt, Rose (2014) asserts that totalitarian regimes hate new beginnings. New beginnings, precarious attempts to reach for different states of mind built on altered relations between self and other, and changed understandings of the persistence of the past in the present have to be oppressed out of existence. It is therefore 'each new birth that totalitarianism hates', writes Rose, who goes on to argue that terror is needed in order to ensure the continued existence of the status quo and to quell any dissent (2014: 4). The new threatens the regime and puts pressure on corrupt socio-political-emotional structures. We are all contaminated by inhabiting immoral societies, whether through fear, the need for status and material security, indifference and/or violent repudiations of vulnerability.

My father cried copiously over the failure of the 1952 revolution, and I suspect his tears were due to his broken dreams, hopes and overwhelming sense of loss. I imagine that his state of mind, and he was certainly not alone, echoes a similar view that is dominant at this period of time in Egypt. The following is a description that I am too inside of to be able to stand back from and it is a repetition of what I have described previously (2015). Alas, the description is still apt and I can only apologise that I cannot find a more optimistic account as the socio-political conditions are so resolutely ingrained. It is the summer of 2016 and I am in my home in Cairo where I live part of the time. The air is heavy with dust and sand so that it is difficult to breathe. I feel as if I am living in a fog. People seem to be walking on eggshells and are unusually subdued, withdrawn and thin skinned. Everyday life is freighted. We comment to one another that we 'do not know Cairo', 'people are not the same' and we 'do not quite recognise where we are' (we mean this metaphorically). We do not quite linger on these comments, as if we are fearful to follow through on these asides, and cannot quite bear to know the implications of our perceptions and feelings. I want to leave; I am struggling to be here because I cannot bear the loss of a Cairo I once loved. Our conversations focus relentlessly and hopelessly on the socio-political situation and on imagining the future. Persistent political upheaval can make it difficult to know where, and to whom, you belong as it throws the self and all that can be taken for granted off balance.

Bibliography

Abaza, M. (2001) 'Shopping malls, consumer culture and the reshaping of public space in Egypt', *Theory, Culture & Society*, 18(5): 97–122.

Abouelnaga, S. (2016) *Women in Revolutionary Egypt: Gender and the New Geographics of Identity*. Cairo/New York: The American University in Cairo Press.

Abraham, N. and Torok, M. (1994) *The Shell and the Kernal: Renewals of Psychoanalysis*. Vol.1. Chicago: University of Chicago Press.

Abudi, D. (2011) *Mothers and Daughters in Arab Women's Literature*. London and Boston: Brill.

Abu-Lughod, L. (2013) *Do Muslim Women Need Saving?* Cambridge, MA: Harvard University Press.

Abou, D. S. and Zaazou, Z. (2013) 'The Egyptian revolution and post-socio-economic impact', *Topics in Middle Eastern and African Economics*, 15(1): 92–114.

Aciman, A. (1997) *Out of Egypt: A Memoir*. New York: Picador.

Ackerman, D. (1990) *A Natural History of the Senses*. New York: Vintage.

Ahmed, L. (1999) *A Border Passage: From Cairo to America–A Woman's Journey*. New York: Farrar, Straus and Giroux.

Ahmed, S. (2004) *The Cultural Politics of Emotions*. Edinburgh: Edinburgh University Press.

Alexander, A. (2005) *Nasser: His Life and Times*. Cairo/New York: American University in Cairo Press.

Alexander, S. (1994) *Becoming a Woman: And Other Essays in 19th and 20th Feminist History*. London: Verso.

Alkhamissi, K. (2006) *Taxi*. Doha: Bloomsbury Qatar Foundation Publishing.

Althusser, L. (1971) *Lenin and Philosophy and Other Essays*. New York/ London: Monthly Review Press (transl. B. Brewster).

Al Aswany, A. (2009) *Friendly Fire*. Cairo/New York: American University in Cairo Press.

Amin, G. (2006) *The Illusion of Progress in the Arab World*. Cairo: American University of Cairo Press.

Al-Ali, N. (2000) *Secularism, Gender and the State in the Middle East: The Egyptian Women's Movement*. Cambridge: Cambridge University Press.

———. (2014) 'Reflections on (counter) revolutionary processes in Egypt', *Feminist Review*, 106(1): 122–128.

Al-Nowaihi, M.M. (1999) 'Constructions of masculinity in two Egyptian novels', in Joseph, S. (ed.) *Intimate Selving in Arab Families: Gender, Self, and Identity*. Syracuse, NY: Syracuse University Press, 235–266.

Al-Zayyat, L. (2005) *The Open Door*. Cairo and New York: American University in Cairo Press (transl. M. Booth). Originally published (1960) as Al-Bab Al Maftah.

Anderson, B. (2009) 'Affective Atmospheres', *Emotion, Space and Society*, 2: 77–81.

Andrijasevic, R., Hamilton, C. and Hemmings, C. (2014) 'Editorial: re-imagining revolutions', *Feminist Review*, 106: 1–28.

Arendt, H. (1958) *The Human Condition*. Chicago: Chicago University Press.

———. (1968) *Men in Dark Times*. New York: Harcourt, Brace and World.

———. (1973) *On Revolution*. London: Penguin (first published 1963 Viking Press USA).

———. (1978) *Life of the Mind, Vol. 1*. San Diego: Harcourt, Inc.

———. (2003) *Responsibility and Judgement*, J. Kohn (ed). New York: Schoken Books

———. (2004a) *The Origins of Totalitarianism*. New York: Schoken Books (first published 1951).

———. (2004b) *On Violence*. Orlando/Austin/New York/San Diego/London: Harcourt, Inc. (first published in 1969).

Arenfeldt, P. and Al-Hassan Golley, N. (eds) (2012) *Mapping Arab Women's Movements: A Century of Transformations from Within*. Cairo and New York: American University in Cairo Press.

Back, L. (2003) 'Sounds in the crowd', in Bull, M. and Back, L. (eds) *An Auditory Culture Reader*. Oxford: Berg, 311–328.

Barthes, R. (1977) *Image, Music, Text*. London: Harper and Collins.

Baron, B. (1994) *The Women's Awakening in Egypt: Culture, Society, and the Press*. New Haven: Yale University Press.

Beinin, J. (2012) 'The Working Class and the Popular Movement in Egypt' in *The Journey to Tahrir: Revolution, Protest, and Social Change in Egypt*. London/New York: Verso, 92–106.

Benjamin, J. (1990) *The Bonds of Love: Psychoanalysis, Feminism and the Problem of Domination*. London: Virago Press.

———. (1995) *Like Subjects, Love Objects: Essays on Recognition and Difference*. New Haven/London: Yale University Press.

———. (1998) *In the Shadow of the Other: Intersubjectivity and Gender in Psychoanalysis*. New York/London: Routledge.

Berlant, L. (2011) *Cruel Optimism*. Durham: Duke University Press.

Bhattacharyya, G. (2008) *Dangerous Brown Men: Exploiting Sex, Violence and Feminism in the War on Terror*. London/New York: Zed Books.

Blunt, A. and Dowling, R. (2006) *Home: Key Ideas in Geography*. Abingdon: Routledge.

Bollas, C. (1987) *The Shadow of the Object: Psychoanalysis of the Unthought Known*. London: Free Association Books.

———. (2011) *The Christopher Bollas Reader*. London: Routledge.

Booth, M. (1997) 'May her likes be multiplied', *Signs*, 22(4): 827–890.

———. (2005) 'Introduction', in Al-Zayyat, L. *The Open Door*. Cairo and New York: American University in Cairo Press.

Bourdieu, P. (1991) *Language and Symbolic Power*. Cambridge, Massachusetts: Harvard University Press (transl. G. Raymond and M. Adamson).

———. (2001) *Masculine Domination*. Cambridge: Polity Press (transl. R. Nice).

Bourdieu, P. et al. (2016) *The Weight of the World: Social Suffering in Contemporary Society*. Cambridge: Polity Press (first published 1999).

Bradley, J. (2009) *Inside Egypt: The Land of the Pharaohs on the Brink of a Revolution*. New York: St Martin's Griffin.

Brown, W. (1995) *States of Injury: Power and Freedom in Late Modernity*. Princeton, New Jersey: Princeton University Press.

Bull, M. and Back, L. (eds) (2003) *An Auditory Culture Reader*. Oxford: Berg.

Butler, J. (1997a) *The Psychic Life of Power: Theories in Subjection*. Stanford: Stanford University Press.

———. (1997b) *Excitable Speech: The Politics of the Performative*. London and New York: Routledge.

———. (2003) 'Afterword: After Loss: What Then?' in Eng, D. L. and Kazanjian (eds) *Loss, The Politics of Mourning*. Berkeley/Los Angeles/London: University of California Press, 467–473.

———. (2004) *Precarious Life: The Power of Mourning and Violence*. London: Verso Books.

———. (2005) *Giving an Account of Oneself*. New York: Fordham University Press.

———. (2015) *Senses of the Subject*. New York: Fordham University Press.

Calhoun, C. (2011) *Rethinking Secularism*. Oxford: Oxford University Press.

Campbell, K. (2004) *Jacques Lacan and Feminist Epistemology*. London/New York: Routledge

Cavarero, A. (2000) *Relating Narratives: Storytelling and Selfhood*. London: Routledge.

Caygill, A. (2013) *On Resistance: A Philosophy of Defiance*. London: Bloomsbury.

Celello, K. and Khouloussy, H. (eds) (2016) *Domestic Tensions, National Anxieties*. Oxford: Oxford University Press.

Césaire, A. (1955) *Discours sur le colonisisme*. Paris: Éditions PRÉSENCE AFRICAINE.

Chatham House (2012) *Defining and Tackling Corruption: Summary of Egypt Dialogue Workshop*. London: Chatham House.

Civantos, C. (2013) 'Reading and writing the turn-of-the-century Egyptian woman intellectual: Nabawiyya Musa's Ta'rikhi Bi-Qalami', *Journal of Middle East Women's Studies*, 9(2): 4–31.

Connor, S. (2004) *The Book of Skin*. London: Reaktion Books.

Cook, S.A. (2012) *The Struggle for Egypt: From Nasser to Tahrir Square*. Cairo: The American University in Cairo Press.

Dabashi, H. (2012) *The Arab Spring: The End of Postcolonialism*. London/New York: Zed Books.

Davidson, S. and Rutherford, J. eds (2011) *The Neoliberal Revolution: A Special Issue of Soundings*. Vol. 48. London: Lawrence and Wishart.

De Alwis, M. (2009) 'Tracing absent presence', in Chatterjee, P., Desai, M. and Roy, P. (eds) *States of Trauma: Gender and Violence in South Asia*. Cambridge: Cambridge University Press.

De Certeau, M. (1984) *The Practice of Everyday Life*. Berkeley: University of California Press.

DuBois, W.E.B. (1989 [1903]) 'Double consciousness and the veil', in DuBois, W.E.B. *The Souls of Black Folk*. New York: Bantam, 1–9.

De Koning, A. (2006) 'Café latte and caesar salad: cosmopolitan belonging in Cairo's coffee shops', in Singerman, D. and Amer, P. (eds) *Cairo Cosmopolitan: Politics, Culture and Urban Space in the new Globalized Middle East*. Cairo and New York: The American University in Cairo Press, 221–234.

Edwards, J.D. (2008) *Postcolonial Literature*. Basingstoke: Palgrave Macmillan.

Ellman, M. (2005) 'Introduction – bad timing', in Freud, S. *On Murder, Mourning and Melancholia*. London: Penguin Books, vii–xxix.

Fanon, F. (1986) *Black Skin, White Masks*. London: Pluto Press.

Ferguson, J. (2013) 'Declarations of dependence: Labour, personhood, and welfare in South Africa', *Journal of the Royal Anthropological Institute*, 19(2): 223–242.

Frankel, J. (2015) 'The traumatic basis for the resurgence of right-wing politics among working Americans'. *Psychoanalysis, Culture and Society*, 20(4): 359–378.

Freeman, M. (2010) 'Telling stories: Memory and narrative', in Radstone, S. and Schwarz, B. (eds) *Memory: Histories, Theories, Debates*. New York: Fordham University Press, 263–280.

Freud, S. (1915) 'Instincts and their vicissitudes', *Standard Edition*, 14: 117–140.

———. (1917) 'Mourning and Melancholia', *Standard Edition*, 14: 237–258.

———. (1920) 'Beyond the Pleasure Principle', *Standard Edition*, 18: 3–64.

———. (1989) *Totem and Taboo*. London: WW Norton (first published 1913).

Frosh, S. (2002a) *Key Concepts in Psychoanalysis*. London: British Library.

———. (2002b) 'The other', *American Imago*, 59(4): 389–407.

———. (2013a) *Hauntings: Psychoanalysis and Ghostly Transmissions*. Basingstoke: Palgrave Macmillan.

———. (2013b) 'Psychoanalysis, Colonialism, Racism', *Journal of Theoretical and Philosophical Psychology*, 33(3): 141–154.

———. (2015) 'Endurance', *American Imago*, 72(2): 157–175.

Fuss, D. (1995) *Identification Papers: Readings on Psychoanalysis, Sexuality, and Culture*. London: Routledge.

Gill, A.K., Heathcote, G. and Williamson E. (2016) 'Violence', *Feminist Review*, (112): 1–8.

Gilroy, P. (2006) 'Multiculture in times of war: An inaugural lecture given at the London School of Economics', *Critical Quarterly*, 48(4): 28–45.

Go, J. (2013) *Postcolonial Sociology*. Bingley: Emerald.

Goffman, E. (1952) '*On cooling the mark out: Some aspects of adaption to failure*', http://www.tau.ac.ul/-algazi/mat/Goffman--Cooling.htm, accessed March 5, 2012.

Gordon, A. (1997) *Ghostly Matters: Haunting and the Sociological Imagination*. Minneapolis: University of Minnesota Press.

———. (2008) *Ghostly Matters: Haunting and the Sociological Imagination*. Minneapolis: University of Minnesota Press (2nd edition).

Graeber, D. (2014) *Debt: The first 5,000 years*. Brooklyn/London: Melville House.

Hall, C. (2002) *Civilising Subjects: Metropole and Colony in the English Imagination*. Cambridge: Polity Press.

Hall, S. (1996a) 'The after-life of Frantz Fanon: Why Fanon? Why now? Why Black Skin, White Masks?', in Read, A. (ed.) *The Fact of Blackness: Frantz Fanon and Visual Representation*. London: Institute of Contemporary Arts and International Visual Arts, 12–37.

———. (1996b) 'Introduction: who needs "identity"?' in Hall, S. and du Gay P. (eds) *Questions of Cultural Identity*. London and New York: Sage, 1–17.

Hallward, P. (2014) 'Defiance or Emancipation', *Radical Philosophy*, (183): 21–32.

Hatem, M. (1987) 'Toward the study of the psychodynamics of mothering and gender in Egyptian families', *International Journal of Middle East Studies*, 19(3): 287–305.

Hemmings, C. (2011) *Stories that Matter: The Political Grammar of Feminist Theory*. Durham, NC: Duke University Press.

Hemmings, C. and Treacher Kabesh, A. (2013) 'The feminist subject of agency: Recognition and affect in encounters with "the Other"', in Madhok, S., Phillips, A., Wilson, K. and Hemmings, C. (eds) *Gender, Agency and Coercion*. Basingstoke: Palgrave Macmillan, 29–46.

Highmore, B. (2010) *Ordinary Lives, Studies in the Everyday*. London/New York: Routledge.

Hoffman, E. (2010) 'The long afterlife of loss', in Radstone, S. and Schwarz, B. (eds) *Memory: Histories, Theories and Debates*. New York: Fordham University Press, 406–415.

Hook, D. (2005) 'A critical psychology of the postcolonial', *Theory and Psychology*, 15(4): 475–503.

———. (2012) *A Critical Psychology of the Postcolonial, The mind of Apartheid*. Hove/ New York: Routledge.

———. (2015) 'Indefinite delay: on (post)apartheid temporality', in Frosh, S. (ed) *Psychosocial Imaginaries, Perspectives on Temporality, Subjectivities and Activism*. Basingstoke: Palgrave, 48–71.

Howe, A. (1991) 'The problem of privatized injuries: feminist strategies for litigation', in Albertson Fineman, M. and Sweet Thomadsen, N. (eds) *At the Boundaries of Law: Feminism and Legal Theory*, Vol. 1. New York: Routledge, 148–168.

Iskander, A. (2013) *Egypt in Flux: Essays on an Unfinished Revolution*. London/New York: The American University in Cairo Press.

Joseph, S. (ed) (1999) *Intimate Selving in Arab Families: Gender, Self, and Identity*. Syracuse, NY: Syracuse University Press.

Joseph, S. and Rieker, M. (2008) 'Introduction: Rethinking Arab family projects', in Arab Families Working Group (eds) *Framings: Rethinking Arab Family Projects*. Davis, CA: University of California Davis, 35–64.

Joseph, S. (2012) 'Thinking intentionality: Arab women's subjectivity and its discontents', *Journal of Middle East Women's Studies*, 8(2): 1–25.

Kandiyoti, D. (1988) 'Bargaining with patriarchy', *Gender and Society*, 2(3): 274–290.

Kandil, H. (2012) *Soldiers, Spies, and Statesmen: Egypt's Road to Revolt*. London/New York: Verso.

———. (2014) 'Sisi's turn', *London Review of Books*, 36(4): 15–17.

Kennedy, R. (2010) 'Memory and the unconscious', in Radstone, S. and Schwarz, B. (eds). *Memory: Histories, Theories and Debates.* New York: Fordham University Press, 179–197.

Khanna, R. (2007) 'Indignity', *Ethnic and Racial Studies*, 30(2): 257–280.

Kuhn, A. (2005) 'Thresholds: film as film and the aesthetic experience', *Screen*, 46(4): 401–414.

Lacan, J. (1998) *The Four Fundamentals of Psychoanalysis.* London: W.W Norton (transl. A. Sheridan).

LaCapra, D. (2001) *Writing History, Writing Trauma.* London: John Hopkins University Press.

Laplanche, J. (1989) *New Foundations for Psychoanalysis.* Cambridge, Massachusetts: Basil Blackwell (transl. D. Macey).

Layton, L. (2002) 'Cultural hierarchies, splitting, and the heterosexist unconscious', in Fairfield, S. Layton, L. and Stack, C. (eds) *Bringing the Plague: Toward a Postmodern Psychoanalysis.* New York: Other Press, 195–223.

Lewis, L. (2012) 'Convergences and divergences: Egyptian women's activisms over the last century', in Arenfeldt, P. and Al-Hassan Golley, N. (eds) *Mapping Arab Women's Movements: A Century of Transformations from Within.* Basingstoke: Palgrave Macmillan, 43–63.

Lloyd, D. (2003) 'The memory of hunger', in Eng, D. and Kazanjian, D. (eds) *Loss: The Politics of Mourning.* Berkeley: University of California Press, 205–228.

Lucey, H., Osvold, A. and Aarseth, H. (2016) 'Working-class fathers and daughters: Thinking about desire, identification, gender and education', *Psychoanalysis, Culture and Society*, 21(2): 128–146.

Macpherson, C.B. (1962) *The Political Theory of Possessive Individualism: Hobbes to Locke.* Oxford: Oxford University Press.

McNay, L. (1999) 'Subject, psyche and agency: The work of Judith Butler', *Theory, Culture, Society*, 16(2): 175–193.

Madhok, S., Phillips, A., Wilson, K. and Hemmings, C. (eds) (2013) *Gender, Agency and Coercion.* Basingstoke: Palgrave Macmillan.

Mahfouz, N. (1985) *The Beginning and the End.* Cairo/New York: American University in Cairo Press (transl. R. Awad).

Mahmood, S. (2005) *Politics of Piety: The Islamic Revival and the Feminist Subject.* Princeton and Oxford: Princeton University Press.

Marangou, N. (2001) *Selections from the Divan.* Nicosia: Kochlias Publications (transl. S. Stephanides).

Matar, H. (2012) *Anatomy of a Disappearance.* London: Penguin.

Mbembe, A. (2006) 'The intimacy of tyranny', in Ashcroft, B., Griffiths, G. and Tiffin, H. (eds) *The Post-Colonial Studies Reader.* London: Routledge, 66–70.

———. (2013) 'Consumed by our lust for lost segregation', *Mail and Guardian* (March 28 to April 4): 29.

———. (2015) 'The state of South African political life', *Africa is a Country*, September 19. Available at: http://africasacountry.com/2015/09/achille-mbembe-on-the-state-of-south-african-politics/ (last accessed July 6, 2016).

Mendelsohn, D. (2007) *The Lost: In Search for Six of the Six Million*. London: Harper Collins.

Mitchell, T. (1991) *Colonising Egypt*. London: University of California Press.

———. (2002) *Rule of Experts: Egypt, Techno-Politics, Modernity*. Berkeley: University of California Press.

Naguib, S. (2012) *The Egyptian Revolution: A Political Analysis and Eyewitness Account*. London: Bookmarks Publications.

Nandy, A. (1983) *The Intimate Enemy: Loss and Recovery of Self Under Colonialism*. Delhi/Oxford: Oxford University Press.

Nelson, C. (1991) 'Biography and women's history: On interpreting Doria Shafik', in Keddie, N.R. and Baron, B. (eds) *Women in Middle Eastern History: Shifting Boundaries in Sex and Gender*. New Haven and London: Yale University Press, 330–333.

Ngai, S. (2005) *Ugly Feelings*. Cambridge, Mass: Harvard University Press.

Nussbaum, M. (2008) *Upheavals of Thought: The Intelligence of Emotions*. Cambridge: Cambridge University Press (first published 2001).

Olick, J.K. (2007) *The Politics of Regret, On Collective Memory and Historical Responsibility*. New York/London: Routledge.

Osman, T. (2010) *Egypt on the Brink: From Nasser to Mubarak*. New Haven: Yale University Press.

Pamuk, O. (2005) *Istanbul: Memories of a City*. London: Faber & Faber (transl. M. Freely).

Passerini, L. (2003) 'Memories between silence and oblivion', in Hodgkin, K. and Radstone S. (eds) *Contested Pasts: The Politics of Memory*. London: Routledge, 238–254.

Patterson, O. (1982) *Slavery and Social Death: A Comparative Study*. Cambridge, Massachusetts/London: Harvard University Press.

———. (2010) 'The mechanisms of cultural reproduction: Explaining the puzzle of persistence', in Hall, J.R., Grindstaff, L. and Lo, M.-C. (eds) *Handbook of Cultural Sociology*. New York: Routledge, 139–151.

Perri, 6., Radstone, S., Squire, C. and Treacher, A. (eds) (2007) *Public Emotions*. Basingstoke: Palgrave Macmillan.

Phillips, A. (1994) *On Flirtation*. London: Faber and Faber.

———. (2012) 'Keeping our distance', in Alexander, S. and Taylor, B. (eds) *History and Psyche: Culture, Psychoanalysis and the Past*. Basingstoke: Palgrave Macmillan, 211–217.

————. (2015) 'Against Self-Criticism', *London Review of Books*, 37(5): 13–16.

Poole, R. (2009) 'Two ghosts and an angel: Memory and forgetting in Hamlet, Beloved, and the Book of Laughter and Forgetting', *Constellations* 16(1): 125–149.

Probyn, E. (1996) *Outside Belongings*. London: Routledge.

Proust, M. (1932) *The Past Recaptured*. California: The Modern Library.

Radstone, S. (2007a) 'Theory and affect: Undivided worlds' in Perri, 6., Radstone, S., Squire, C. and Treacher, A. (eds) *Public Emotions*. Basingstoke: Palgrave Macmillan.

————. (2007b) *The Sexual Politics of Time: Confession, Nostalgia, Memory*. London: Routledge.

Radway, J. (2008) 'Foreword', to Gordon, A. *Ghostly Matters: Haunting and the Sociological Imagination*. Minneapolis: University of Minnesota Press (2nd edition), vii–xiii.

Roberts, H. (2013) 'The Revolution That Wasn't', *London Review of Books*, 35(17): 3–9.

Rose, J. (1998) *States of Fantasy*. Oxford: Clarendon Press.

————. (2003a) *On Not Being Able to Sleep: Psychoanalysis and the Modern World*. London: Chatto and Windos.

————. (2003b) 'Response' in Said E., *Freud and the Non-European*. London: Verso.

————. (2004) 'Returning to Ourselves', Interview with Edward W. Said in Viswanathan, G. (ed) *Power, Politics and Culture: Interviews with Edward W. Said*. London: Bloomsbury (first published 2001), 419–431.

————. (2013) *The Last Resistance*. London: Verso (first published 2007).

————. (2014) *Women in Dark Times*. London: Bloomsbury.

Rothberg, M. (2009) *Multidirectional Memory: Remembering the Holocaust in the Age of Decolonization*. Stanford: Stanford University Press.

Said, E. (2004a) *Humanism and Democratic Criticism*. New York: Columbia University Press.

————. (2004b) 'Returning to Ourselves', Interview with Edward W. Said in Viswanathan, G. (ed) *Power, Politics and Culture: Interviews with Edward W. Said*. London: Bloomsbury (first published 2001).

Salmawy, M. (2014) *Butterfly Wings*. Cairo: American University in Cairo Press (transl. R. Cohen).

Schwartz, B. (2000) 'Becoming postcolonial', in Gilroy, P., Grossberg, L. and McRobbie, A. (eds) *Without Guarantees: In Honour of Stuart Hall*. London and New York: Verso, 268–281.

————. (2011) *Memories of Empire, The White Man's World (Vol. 1)*. Oxford: Oxford University Press.

Scott, D. (2009) 'The paradox of beginnings', *Small Axe*, 13(1): vii–xiv.

Scott, J. (2012) 'The incommensurability of psychoanalysis and history', *History and Theory*, 51(1): 63–83.

Segal, J. (2000) *Phantasy: Ideas in Psychoanalysis*. Cambridge: Icon.

Seshadri-Crooks, K. (2000) *Desiring Whiteness: A Lacanian Analysis of Race*. London/New York: Routledge.

Shechter, R. (2008) 'The cultural economy of development in Egypt: Economic nationalism, hidden economy and the emergence of mass consumer society during Sadat's Infitah', *Middle Eastern Studies*, 44(4): 571–583.

Sirman, N. (2005) 'The postcolonial through the prism of love: Emotions and the constitution of the modern subject', in Gülerce, A., Hofmeister, A., Staeuble, I., Saunders, G. and Kaye, J. (eds) *Contemporary Theorizing in Psychology: Global Perspectives*. Ontario: Captus Press, 346–354.

Soueif, A. (1992) *In the Eye of the Sun*. London: Bloomsbury.

———. (2012) *Cairo: My City, Our Revolution*. London: Bloomsbury.

Spivak, G. (1998) 'Can the Subaltern Speak', in Nelson, C. and Grossberg, L. (eds) *Marxism and the Interpretation of Culture*. Chicago: University of Illinois Press.

Stewart, K. (2007) *Ordinary Affects*. Durham and London: Duke University Press.

Sullivan, S. (2006) *Revealing Whiteness: The Unconscious Habits of Racial Privilege*. Bloomington and Indianapolis: Indiana University Press.

Thapar-Björkert, S., Samelius, L., Sanghera, G. (2016) 'Exploring symbolic violence in the everyday: Misrecognition, condescension, consent and complicity', *Feminist Review* 112: 144–162.

Treacher, A. (2006) 'Something in the air: Otherness, recognition and ethics', *Journal of Social Work Practice*, 2(1): 27–37.

———. (2007) 'Matters of belonging to place and the nation', *The Psychology of Women*, 9(1): 13–23.

Treacher Kabesh, A. (2011) *On Being Haunted by the Present*. Borderlands, 10(2): 1–21.

———. (2013a) *Postcolonial Masculinities: Emotions, Histories and Ethics*. Farnham: Ashgate.

———. (2013b) 'Soundspace', in Kuhn, A. (ed) *Little Madnesses: Winnicott, Transitional Phenomena and Cultural Experience*. London: I.B. Tauris, 65–76.

———. (2015) 'Political upheaval in Egypt: Disavowing troubling states of mind', *Psychoanalysis, Culture and Society*, 20(4): 343–358.

———. (2016) 'The Egyptian economic crisis: Insecurity, affect, nostalgia', in Karner, C. and Weicht, B. (eds) *The Commonalities of Global Crisis: Markets, Communities and Nostalgia*. Basingstoke: Palgrave Macmillan, 323–344.

UN. (2014) *The World Food Programme in 2014: Facts and Figures.* Rome: United Nations: http://documents.wfp.org/stellent/groups/public/documents/communications/wfp274971.pdf?_ga=1.141105457.2031134935.14682316 70 (last accessed July 11, 2016).

———. *United Nations Development Report: Sustaining human progress: reducing vulnerabilities and building resilience.* New York: United Nations.

Viswanathan, G. (2004) *Power, Politics and Culture: Interviews with Edward W. Said.* London: Bloomsbury (first published 2001).

Walcott, D. (1994) 'The Muse of History', in Coombs, O. (ed) *Is Massa Day Dead?* New York: Anchor.

Walkerdine, V. and Jimenez, L. (2012) *Gender, Work and Community after De-Industrialisation.* Basingstoke: Palgrave Macmillan.

Whidden, J. (2005) 'The generation of 1919', in Goldschmidt, A., Johnson, A.J. and Salmoni, B.A. (eds) *Re-Envisioning Egypt 1919–1952.* Cairo: American University in Cairo Press, 19–45.

Wilkinson, R. and Pickett, K. (2010) *The Spirit Level: Why Equality is Better for Everyone.* London: Penguin.

Winnicott, D. (1965) *The Maturational Processes and the Facilitating Environment: Studies in the Theory of Emotional Development.* London: The Hogarth Press and The Institute of Psychoanalysis.

Winnicott, D.W. (1990) *Home Is Where We Start From: Essays by a Psychoanalyst.* London: Norton.

Young-Bruehl, E. (1998) *Subject to Biography, Psychoanalysis, Feminism, and Writing Women's Lives.* Cambridge, Massachusetts/London: Harvard University Press.

———. (2006) *Why Arendt Matters.* New Haven/London: Yale University Press.

Yuval-Davis, N. (2006) 'Belonging and the politics of belonging', *Patterns of Prejudice,* 40(3): 197–214.

Zagajewski, A. (2001) 'Try to Praise the Mutilated World', *The New Yorker,* September 24 (transl. C. Cavanagh).

Žarkov, D. (2016) 'Co-option, complicity, co-production: Feminist politics on war rapes', *European Journal of Women's Studies,* 23(2): 119–123.

Index

Abouelnaga, Shereen, 146
absent presences, 50
Abudi, Dalya, 109
Abu-Lughod, Lila, 100, 103, 114–16
Aciman, André, 54
Ackerman, Diane, 60
ahawi baladi (traditional, male
    dominated cafés), 40
Ahmed, Sara, 136, 151, 158, 160
Ahzan Madina (Al-Nowaihi), 64
'aila' (family), 55
Al-Ali, Nadje, 94, 100, 104
*Al-Bab Al-Maftuh. see The Open
    Door* (Al-Zayyat)
Alexander, Sally, 54, 75
Al-Garf, Azza, 147
Al-Ghazali, Zainab, 112
Al-Hassan Golley, N., 111
alienation, 95, 136, 142
Al-infitah (opening up), 27, 83
Alkhamissi, K., 38
Al-Qaeda, 9, 134
Al-Sisi, Abdul Fattah, 3, 9–10, 25,
    36, 84–87, 95, 126, 137, 139
Althusser, L., 63
Al-Wafd party, 73, 81–82

Alwis, De, 50
Anatomy of a Disappearance
    (Matar), 66
Anderson, Ben, 123
Anglo-Egyptian Treaty (1936), 82
anti-imperialism, 86–87, 89
anxiety, 2, 5, 13, 15, 20, 23, 31–32,
    41–44, 51, 78, 96, 116, 117,
    126, 135, 142, 157
apathy, 123–24
Arabic Popular Movement, 144
Arab Spring, 18
Arendt, Hannah, 12, 19, 78, 137,
    149–50, 153–54, 164
Arenfeldt, P., 111
autonomy, and feminism, 109

Back, Les, 54
'Bargaining with patriarchy' (article),
    102, 118
Baron, Beth, 111
Barthes, R., 60
Battle of the Camels, 131
The Beginning and the End
    (Mahfouz), 12, 23, 37
Beinin, J., 144

'*beit*' (household), 55
belonging and connectedness, 54–62,
    162–63
Benjamin, Jessica, 58, 97n2, 107,
    121–22
Berger, John, 54
Berlant, Lauren, 50
Beyond the Pleasure Principle
    (Freud), 79
Bint-al Nil (Daughters of the
    Nile), 113
Bollas, Christopher, 52, 95, 96, 161
Booth, Marilyn, 68, 108
A Border Passage (Ahmed), 12
Bourdieu, Pierre, 16, 69, 118
Bradley, John, 133
Bread Riots, 145
British Protectorate, 73, 81
Brown, Wendy, 151
Butler, Judith, 117, 121, 136–37,
    151, 161–62, 164
Butterfly Wings (Salmawy), 12, 48,
    107–10, 119

Cairo Fire, 82, 145
Campbell, Kirsten, 162
Castro, Fidel, 86
Cavarero, A., 154
Caygill, H., 163
Celello, K., 71n3
Civantos, C., 117–18, 122n3
colonial boomerang, 78
colonialism/colonisation, 6, 17–18,
    21, 26, 29–30, 36, 39–40,
    47, 49–50, 64, 68–70, 75–76,
    78–80, 85–86, 89–91, 93–95,
    134–35, 139–44, 152
communication, 13, 44, 59, 62, 65
Communist Party, 95
compassion, 156, 160
complex personhood, 62–66
Constitution Party, 144

'Consumed by our lust for lost
    segregation' (Mbembe), 79
Copts, 132
corruption, 2, 8–10, 20–26, 29, 32–33,
    35–37, 73–74, 79, 82, 130, 145,
    150, 152, 153, 160, 165
cruel optimism, 50
cultural authority, 69

Day of Rage, 130
death drive, 79
decolonization, 10, 27, 70, 74,
    140–41
Deep State, 11, 13, 95, 126–28, 150
de Koning, Anouk, 40
denigration, 29–34, 94
dependency, 31;
    responsibility and, 38–42
desires, *passim*
Desiring Whiteness (Seshadri-
    Crooks), 142
'the Devil take the English'
    slogan, 82
'Dignity for Egyptians,' 83, 85
disidentification, and identification,
    66–70
double consciousness, 52, 65
DuBois, W.E.B., 52

Eden, Anthony, 86
Edwards, Justin, 61
EFU. *see* Egyptian Feminist Union
    (EFU)
ego, 58–59, 107
Egypt Against Terrorism, 95
Egypt/Egyptians, *passim*;
    belonging and connectedness,
        54–62, 162–63;
    corruption in, 2, 8–10, 20–26,
        29, 32–33, 35–37, 73–74, 79,
        82, 130, 145, 150, 152, 153,
        160, 165;

denigration, 29–34, 94;
economic conditions, 36–38;
exploitation, 29–34;
feminism in, 99–122;
and gender role, 93–95;
indifference, 154–61;
material conditions, 34–45;
neo-liberal subjectivity, 104–11;
oppression in, 2, 3, 9, 11, 13, 32,
    74, 77, 79, 80, 85, 91, 101,
    105, 109, 115, 116, 118, 124,
    126–34, 150;
political liberation, 80–85;
political power and repression,
    134–44;
poverty and insecurity, 20, 23–25,
    31–34, 37, 43–44, 78;
repetition recognition/mis-
    recognition, 89–97;
resistance, 96, 116–22;
responsibility and dependency,
    38–42;
as 'state of emergency,' 127–28;
violence in, 3, 9–10, 29–30, 35,
    39, 47, 52, 65, 68–70, 77, 79,
    90, 100–101, 103, 124–25,
    137–38, 140–41, 147, 156–60;
vulnerability, 6, 31, 34–45, 59,
    66, 67, 92, 93, 121, 122, 137,
    143, 154, 158, 165;
women in (*see* women, in Egypt)
Egyptian Constitution Party, 99
Egyptian Feminist Union (EFU),
    112, 117
Egyptian Royal Family, 82
Egypt Reform Party, 144
Ellman, Maud, 93
El-malek Farouk, 80
El-Nadeem Centre for Rehabilitation
    of Victims of Violence and
    Torture, 147
embedded introjections, 90, 92

Emergency Law of 1958, 84, 130, 145
emotions, *passim. see also specific*
    types
enlarged mentality, 22, 149
Excitable Speech (Butler), 117
'extraordinary renditions,' 146

family life, in Egypt, 54–62;
    and parenting, 66–70;
    and religion, 63
Fanon, Frantz, 6, 17, 49, 68–70, 79,
    91, 150
fantasy(ies), 4, 6, 12–13, 15, 18–20,
    33, 43, 51, 53, 74–77, 86, 88,
    93, 97n1, 126, 136, 151, 153,
    154, 156–58
fault lines, 77, 125, 131
fear, 95, 135–36
feminism, in Egypt, 99–122
Ferguson, James, 30, 135
freedom, and feminism, 108–9
Freedom and Justice Party, 144, 146
Free Officers movement, 77, 128
Freud, S., 13, 58, 75, 79, 96, 124,
    138, 139, 152
Friendly Fire (Al Aswany), 12
Frosh, Stephen, 13, 51, 58, 92,
    142, 164
Fuss, Diana, 51, 62, 68, 80, 90,
    138, 139
fuul (stewed brown beans), 42

Gender, Agency and Coercion
    (Madhok), 104
Gender, Work and Community
    after De-Industrialisation
    (Walkerdine and Jimenez), 19
gender role, and Egypt, 93–95
geopolitical regions, 36, 50, 102, 104
Ghostly Matters: Haunting and the
    Sociological Imagination
    (Gordon), 13, 50, 62

Gill, A. K., 138
Giving an Account of Oneself
    (Butler), 161
'Glory be to Egypt,' 83, 85
Go, Julian, 10, 27, 140
Goffman, E., 143
Gordon, Avery, 12, 13, 50, 62–65,
    70, 154
Graeber, David, 29
Great Powers, 82

Hall, Catherine, 91
Hall, Stuart, 6, 47, 49, 52
Hallward, P., 163
Harassmap, 147
Hard Talk (TV show), 99
Heathcote, G., 138
Heikel, Mohammed, 28
Hemmings, Clare, 105, 118, 122n1
Highmore, Ben, 125
hijab (veil)/*hegab/hejab,* 9, 120, 146
homes, 3, 33, 38–39, 42–43, 53–54,
    57, 60–61, 78, 80, 88, 114,
    116, 119, 122, 129, 135, 146,
    147, 165
Hook, Derek, 65, 97n3, 126, 135
humiliation, 10, 20, 21, 32, 34,
    37, 41–45, 69, 74, 140,
    143–44, 146

Ibrahim, Samira, 132
identification, *passim*;
    and disidentification, 66–70;
    and personhood, 62–66
inferiority, 17, 49, 68, 91, 94, 95,
    103, 141
insecurity and poverty, 20, 23–25,
    31–34, 37, 43–44, 78
interdependence, 30
intergenerational transmission, 87
International Monetary Fund (IMF),
    32, 145

In the Eye of the Sun (Soueif),
    12, 137
Islam, 9, 26, 27, 34–35, 43, 56,
    63, 73, 81–83, 111, 113–17,
    119–20, 145–47
Islamic movements, 34–35, 113, 114,
    116, 147
Islamic Revival, 114

January 2011 Revolution, 23
'Jehan's Law', 113
Jimenez, L., 19, 29, 31
Joseph, Suad, 55, 56, 58, 62, 71n4,
    103, 107
Justice Party, 144

Kandil, Hazim, 4, 83, 127–28
Kandiyoti, Deniz, 102, 118
Keeping Our Distance (Phillips), 12
Khouloussy, H., 71n3
khwagga complex, 68
Kifaya (Enough), 130, 145
King Farouk, 79–80, 83
Klein, Melanie, 97n1
Kuhn, Annette, 53

Lacan, J., 108
LaCapra, Dominic, 141
Laplanche, J., 58–60
Layton, Lynne, 71n5, 120
Lewis, Leslie, 112, 114
The Life of the Mind (Arendt), 19, 79
Lloyd, David, 35, 45
Lucey, H., 57, 66

Mahfouz, N., 23, 37
Mahmood, S., 105, 106, 115, 120
Mamelukes, 134
The March of the Millions
    (1 February), 130
Marxism, 87
Matar, Hisham, 66

material support, 24–25, 37
Mbembe, Achille, 4, 70n1, 79, 90
Memories of Empire (Schwarz), 86
Mendelsohn, Daniel, 15
Men in Dark Times (Arendt), 155
Midan Tahrir (Liberation Square), 7, 23
Mitchell, Timothy, 29, 39
Morsi, Muhammad, 2, 8–9, 157
Mubarak, Gamal, 8, 130
Mubarak, Hosni, 8, 11, 23, 26, 28, 32, 73, 79–80, 84–85, 113, 126, 130–31, 139, 144–46
'Mubarak, irhal' ('Mubarak, go'), 131
Musa, Nabawiyya, 111, 116–20, 122n3
Muslim Brotherhood, 2–4, 8–9, 11, 18, 94–96, 112, 114, 125, 127, 129, 135, 157, 159, 162
Muslim Women's Association, 112

Nabarawi, Saiza, 112
Naguib, Mohammed, 77
Nahda, Midan, 4
Nandy, Ashis, 152
narratives, *passim*
Narzra for Feminist Studies and the New Women's Research Centre, 147
Nasif, Malak Hifni, 111, 112
Nasser, Gamal Abdul, 10, 23, 35, 78–80, 83, 85–87, 89, 95, 113, 129, 137, 139, 157, 162
Nasserite era, 79, 82, 85
National Council of Women, 113
National Democratic Party, 132
Nationalist Congress, 112
nation state, 81, 146
Nelson, Cynthia, 112
neo-liberalism, 29–31, 34–35
neo-liberal subjectivity, 104–11, 124

Ngai, S., 59, 68, 124
1952 Revolution, 74, 77, 82, 165
1919 Revolution, 74, 81
normative unconscious, 120
nostalgia, 45n1, 80
Nussbaum, Martha, 155, 160

Obama, Barak, 84–85
object relations, 59, 107, 122n2
Olick, J. K., 152–53
On Violence (Arendt), 137
The Open Door (Al-Zayyat), 12, 88, 107–10, 140, 163
Operation Anti-Sexual Harassment (OpAnti-SH), 147
oppression, 2, 3, 9, 11, 13, 32, 74, 77, 79, 80, 85, 91, 101, 105, 109, 115, 116, 118, 124, 126–34, 150
Ottoman Empire, 134
Out of Egypt (Aciman), 54

Palestinian–Israeli conflict, 26
Pan-Arab Union and, 89
parenting, in Egypt, 66–70
Passerini, Luisa, 152
passionate attachments, 137
patriarchy, and feminism, 118–19
Patterson, Orlando, 69, 90
Personal Status Law, 112, 113
personhood, 56, 62–66
petrification, 79, 97n3, 139
phantasy(ies), 3, 5, 47–53, 55, 61, 64, 74, 75, 88, 97n1, 102, 105, 116, 158–59
Phillips, Adam, 12, 64, 156
Picket, Kate, 44
political liberation, in Egypt, 80–85
political power, and repression, 134–44
Poole, Ross, 153
Popular Current movement, 144

postcolonialism, 4, 6, 7, 10, 13–15,
    18, 20–22, 31, 47, 50, 65, 68,
    102, 104, 141
poverty and insecurity, 20, 23–25,
    31–34, 37, 43–44, 78
Press Syndicate, 113
Probyn, Elspeth, 71n2, 163
Prophet Mohammed, 35
protective secrets, 92–93
The Psychic Life of Power
    (Butler), 136
psychoanalysis, 5–6, 13, 49, 58, 104,
    107, 122n2, 151
psychopolitical subjectivities, 6, 47
Public Emotions, 11

qalam (pen), 117
Qur'an, 56

Rabaa, Midan, 4
Rabaa al-Adawiya mosque, 9
Radstone, Susannah, 15
religion, 7, 21, 25, 38, 42–43, 55, 63,
    67, 101–103, 109, 114–118,
    120, 131, 139–140, 150–151,
    153, 161, 163–164
repetition, *passim*;
    recognition/mis-recognition,
    89–97
repression, 50, 63, 70, 84, 126–34,
    136, 150;
    and power, 134–44
resistance, 13, 18, 19, 21, 30, 34, 77,
    81, 87, 92, 96;
    problematising, 116–22
Revolutionary Socialists, 130
Revolution of 2011, 1–3, 7, 8, 11,
    23, 24, 130–31, 146, 153
Rieker, Martina, 55, 62
Roberts, Hugh, 131
Rose, Jacqueline, 5, 65, 95–96, 134,
    141, 151–53, 164–65

Sadat, Anwar, 23, 80, 83, 113, 139
Said, Edward, 4, 6, 33, 137, 154
Salafi movement, 35, 36, 144
Samelius, L., 138
Sanghera, G., 138
SCAF. *see* Supreme Council of
    Armed Forces (SCAF)
Schwarz, Bill, 86, 93, 96
Second World War, 112
Segal, Julia, 51
selfhood, 50, 52, 56–59, 63, 91, 92,
    126, 155
Seshadri-Crooks, Kalpana, 142–43
Shafik, Doria, 113
Shah of Iran, 27
Sha'rawi, Huda, 112
Shechter, R., 35
shisha (the traditional water pipe), 39
Shukrallah, Hala, 99–100
Sirman, Nüket, 57, 70
6 April Youth Movement, 'We are
    all Khaled Saeed,' 130
social and psychic illusion, 122
social death, 69
social membership, 39, 135
socio-political-emotional events,
    passim
Soueif, Adhaf, 1, 7, 137
soundscape, 60–61
Spivak, G., 121
States of Fantasy (Rose), 151
Stewart, Kathleen, 5, 52
Stolen Revolution, 9
'The Stolen Revolution,' 131
subjection:
    and psychic life, 151;
    and subjugation, 136;
    and subordination, 135
subjectivation, 106
subjectivity, *passim*
Suez Canal, 10, 26, 36, 81, 82, 85–86
Suez War, 10, 88

Sulayman, Muhammed Effendi, 140
Sullivan, S., 60, 87
Supreme Council of Armed Forces
    (SCAF), 2, 8, 131–32
symbolic violence, 30, 69, 138

Tahrir Bodyguards, 147
Tahrir Midan, 130–31
Tamarrod (revolt/rebellion), 130
tamiyya (the Egyptian version of
    falafel), 42
Ta'Rikhi Bi-Qalami' (Civantos), 117
Taxi (Alkhamissi), 38
temporalities, 13, 18, 20, 48, 61, 75,
    96, 97n3
terrorism, 95, 133–34
Thapar-Björkert, S., 138
Theory and Affect: Undivided Worlds
    (Radstone), 15
Totem and Taboo (Freud), 138
transmissions, 44, 64
Tripartite Aggression, 87–89

Umm Kulthum concert, 80
unconscious subjectivity, 106–7, 110
unconscious time, 75
unemployment, 8, 24–25, 28, 32, 41,
    101, 130
Union (Ittihad) Party, 81
United Nations Development
    Report, 25
Upheavals of Thought (Nussbaum), 14
'usra' (kin), 55

violence, 3, 9–10, 29–30, 35,
    39, 47, 52, 65, 68–70,
    77, 79, 90, 100–101, 103,
    124–25, 137–38, 140–41,
    147, 156–60
voice-bodies, 60
vulnerability, 6, 31, 34–45, 59, 66,
    67, 92, 93, 121, 122, 137, 143,
    154, 158, 165

Walkerdine, V., 19, 29, 31
Whidden, James, 81
Wilkinson, Richard, 44
Williamson, E., 138
Winnicott, D., 155
women, in Egypt, 99–122;
    and employment, 37–38;
    humiliation of, 32, 93–94,
        132–33, 146–47;
    necessity of struggle, 111–16;
    neo-liberal subjectivity, 104–11;
    problematising resistance,
        116–22;
    responsibility and dependency,
        38–42

Young-Bruehl, Elisabeth, 101,
    159–60
Youth for Egypt, 144
Yuval-Davis, Nira, 53

Zaghlul, Sa'd, 118–19
Žarkov, D., 100

About the Author

Dr. Amal Treacher Kabesh is an Associate Professor in the School of Sociology and Social Policy (University of Nottingham). She has published extensively on subjectivity (specifically gender, ethnicity and postcolonial subjectivity). She draws on postcolonial theory and psychoanalysis to theorise subjectivity and identity. Her previous monograph, *Postcolonial Masculinities: Emotions, Histories and Ethnics,* was published in 2013.

www.ingramcontent.com/pod-product-compliance
Lightning Source LLC
Chambersburg PA
CBHW021817270326
41932CB00007B/225